Memory Matters

This book is grounded in the debates of the 1980s and 1990s that surrounded recollections of childhood sexual abuse, particularly those that emerged in the context of psychotherapy. When growing numbers of therapists claimed that they were recovering deeply repressed memories of early sexual violations in their female clients, a wave of alarmed critics countered that therapists were implanting the very memories they were discovering. In looking back at this volatile and heated controversy, *Memory Matters* takes up disturbing questions that linger concerning memory, sexuality, and childhood.

Beginning with a re-analysis of cases from the recovered memory era, the volume goes on to offer fresh perspectives on recollections of childhood sexual abuse. Informed by feminist and critical perspectives within psychology, contributing authors introduce examples from their own qualitative research on processes of remembering. They offer rich examples from a wide range of applied settings, from the courts, psychotherapy, institutions for the disabled, to self-help groups and the media.

A shared set of questions is addressed by each of the authors to create a dialogue with the reader on recurring motifs. *Memory Matters* is an ideal resource for advanced undergraduate and postgraduate students in the social sciences and legal studies, as well as practitioners in the fields of mental health, crisis services, and the law. Scholarly and accessible in tone, the book also offers helpful insights for professionals working with childhood memory.

Janice Haaken is Professor of Psychology at Portland State University, a clinical and community psychologist, and a documentary filmmaker. She has published extensively in the areas of psychoanalysis and feminism, the history of gender and diagnostic categories, group responses to violence and trauma, gender and collective remembering, storytelling, and the psychology of social change.

Paula Reavey is a Senior Lecturer in Psychology at London South Bank University. Her research interests are around social remembering, embodiment and distress across a variety of therapeutic, everyday and psychiatric settings. These include the study of everyday recollections of child sexual abuse, therapeutic understanding of gender and memory and the use of memory work with service users.

Memory Matters
Contexts for Understanding Sexual
Abuse Recollections

Edited by Janice Haaken and Paula Reavey

LONDON AND NEW YORK

First published 2010
by Routledge
27 Church Road, Hove, East Sussex BN3 2FA

Simultaneously published in the USA and Canada
by Routledge
270 Madison Avenue, New York, NY 10016

Routledge is an imprint of the Taylor & Francis Group, an Informa business

© 2010 Psychology Press

Typeset in Times by RefineCatch Limited, Bungay, Suffolk
Printed and bound in Great Britain by
TJ International Ltd, Padstow, Cornwall
Cover design by Design Deluxe

All rights reserved. No part of this book may be reprinted or reproduced or utilised in any form or by any electronic, mechanical, or other means, now known or hereafter invented, including photocopying and recording, or in any information storage or retrieval system, without permission in writing from the publishers.

This publication has been produced with paper manufactured to strict environmental standards and with pulp derived from sustainable forests.

British Library Cataloguing in Publication Data
A catalogue record for this book is available from the British Library

Library of Congress Cataloging-in-Publication Data
Memory matters : contexts for understanding sexual abuse recollections / edited by Janice Haaken and Paula Reavey.
    p. cm.
  Includes bibliographical references and index.
  ISBN 978-0-415-44491-0 (hbk.)
  1. Recovered memory. 2. Child sexual abuse.   I. Haaken, Janice, 1947– II. Reavey, Paula.
  RC455.2.F35M46 2010
  616.85′83690651–dc22
                                                 2009003514

ISBN: 978-0-415-44491-0 (hbk)

This book is dedicated to the memory of my late mother, Jeanne Reavey. Her bizarre and hilarious ways of remembering have greatly influenced my interest in memory and storytelling and her vivacity and strength are qualities I shall never forget and continually miss. (PR)

For my mother and first teacher in life, Leah Hawkinson Torkelson. (JH)

Contents

List of contributors ix
Acknowledgements xiii

1 **Why memory still matters: disturbing recollections** 1
 JANICE HAAKEN AND PAULA REAVEY

SECTION 1
Looking back on the recovered memory debate: claims and counter-claims 15

2 **On changing one's mind twice: the strange credibility of retracting recovered memories** 17
 MALCOLM ASHMORE AND STEVEN D. BROWN

3 **Reconstructing Bartlett and revisiting retractions of contested claims of abuse** 41
 JAMES OST AND KARL NUNKOOSING

4 **Speaking up against justice: credibility, suggestibility and children's memory on trial** 63
 JOHANNA F. MOTZKAU

5 **Transformations of public and private knowledge: audience reception, feminism and the experience of childhood sexual abuse** 86
 JENNY KITZINGER

6 **'Alternative memories' and the construction of a sexual abuse narrative** 105
 JO WOODIWISS

SECTION 2
Widening the lens: cultural contexts for remembering child sexual abuse — 129

7 **The spaces of memory: rethinking agency through materiality** — 131
PAULA REAVEY

8 **'Truth', memory and narrative in memoirs of child sexual abuse** — 142
KATHRYN ROBSON

9 **Memory, sexual abuse and the politics of learning disability** — 157
RACHEL FYSON AND JOHN CROMBY

10 **Memory, truth, and the search for an authentic past** — 175
SUE CAMPBELL

11 **Therapy as memory-work: dilemmas of discovery, recovery and construction** — 196
ERICA BURMAN

12 **Transformative remembering: feminism, psychoanalysis, and recollections of abuse** — 216
JANICE HAAKEN

Index — 230

Contributors

Malcolm Ashmore is author of *The Reflexive Thesis* (University of Chicago Press, 1989) and co-author of *Health and Efficiency* (Open University Press, 1989). Interested in the sociodiscursive analysis of science and expertise, he researches the debunking of scientific fraud, the false/recovered memory controversy, the visuality of text, the ironies of document authentication, and the knowledges of love.

Steven D. Brown is Professor of Social and Organizational Psychology at the University of Leicester, UK and Visiting Professor at the Universiteit voor Humanistiek, Utrecht, NL. His research interests are around the mediation of social remembering across diverse settings. These include commemoration of the 2005 London bombings; personal, familial and institutional recollection of childhood traumas and challenges; self-archiving in virtual social networking. He is author of *The Social Psychology of Experience: Studies in Remembering and Forgetting* (with David Middleton, 2005, Sage Publications) and *Psychology without Foundations: Constructionism, Mediation and Critical Psychology* (with Paul Stenner, 2009, Sage Publications).

Erica Burman is Professor of Psychology and Women's Studies at Manchester Metropolitan University, where she co-directs the Discourse Unit and the Women's Studies Research Centre. Her recent books are *Deconstructing Developmental Psychology* (Routledge, 2nd edition, 2008), and *Developments: Child, Image, Nation* (2008, Routledge). She is also a group analyst. Her current projects address consequences of connections between national and international asylum, immigration and domestic violence policies, and the child–woman relationship.

Sue Campbell is Professor of Philosophy and Gender and Women's Studies at Dalhousie University in Halifax, Nova Scotia. Her research is in moral and political psychology, primarily on politically adequate conceptualizations of memory and emotion. She is the author of *Relational Remembering: Rethinking the Memory Wars* (Rowman and Littlefield, 2003) and *Interpreting the Personal: Expression and the Formation of Feelings* (Cornell,

1997), and the co-editor of *Embodiment and Agency* (Penn State University Press, 2009), and *Racism and Philosophy* (Cornell, 1999).

John Cromby's PhD work was with children attending a school for students with learning disabilities, and in many ways this was the beginning of a lengthy engagement with the way that bodies and social influence come together to constitute experience. Since then, he has pursued this interest in relation to embodiment, emotion, and 'mental illness'. Currently, he is a Psychologist in the Department of Human Sciences at Loughborough University.

Rachel Fyson is currently a Lecturer in Social Work in the School of Sociology and Social Policy, University of Nottingham, UK. She has previously worked as a Research Fellow for the Ann Craft Trust (a national charity which works to prevent the abuse of people with learning disabilities) and the Norah Fry Research Centre, University of Bristol (a national centre of excellence in learning disability research). Prior to becoming an academic she worked for many years with both children and adults with learning disabilities. Her research interests include sexual abuse, learning disability, interagency working and policy implementation.

Janice Haaken, PhD, is Professor of Psychology at Portland State University, a clinical and community psychologist, and a documentary filmmaker. Haaken has published extensively in the areas of psychoanalysis and feminism, the history of gender and psychiatric diagnosis, group responses to violence and trauma, and the psychology of storytelling. She is author of *Pillar of Salt: Gender, Memory, and the Perils of Looking Back* (1998), co-author of *Speaking Out: Women, War and the Global Economy* (2005), and author of the forthcoming *Hard Knocks: Domestic Violence and the Psychology of Storytelling*. Her films include *Diamonds, Guns, and Rice*, *Queens of Heart: Community Therapists in Drag*, and *Moving to the Beat*.

Jenny Kitzinger is Professor of Media and Communications Research at Cardiff University. Her recent books include: *Framing Abuse: Media Influence and Public Understandings of Sexual Violence against Children* (Pluto, 2004) and *Human Cloning in the Media: From Science Fiction to Science Practice* (Routledge, 2008) (co-author). Her work is particularly concerned with questions of media power, influence and audience reception. She has also written extensively about focus group research methods. Her research which focuses on sexual violence includes examining the emergence of child sexual abuse as a public issue, the representation of social work intervention scandals, the discovery of 'false memory syndrome', responses to a feminist social awareness advertising campaign and the development of anti-violence initiatives in schools.

Johanna F. Motzkau is Lecturer in Psychology at the Faculty of Social Sciences, the Open University, UK. She has a background in philosophy,

German Kritische Psychologie, theoretical psychology, developmental psychology and forensic psychology. She is interested in epistemological and methodological issues, post-structuralist philosophy, children's rights, gender, sexual violence, and the efficacy of psychological knowledge in international legal contexts. Previous work has drawn on the writings of Gilles Deleuze to examine the 'language of deconstruction'. Recent work has focused on theoretical and practice issues around suggestibility, memory and credibility. Current research draws on the work of G. Deleuze, M. Foucault and I. Stengers to examine the history and theory of suggestibility research in relation to child witness practice in England and Germany.

Karl Nunkoosing is a Principal Lecturer at the Department of Psychology, University of Portsmouth, UK. He teaches the social construction of disability, qualitative methods and critical discourse analysis. His research includes the experiences of fathers of disabled sons and daughters; he is interested in stories and narratives, gender, culture and in the serious business of playfulness.

James Ost is a Senior Lecturer at the Department of Psychology, University of Portsmouth (UK) and a Chartered Psychologist. He teaches cognitive psychology and the psychology of trauma and memory. His research interests include the social nature of remembering and remembering in forensic contexts. He is on the scientific advisory board of the British False Memory Society (BFMS).

Paula Reavey is a Senior Lecturer in Psychology at London South Bank University. Her research interests are around social remembering, embodiment and distress across a variety of therapeutic, everyday and psychiatric settings. These include the study of everyday recollections of child sexual abuse, therapeutic understandings of gender and memory and the use of memory-work with service users. She is co-editor of *New Feminist Stories of Child Sexual Abuse: Sexual Scripts and Dangerous Dialogue* (with Sam Warner, 2003, Routledge), *From Disorder to Experience: Beyond Abnormal Psychology* (with Richard Bentall, John Cromby and Dave Harper, forthcoming, Palgrave) and the editor of a forthcoming volume *Visual Psychologies: Using and Interpreting Images in Qualitative Research* (Routledge).

Kathryn Robson is a Lecturer in French at Newcastle University. She is the author of *Writing Wounds: The Inscription of Trauma in post-1968 French Women's Life-Writing* (Rodopi, 2004) and numerous articles on trauma, loss and sexual abuse in the context of contemporary fiction and life-writing.

Jo Woodiwiss is Senior Lecturer in Sociology at the University of Huddersfield, having previously taught at Leeds Trinity and UEA. Her current teaching includes the sociology of the body and inequality and difference. Her research interests include narratives and self/identity, self-help culture and narratives of childhood sexual abuse, and women's health and well-being. She has written a number of articles and presented conference papers on women's engagement with narratives of childhood sexual abuse and 'alternative memories' and a forthcoming book *Contesting Stories of Childhood Sexual Abuse* (Palgrave).

Acknowledgements

Paula: I would like to thank the following people for their help and support in writing and preparing this book. First of all, thank you to a number of very important and cherished friends and colleagues who have engaged in wonderfully complex discussions about the nature of memory and the application of theories of memory in psychological and community practice. These include Sam Warner, Marcia Worrell, Elanor Cowland and last but not least, Steve Brown, who has provided marvellous entertainment as a background to these tricky discussions. A great many thanks go to my participants, whose stories regarding their own (often painful, always brave) accounts of their experiences and lives have provided such rich and insightful material for me to follow and work with over the years. Finally, I would like to sincerely thank Alex John, my partner, for his continuing and loving support, during bereavement and far far beyond what I could have ever expected. This gratitude extends to my son Oskar, who is a joy to live with, who never stops talking and asking those all important questions.

Janice: My deepest appreciation goes to my partner, Tom Becker, and for his unflagging support and critical readings of manuscripts. Many colleagues contributed to my thinking about the concept of transformative remembering described in these works, most notably Johanna Brenner, Friderike Heuer, Frann Michel, Debbie Nathan, and Astrid Schlaps. I also want to thank Adrienne Harris, Victor Wolfenstein, Claire Kahane, Sue Grand, Gerald Fogel, and Sheila Namir for their astute commentary on *Pillar of Salt* in the special issue of *Studies in Gender and Sexuality* (vol 4, April, 2003). And finally, I wish to express gratitude to my students and colleagues at Portland State University and to my patients, whose reflections on the past have guided my own efforts to understand when and how memories come to matter to people.

Finally, we would like to acknowledge London South Bank University, which continues to financially support our working relationship. In particular, thank you to Ian Albery, a great colleague and friend who has been instrumental in supporting this collaboration at the departmental level.

1 Why memory still matters
Disturbing recollections

Janice Haaken and Paula Reavey

The capacity to generate mental representations of past events – to remember – remains one of the most mystifying aspects of human consciousness. Although research has advanced on the neurological side of memory processes, scientific understanding of how and why particular recollections come to matter to people remains more elusive. Memories may or may not matter, depending on the emotional and social investments attached to particular versions of the past.

This book grew out of a heated debate that raged in the 1980s and 1990s over recollections of childhood sexual abuse (CSA), and specifically recollections that emerged in the context of psychotherapy, mainly in Europe and the United States. The feminist movement of the 1970s opened up a cultural space for women to speak publicly about intimate forms of violence, from incest and domestic violence to sexual harassment and date rape. By the late 1980s, however, many women (and some men) who had no prior knowledge of having been sexually abused as children began to recall such experiences, typically with the assistance of therapists schooled in techniques for uncovering traumatic memory. Clinical symptoms from eating disorders to depression were identified as disguised indicators of abuse, as therapists advanced what many felt to be a moral mandate to expose hidden histories of sexual abuse, and particularly those behind the everyday maladies of women.

These 'recovered' recollections of abuse – which often departed from a prior autobiographical record – captured centre stage in the media, from television, films, and chat shows to newspaper articles and the tabloids. Celebrities and everyday people recounted increasingly lurid stories of incestuous abuse to rapt audiences. As increasing numbers of young women began to identify as child sexual abuse survivors based on the uncovering of such memories, a backlash set in. Researchers and critics also seized the stage, asserting that over-zealous therapists unwittingly found the very sexual scenes that they were seeking in the dark visages of memory. More than any other issue in the late twentieth century, the recovered memory debate polarized the mental health field and legal community, with feminists – both in academia and in service work – heavily aligned with the recovered memory side of the controversy.

In looking back on this battlefield of recollections, *Memory Matters* takes up questions about memory, sexuality, and childhood that have lingered, even as the embers have cooled in most quarters of academia and popular culture. Not unlike other passionate situations of conflict, the subsiding of open conflict may register weariness over fighting as much as it does resolution of basic differences. But the reduced emotional intensity may create possibilities for moving beyond old stalemates and for re-assessing the cultural ground that has been both won and lost. This book grew out of an effort to collectively reflect on this period of controversy, and to sort through the issues from the vantage point of some historical distance.

In this book we argue that neither of the dominant positions in the 'war' over memory – the true versus false memory positions – decisively prevailed in public or academic discourse over childhood memory. Although some softened hardline positions, others turned away entirely from the issues because of the bitter acrimony generated by moral claims on both sides. We began this collection of papers with the premise that memory may 'matter' more or less, given a specific context, and that there are many 'matters' concerning everyday contexts shaping processes of remembering that have yet to be addressed (Campbell, 2003; Haaken, 2003; Motzkau, 2007; Reavey and Brown, 2006).

The politics of remembering

A primary aim of this volume is to bring into focus key historical dynamics and contests over power that shape the terms of storied forms of remembering, and particularly in matters concerning sexuality and childhood. Of the various campaigns of the women's movement of the 1970s, childhood sexual abuse garnered the most passionate support as a collective form of storytelling. Unlike other insults and injuries girls suffered in the course of development, child sexual abuse, and particularly incest, drew political strength from the very revulsion that had kept the issue so shrouded in secrecy. By the late 1980s, mandatory child abuse reporting laws were passed throughout the United States and Canada as well as Europe and the United Kingdom, with most enforcement efforts focused on reported cases of sexual abuse. More than physical assaults or neglect of children, sexual violations emerged as the paradigmatic trauma of childhood.

Much of the heat of the recovered memory controversy centred on the question of why growing numbers of female patients were identifying as sexual abuse survivors. Armies of experts offered scientific explanations for how important events in childhood could be forgotten and later remembered. In response, experts on the other side of the battle zone insisted that memory was highly malleable and that many therapists were unwittingly implanting memories of abuse in vulnerable patients. By the early 1990s an organization formed in the United States, the False Memory Syndrome Foundation, which mounted a campaign to establish the role of suggestibility in producing evidence of 'false' memories. Research on memory – often carried out in controlled and dry laboratory conditions – aroused passionate interest as groups on both sides of the controversy sought scientific findings to support their positions.

For feminist-informed therapists and academics, the political mandate to 'believe women' and to 'validate' recovered memories acquired a palpable moral urgency. Questions concerning the scientific and forensic evidence in support of recovered memory claims were often dismissed as forms of colluding with perpetrators. Most critics of recovered memory therapy, an approach that centred on the uncovering of childhood trauma, drew a line between incest survivors who had continuous knowledge of having been abused (cases thought to be non-problematic), and those women who 'found' their memory through therapy or a recovery group experience. The scientific critiques generally focused on these latter cases, where hypnosis or other social influences were thought to account for the emergence of memories of abuse.

Just as the recovered memory campaign erupted on the cultural stage with fierce intensity, so, too, did the crisis drop precipitously from public view. If there was repression and recovery of memory about childhood sexual abuse operating on a social level, the process of repression reasserted itself as the recovered memory debate receded from public consciousness.

Memory Matters represents an effort on the part of contributing scholars to resist such forces of social repression – and to hold onto the important lessons of this contentious era that divided families and communities. We are in no way nostalgic for the era prior to the feminist movement of the 1970s, when cultural silence around child sexual abuse was pervasive, nor for a time when incest was thought to be a problem primarily associated with working class and poor families. The mass mobilization of women during this period presented a fundamental challenge to the social order and to the terms under which women negotiated their fates under patriarchy. But we do lament the hardline position that fused feminism with literalist views of memory, and a feminist politics based on rallying around the utterances of women, without regard to the source of those utterances. The literalist position on memory stripped women's recollections of complexity and reduced exploratory space for understanding why sexual abuse emerged as the dominant story of childhood distress for many women in the late twentieth century. In recovering terrain for exploring the social symbolic loadings of recovered scenes of sexual abuse, we take the view that the debate itself was symptomatic of broader crises in the Western world over sexuality, gender, and authority – crises that will be taken up throughout this volume.

Contributors to *Memory Matters* provide frameworks for looking back on the memory wars, aided by the vantage point of historical distance. In our effort to understand what was at stake for various participants in the recovered memory debate, we rework emotionally charged accounts of the past. Although some critics of recovered memory characterize the climate of the debate as one of social hysteria (e.g. Loftus & Ketcham, 1994; Showalter,

1997), this 'diagnosis' of the irrationality that prevailed may readily obscure key issues. The concept of social hysteria may be descriptive of the emotionally charged tenor of embattled participants, and how group anxieties may overtake capacities to reason. But inevitably there are historical and cultural variations in the available social space for thoughtful discussion on charged social topics.

Contributors here share an interest in how power dynamics shape the versions of the past that survive and are transmitted. Narrative forms of remembering, whether through stories of sacrifice, heroic tales of courageous deeds, or testimonials of traumatic suffering, bind each generation to the next. While stories vary in content and form, all human cultures create them as a means of binding individuals to the social order, both emotionally and cognitively. Periods of social change and transformation always involve contests over how the past is preserved and the moral lessons to be drawn from the dramas that shape individual and collective life.

Women's recovered memories of child sexual abuse called into question the sanctity of culturally valued institutions, such as the church and family, in that many of the perpetrators were respected members of institutions that claimed to protect women. Testimonials based on recovered memories also precipitated longstanding tensions between disciplines guided by different procedural approaches to evaluating truth claims. The courts and the broader legal arena, for example, are based on the premise of a juridical truth – the extent to which available physical or other material evidence supports specific claims. Although motives and states of mind enter into legal reasoning, the primary aim is to establish whether available facts support assertions concerning alleged events.

Feminist scholars have identified how patriarchal representations of femininity shape legal judgements of women – as passive, suggestible and unreliable as witnesses – and how these stereotypes contribute to the extremely low rate of abuse convictions among accused male sex offenders (Smart, 1992). Yet this critical point side-steps the many uncertainties that arise when legitimate arguments are made concerning the capacities of witnesses, such as cases involving retraction (where a person changes their mind about a claim), or cases where the capacities of the testifier are limited or impaired in some way, or cases involving children's testimonies in courts.

Feminism and psychotherapeutic culture

The feminist movement of the 1970s subverted the dominant cultural romance that cast women as dependents and men as benevolent protectors. Refusing the seductive fairy tales of childhood, where the princess secures her fate by finding the right prince, feminists insisted on more truthful accounts of female experiences in the patriarchal family. Rather than cautionary tales of sexual threats lurking in dark alleys, a new genre of riveting stories centred on the dangers to girls under the covers of their own beds.

It is not surprising that many feminists aligned themselves with the recovered memory movement in that women have themselves been hidden behind a veil of silence in patriarchal societies. Sigmund Freud brought childhood sexuality into public consciousness, introducing as well through his early clinical work links between forgotten sexual events in childhood and neurotic symptoms in adulthood, particularly symptoms associated with hysteria. Freud later abandoned his early 'seduction theory' that traced hysteria in women to early sexual violations, moving to the position that sexual repression played a larger role in adult neurosis than did sexual abuse (see Masson, 1990; Herman, 2001).

Although he has been critiqued by feminists for abandoning the seduction theory of hysteria, Freud did shift to a more complex view of the relationship between anxiety, prohibitions and early sexual experience (see Haaken, 1998). Further, Freud placed gender and sexuality at the centre of a theory of development that emphasized the dynamic complexity of subjective experience. In patriarchal societies, girls confront different obstacles than do boys in becoming aware of and making use of active desires. Normative heterosexuality also positions girls and women as passive receptors for male desire – a position that contributes to the sexual victimization of women, but also to female discomfort with genital sexuality in general (Benjamin, 1988; Rose, 1986).

Much of the work of therapy centres on reworking memory, and on achieving new insights into past events. Clinical listening involves attending to the recurring motifs and subtexts of memory and to the emotional investments attached to particular childhood experiences. For psychodynamic therapists, particularly, stories about various protagonists in childhood are, in part, stories about the self. Objects in the schemata of memory may emerge as symbolic markers of zones of conflict, or they may concretize more elusive aspects of mind. The therapeutic process of understanding how the patient invokes the past – how a scene from memory may acquire a range of meanings over time – runs counter to forensic reasoning. Because the therapeutic process involves moving beyond the literal content of memory to identify underlying motifs, this process can be mystifying.

The therapeutic structuring of stories about the past are shaped by the convergence of the individual life experience of the patient and the theoretical orientation of the clinician. But the narratives of the self that emerge in therapy also are shaped by the wider socio-cultural worlds that both the patient and therapist inhabit.

Memory matters across the social sciences

The problem of traumatic memories – those registers of past events that potentially impair human capacities – has been taken up across a range of disciplines, including anthropology (Antze and Lambek, 1996; Douglass and Vogler, 2003), feminist studies (Campbell, 2003; Champagne, 1996), sociology (Misztal, 2003), philosophy (Hacking, 1995; Margalit, 2002), and psychology (Conway, 1997; Haaken, 1998; MacMartin, 1999; Reavey and Warner, 2003). As psychologists and co-editors of this volume, we are concerned with how our own discipline intervened in the debate, and particularly with the dominance of scientific procedures that equate empirical inquiry with quantitative methods. Hypothesis-testing has typically involved behavioural observations under conditions not conducive to the therapeutic conditions of many of the recovered memory accounts. Further, psychologists trained in this experimental tradition tend to evaluate the credibility of a perception or belief by seeking its direct correspondence to an external phenomenon or objectifiable reality.

While differing in key areas, many psychoanalytic, feminist and social constructionist psychologists share a critique of this over-objectifying approach to a science of mind. These psychologists insist that memory and other aspects of mental life are fluid and dynamic. Further, the 'truth' of a memory is continually open to negotiation, questioning and reconstruction, depending on the context of its use (Haaken, 1998; Conway, 1997; Campbell, 2003; Reavey and Brown, 2006).

There are important areas of widening agreement, however, among researchers and clinicians concerning memory processes. First, there is a shift from memory as a faculty of mind that produces discrete imprints of past events to a concern with remembering as a socially structured human activity. Contemporary practitioners and researchers are more apt to emphasize the social contexts that shape the construction of memories. Personal recollections may be co-constructed and undergo elaboration as they are transmitted through a social field of experience. Second, there is widening recognition that representations of the past are open to an array of interpretations. Power dynamics – on interpersonal and societal levels – do shape the stories that come to constitute personal identity. Contemporary dilemmas also shape the areas of the past that are remembered and the social uses of memories. As a result, the accuracy of recollections may be less crucial than are the social contexts in which such recollections circulate. Third, there is broad awareness in the field of memory studies of the ethical aspects of both remembering and forgetting, from the call to bystanders to 'bear witness' to traumatic suffering to testimonials and memorials that preserve accounts of past suffering and address questions of responsibility, accountability, and demands for reparation.

In this volume, we bring qualitative research on memory – and specifically, on recollections of sexual abuse – into our analysis of lingering issues in the recovered memory debate. We also extend the boundaries of psychology to include interdisciplinary perspectives on memory, and foreground social psychology as a key site for bridging disciplines that take up the *collective* or *social* aspects of representations of the past. Even as there are areas of agreement among contributors concerning the fluid boundaries between 'true' and 'false' memories, *Memory Matters* takes up the knotty questions that remain over how to go about assessing degrees of truth or falsehood, as well as how to assign responsibility for injurious experiences in the past.

Organization of the volume

Although the era of 'post-conflict' in the recovered memory debate allows for the *co-existence* of true and false memories, this volume makes visible the ethical, social, and cultural issues that remain. The contributors address how memories of abuse are received and scrutinized in a range of practice-based and interpersonal settings – from therapy, the media, legal settings, and everyday life – and explain how understandings of memory operate within these diverse arenas of practice. The sources of data are primarily qualitative, rather than quantitative. Contributors combine empirical qualitative data, gathered through interviews, case histories, focus groups and video recordings, published media, legal, autobiographical material, and clinical case studies. They also work in disciplines across the social sciences and humanities, including critical social psychology, literary theory, psychoanalysis, media studies, social work, sociology, and psychology, and draw upon a wide range of theories to inform their interpretations of data.

While they offer a diversity of perspectives, the contributors share a focus on how notions of truth or accuracy of memory are produced in particular locales. They also share traditions of critical inquiry that make use of multiple perspectives on a given social phenomenon. This attentiveness to multiple perspectives on the past and contexts for remembering need not imply relativism, nor does it suggest a disregard for factual claims. Our aim here, rather, is to unpack the range of social investments in versions of the past and to make clearer where and when factual claims do come into play.

Memory Matters is organized into two sections. The first section returns to the more riveting scenes of the recovered memory controversy, revisiting troubling questions that linger far after the debate subsided. The section retraces key discursive moves in the claims and counter-claims that circulated in North America and Europe, from legal settings, psychotherapy, self-help groups to popular culture. The contributors work closely with the stories that took centre stage and offer new readings of those stories. The second section of the book takes a step back from the heat of the debate and attends to cultural influences beyond the immediate heat of the controversy. In working with the broader social context that set many of the claims and counter-claims in motion, contributors suggest that memories of sexual abuse in childhood may be deployed for a wide range of reasons – for rememberers and translators of memories alike – and register broader cultural forces shaping everyday thinking about links between present and past.

Section 1. Looking back on the recovered memory debate: claims and counter-claims

A contentious area of the recovered memory debate concerns cases of retraction, where individuals reversed positions and came to the conclusion that previously 'recovered' memories of sexual abuse were false. In the recovered memory/false memory controversy, 'retractors' gained considerable prominence, even as they stirred palpable uneasiness on both sides. Malcolm Ashmore and Steven Brown introduce Section 1 of the book with a discursive analysis of an interview with the mother of a retractor and also of a video recording produced on behalf of the False Memory Syndrome Foundation (FMSF) featuring a retractor and members of her family. Retractors' stories captured media interest late in the memory debate, as some retractors emerged as the 'prodigal daughters' of the False Memory Syndrome Foundation. The principal deployment of such star retractors appears to be epistemic: they embody a convincing refutation of the reality of repressed memory and of the legitimacy of therapeutic techniques designed to elicit such memories. The sources of the credibility of retractors' accounts include personal experience and the power of conversion. Ashmore and Brown suggest, however, that the credibility of retractors confronts various challenges in securing social legitimacy. In comparing survivors' and retractors' accounts of conflicting memory reports and attending to their differing logical strategies, the authors show how changing one's mind may either weaken or strengthen the case for credibility.

In Chapter 3, James Ost and Karl Nunkoosing turn to the vexing problem of retraction of therapeutically recovered memories of abuse by discussing the case of Nicola, a woman who remembered sexual abuse with her father after a period of severe mental illness and later came to believe this to be a false memory. Drawing on the theory of social remembering rooted in the work of Frederic Charles Bartlett, the authors present a range of contexts for understanding the shifting versions of Nicola's memory. The authors present a discursive analysis of interviews with Nicola to illustrate how she attempts to make sense of a range of competing claims to truth, both in the context of psychiatric treatment and in periods of her recovery where she seeks reconciliation with her parents. Ost and Nunkoosing enlist Bartlett's social theory of remembering to foreground key motivational dynamics associated with remembering, and particularly how making sense of the *past* is rooted in the *present*. This approach suggests that retractors themselves must continually rethink their memories within a contemporary context. The authors attempt to move beyond the truth or falsehood of retractors' reports to describe how these fluctuating accounts register a more general tendency in human processes of remembering.

Johanna Motzkau examines in Chapter 4 the status of children's testimony – another area of troubling uncertainty – and shows how professionals who assessed children's memories in court cases have managed questions over their capacities to testify. As a result of increased awareness of child sexual abuse in the late twentieth century, children were increasingly admitted to court as witnesses, while wariness persisted over the reliability of their memories and their ability to provide accurate testimony in legal proceedings. Motzkau examines the complex dilemmas surrounding the credibility of children's memories as they emerge at the intersection of legal and psychological discourses in England and Wales. Drawing on interviews conducted with police officers, prosecutors, lawyers, judges, and psychological experts in these two countries, Motzkau traces the personal and political rationales, instruments, and practices employed to negotiate the accuracy and credibility of children's legal testimonies concerning sexual abuse. Her analysis suggests how dilemmas surrounding child testimony in courts register broader social anxieties concerning sexuality, the protection of children, and memory credibility. For children to qualify as dependents who require protection from the state, their testimony must meet conventional criteria as virtuous victims. This child protection discourse forecloses, Motzkau concludes, possibilities for understanding the multiple social meanings and uses of child witnesses in the courtroom.

The media represents yet another contested site for competing claims over dramatic revelations of childhood sexual abuse. From tabloids and broadsheets to fictional and non-fictional television programmes and films, the media produced countless reports and programmes that shaped public perceptions and individual experiences of memory and child sexual abuse. In Chapter 5, Jenny Kitzinger introduces a range of media representations of sexual abuse in Britain and the United States during the 1980s and 1990s, when the topic migrated from obscurity to widespread public recognition. She examines how women in survivor groups and other social settings enlisted media representations in naming past experiences as sexual abuse. Her study centres on understanding how the media creates as well as reflects processes of social change. Through an analysis of interviews with women survivors of sexual abuse, she explores how individuals used media knowledge to interpret their memories and to formulate agentic versions of selfhood. Kitzinger notes, however, that the survivor literature's recurring claims of authenticity run the risk of reducing the complexity of memory in its implicit emphasis on straightforward connections between the past and present.

Jo Woodiwiss concludes this section with her analysis of how women survivors of child sexual abuse make use of the self-help recovery literature in complex and conflictual ways. Chapter 6 begins with claims that child sexual abuse inevitably results in long-term psychological damage or trauma, and that healing centres on recovering memory of the abuse, often in the form of 'body memories.' For many women who enter adulthood with no memory of early sexual abuse, this process of recovery relies on accessing non-cognitive memories, such as imagistic memory, body memory, feeling memory, and acting-out memory. Woodiwiss explores the role of these alternative memories for women who came to believe that they were sexually abused in childhood, and how these alternative memories shaped the narratives or life stories they came to tell. She explains how and why some women endorse this explanation for their symptoms, while others came to reject memories that they once believed to be true. Woodiwiss locates recollections of childhood sexual abuse in the context of an increasingly pervasive therapeutic culture, where ideas about healing, recovery, the inner child, and recovered memories inform many aspects of everyday life.

Section 2. Widening the lens: cultural contexts for remembering child sexual abuse

Paula Reavey begins Section 2 by exploring frameworks for remembering, attending to how cultural contexts, specifically everyday spatial locales, register as sites for creative uses of the past. Drawing on her analysis of interviews of women survivors, she attempts to go beyond the relational motifs that dominate the recovered memory literature to focus on the broader imagistic field of these motifs. Reavey offers a corrective to the tendency in the clinical literature, particularly, to focus on traumatic events rather than on the everyday material contexts of memory that structure forms of recall. These material spaces, she argues, contribute to the organization of memory, and in particular as it relates to a personal sense of agency. This focus on how women survivors make use of the material contexts of memory invites richly textured and complex readings of abuse stories, including how feelings of agency and victimization often co-mingle. Attending to how women make use of physical spaces in their memory reports, Reavey contends, creates an opportunity for women to discuss memories that do not conform to conventional notions of (feminine) victimhood.

In Chapter 8 Kathryn Robson continues this exploration of the cultural terrain by analysing two quite different autobiographical accounts widely cited in the recovered memory literature: Sylvia Fraser's *My Father's House* and Janice Williamson's *Crybaby!* Robson offers readings of the two memoirs that move beyond the conventions of the memoir as confessional, with its trope of revealing a disturbing and pathogenic secret. Rather, testifying to child sexual abuse means renegotiating (invoking and also challenging) the very notion of a singular 'truth' about the past. Robson also unpacks these autobiographical texts to show how the absolute demands of the true/false memory debate suture over areas of genuine uncertainty – between narrative and bodily memory, between the present and the past, and between private and public testimonials. Her readings of *My Father's House* and *Crybaby!* locate key sites where links between the past (childhood abuse) and the present (the self-positioning of the narrator as she remembers and writes) take gendered and sexualized forms.

Rachel Fyson and John Cromby in Chapter 9 take up the neglected topic of recollections of sexual abuse among persons with intellectual disabilities and the implications of their own research in this area for working in forensic, therapeutic, and welfare service fields. The authors begin with data on rates of child sexual abuse in learning disability communities and key factors that contribute to this association, including issues of social status and power. In exploring power dynamics related to disability, including how definitions of disability circulate culturally and politically, Fyson and Cromby show how sexually abused individuals with disabilities are often silenced. In the absence of supports for recollecting abuse, expressions of anger that are commonly recognized as sequelae to abuse are often interpreted as symptoms of their disabilities. Further, such behaviours come to be managed through the lens of their disability rather than explored as possible indicators of a history of abuse. Fyson and Cromby also explain how institutional dynamics blunt opportunities for people with disabilities to make sense of their memories or to disclose and work through recollections of abuse.

Widening the lens on childhood memory also invites revisiting ethical dilemmas associated with reports of childhood sexual abuse of uncertain social origins or contested validity. In Chapter 10 Sue Campbell takes up the ethical challenges that remain in the wake of the recovered memory debate. She begins with the argument that any concept of 'truth' is bound up in social relationships and cultural frameworks, but contends that a concretely grounded conception of truth remains vital to preserving cultural space for the credibility of sexual abuse survivors and their sense of personal identity. The empirical basis of memory has special relevance for oppressed groups, she argues, whose recollections are more often scrutinized or discredited. Campbell's central argument is that we need to attend to how the procedures of science and the professions narrow conceptions of truth, and how the literal aspects of memory *do* matter, without reducing memory to forensic accuracy.

In Chapter 11, Erica Burman draws on psychoanalytic social theory to discuss therapeutic constructions of the past and professional practices in the UK in response to the recovered memory controversy. The public scrutiny of memory-making in therapy, Burman suggests, is overdetermined by historical anxieties over the role of professional authority in late capitalism. In response to various assaults on therapeutic expertise, clinical trainees become overly anxious and professional organizations have adopted procedures that translate this anxiety into obsessive guidelines, often counter to what good psychotherapy requires. Burman argues that the movement to tighten professional guidelines fails in its aim of reducing the indeterminacies surrounding therapeutic exploration of memory. Burman also reorients this scrutiny toward attending more carefully to assumptions underlying how psychological knowledge about the past is produced. Drawing on recent (including feminist) analyses of memory as a social practice, Burman concludes that self-reflection and multiple perspectives on the past are what matter most to feminist-informed clinical practices.

In the final chapter, Janice Haaken seeks a rapprochement between recovered memory adherents and their critics by offering a culturally informed approach to understanding therapeutic exploration of sexual scenes from childhood. Enlisting feminist theory as a critical lens for a psychoanalytic reading of memory, she shows how the cultural materials available to both therapist and client shape the versions of the past recovered. As the client recounts his or her personal history, particular events also emerge as prototypical of later conflicts. Haaken explains how scenes of child sexual abuse, and particularly father/daughter incest, acquired social symbolic loadings in the 1980s and 1990s, particularly in the context of shifting gender roles, as they allowed women to give voice to less readily articulated female grievances. Haaken introduces the concept of *transformative remembering* to illustrate the creative side of therapeutic exploration of the past and how the organization of the self and the organization of memory are intertwined. Her focus on *remembering* rather than *memory* – on the verb rather than the noun – foregrounds the search for representations in childhood that support emerging capacities in female development, including resistances to patriarchal control. Haaken also applies the concept of transformative remembering to a case from her clinical practice. Haaken concludes, much as do the other contributors to this section, that literal readings of memory inhibit exploration of the dynamics of remembering, and of the shifting uses of scenes from childhood over time, particularly as new scenes of struggle emerge on the psychological and social horizons to permit new forms of remembering.

References

Antze, P. and Lambeck, M. (eds) (1996) *Tense Past: Cultural Essays in Trauma and Memory*. New York: Routledge.
Benjamin, J. (1988) *The Bonds of Love: Psychoanalysis, Feminism, and the Problem of Domination*. New York: Pantheon Books.
Campbell, S. (2003) *Relational Remembering: Rethinking the Memory Wars*. Lanham, MD: Rowman and Littlefield.
Champagne, R. (1998) *The Politics of Survivorship: Incest, Women's Literature, and Feminist Theory*. New York: New York University Press.
Conway, M. A. (1997) (ed.) *Recovered Memories and False Memories*. Oxford: Oxford University Press.
Douglass, D. A. and Vogler, T. A. (2003) *Witness and Memory: The Discourse of Trauma*. London: Routledge.
Haaken, J. (1998) *Pillars of Salt: Gender, Memory, and the Perils of Looking Back*. London: Free Association Press.
Haaken, J. (2003) 'Traumatic revisions: remembering abuse and the politics of forgiveness', in P. Reavey and S. Warner (eds) *New Feminist Stories of Child Sexual Abuse: Sexual Scripts and Dangerous Dialogues*. London: Routledge.
Hacking, I. (1995) *Rewriting the Soul: Multiple Personality and the Sciences of Memory*. Princeton: Princeton University Press.
Herman, J. L. (2001) *Trauma and Recovery: From Domestic Abuse to Political Terror*. London: Rivers Oram Press/Pandora.
Loftus, E. F. and Ketcham, K. (1994) *The Myth of Repressed Memory*. New York: St Martin's Press.
MacMartin, C. (1999) 'Disclosure as discourse: theorizing children's reports of sexual abuse', *Theory and Psychology* 9(4): 503–32.
Margalit, A. (2002) *The Ethics of Memory*. Cambridge: Harvard University Press.
Masson, J. M. (1990) *Against Therapy*. London: Fontana.

Misztal, B. A. (2003) *Theories of Social Remembering*. Buckingham: Open University Press.

Reavey, P. and Brown, S.D. (2006) 'Transforming agency and action in the past, into the present time: adult memories and child sexual abuse', *Theory and Psychology* 16(2): 179–202.

Reavey, P. and Warner, S. (eds) (2003) *New Feminist Stories of Child Sexual Abuse: Sexual Scripts and Dangerous Dialogues*. London: Routledge.

Rose, J. (1986) *Sexuality in the Field of Vision*. London: Verso.

Showalter, E. (1997) *Hystories: Hysterical Epidemics and Modern Media*. New York: Columbia University Press.

Smart, C. (1992) 'The women of legal discourse', *Social and Legal Studies* 1(1): 29–44.

Further reading

Foucault, M. (1978) *The History of Sexuality: Volume One*. Middlesex: Penguin.

Gavey, N. (2005) *Just Sex? The Cultural Scaffolding of Rape*. London and New York: Routledge.

Haaken, J. (1999) 'Heretical texts: *The Courage to Heal* and the Incest Survivor Movement', in S. Lamb (ed.) *New Versions of Victims: Feminists Struggle with the Concept*. New York: New York University Press.

Huff, N. C. and Rudy, J. W. (2004) 'The amygdala modulates hippocampus-dependent context memory formation and stores cue-shock associations', *Behavioral Neuroscience* 118(1): 53–62.

Kitzinger, J. (2003) 'Creating discourses of "false memory": media coverage and production dynamics', in P. Reavey and S. Warner (eds) *New Feminist Stories of Child Sexual Abuse: Sexual Scripts and Dangerous Dialogues*. London: Routledge.

Loftus, E. F. (2002) 'Memory faults and fixes', *Issues in Science and Technology* 18(4): 41–50.

Loftus, E. F. (2003a) 'Make believe memories', *American Psychologist* 58(11): 867–73.

Loftus, E. F. (2003b) 'Our changeable memories: legal and practical implications', *Nature Reviews: Neuroscience* 4: 231–4.

Middleton, D. and Brown, S.D. (2005) *The Social Psychology of Experience: Studies in Remembering and Forgetting*. London: Sage.

Motzkau, J. F. (2007) 'Matters of suggestibility, memory and time: child witnesses in court and what really happened', *Forum: Qualitative Social Research* 8(1): Art 14. Online: http:www.qualitative-research.net/index.php/fqs/article/view/204.

Ofshe, R. and Watters, E. (1994) *Making Monsters: False Memories, Psychotherapy, and Sexual Hysteria*. Berkeley: University of California Press.

Ost, J. (2003). 'Essay review: seeking the middle ground in the "memory wars"', *British Journal of Psychology* 94: 125–39.

Reavey, P. (2003) 'When past meets present to produce a sexual "other": examining professional and everyday narratives of child sexual abuse', in P. Reavey and S. Warner (eds) *New Feminist Stories of Child Sexual Abuse: Sexual Scripts and Dangerous Dialogues*. London: Routledge.

Reavey, P. and Brown, S. D. (2009, in press) 'The human and non-human participants of memory: exploring the objects and spaces of memories of child sexual abuse in making sense of agency and intention', *Culture and Psychology*.

Wright, D. B., Ost, J. and French, C. C. (2006) 'Ten years after: what we know now that we didn't know then about recovered and false memories', *The Psychologist* 19: 352–5.

Section 1
Looking back on the recovered memory debate
Claims and counter-claims

2 On changing one's mind twice

The strange credibility of retracting recovered memories

Malcolm Ashmore and Steven D. Brown

Introduction

Memory is inseparable from moral judgement. In classical philosophy, remembrance is the drawing together of the past in the present for the purposes of evaluation and making choices. The Roman philosopher Cicero saw memory as integral to prudence – knowledge of good and bad and the differences that lie in between. She or he who speaks publicly of the past enters into a set of obligations about how to act in relation to the events and times they recount (see Yates, 1992; Margalit, 2002). For the past is rarely neutral. It comes with implications about present circumstances and future courses of action. These may appear in the form of continuities or breaks, succession or branching. A consideration of the past rarely indicates directly some future-to-come. It is better thought of as an interpretative puzzle with numerous solutions, all of which have differing consequences for the present.

If classical philosophers infuse recollection with moral judgement, they are less forthcoming on how the work of remembering actually leads to the act of judging. Aristotle, for example, describes how the past leaves very different 'marks' or 'traces' upon us, according to our temperament and our engagement with the business of living (see Krell, 1990). Remembering is then forced to seek external supports and techniques. It is an art, a skilfully developed practice, rather than a mere faculty, as Yates (1992) describes at length in relation to Renaissance thought. So whilst we may be confident in the general relationship between memory and moral judgement, classical philosophy does not deliver clarity on how memory may serve as a clear foundation for making choices, nor on the very nature of memory itself. As John Sutton (1998) observes, the conceptualisation of this aspect of memory is typically the least compelling aspect of a wide range of philosophical systems, from Descartes to Hume to Russell.

It is against this broad historical backdrop that Ian Hacking (1995) describes the emergence in the mid to late nineteenth century of a new nexus of experimental and clinical knowledge about memory. This new knowledge purported to offer an objective account of remembering which could reveal its internal laws and tendencies. Experimental psychologists such as Hermann Ebbinghaus (1885) claimed that they could tidy up the mass of 'unsuitable' metaphors which had previously been used to conceptualise memory through the application of laboratory methods which would be able to reveal the mechanics of memorisation and retention. The physiologist Paul Broca (1861) identified a neuroanatomical location for the faculty of language – the site of the 'memory for words' within the brain (see Matsuda, 1996). Psychiatrists such as Pierre Janet developed powerful accounts of memory pathologies – notably the 'fixed idea' – and corresponding techniques such as hypnosis which could assist in their investigation. The current that runs through all three of these scientific endeavours is the turning away from the idea of remembering as an artful practice (as it had been considered in the philosophical tradition) towards memory as a psychological and/or physiological capacity (as demonstrated in experimental tasks).

Ebbinghaus, Broca and Janet are exemplary practitioners of what Hacking refers to as the then emerging 'sciences of memory' (i.e. psychology, neuropathology and psychoanalysis). These sciences attempted to take charge of remembering as an epistemic concern. Their central concern was no longer the obligations that recollection places on the person, but rather the internal quality of the recollection itself, the extent to which it could be taken as a veridical report of some past event. Understood in this way, remembering is taken to be the exercise of a neuropsychological faculty which operates according to a set of regularities or psychological 'laws'. Accuracy rather than interpretation in relation to the recollected event becomes the principal criterion. However, Hacking notes that the transformation of memory into a scientific object did not entirely erase questions of moral agency. There is a shift away from the *activity* of recollection and towards the *subject* who recalls. What is questioned is no longer the interpretive work, the 'art' of remembering, but whether this subject makes competent use of their memorial faculties. Moral agency is transformed from a public act into a private psychological mechanism.

The consequences of this shift have been routinely debated in the psychological literature throughout the past century. In a classic work, Bartlett (1932) proposed that notions of accuracy were very rarely the sole stakes in everyday instances of remembering (see Middleton and Brown, 2005; Ost and Nunkoosing, Chapter 3 this volume). More recently, the call for an 'ecological' approach to memory (cf. Winograd and Neisser, 1988) advocates the study of the 'social functions' in which various aspects of remembering are embedded. However, the most significant challenge to the consensual character of the 'sciences of memory' has come not from within academic psychology or philosophy, but from a complex set of intense social debates around female adult survivors of child sexual abuse and 'recovered memory' that took place in the final decades of the twentieth century. These debates are sometimes, albeit controversially, referred to as the 'memory wars' (see Schacter, 1996; Haaken, 1998; Campbell, 2003). At issue here is the reality of what is called recovered memory (RM) by one of the warring parties, and false memory syndrome (FMS) by the other. On the RM side (dominant from the mid 1980s to the mid 1990s) the claim is that the trauma of sexual abuse in childhood can result in psychologically traumatic repressed (or dissociated) memories. In therapy these old memories are recovered through techniques such as hypnotic age regression, guided imagery, and incest survivor-group therapy. Recovered memories have been theorised as more reliable than ordinary memories: having been buried and inaccessible, they remain indelible markers of the original event (van der Kolk, 1995). In addition, the fact that they are memories of traumatic events is said to change their character, 'traumatic memory' not obeying the rules of the ordinary variety (Terr, 1994). The opposing view, promoted since the early 1990s most effectively by an American organisation called the False Memory Syndrome Foundation (FMSF), is that memories recovered in such a way are probably false, and the result of implanted suggestions from therapists, at a time when their clients are psychologically fragile, and vulnerable to suggestion. The argument that such memories are not reliable draws on two sources: a general scepticism about the existence of repression or dissociation as mechanisms of forgetting traumatic events (Holmes, 1990); and studies in experimental psychology that argue that 'memories' of fictional events can be implanted and then falsely remembered (Loftus and Pickrell, 1995).

Setting the debates up in this way can result in fundamental issues being obscured. Janice Haaken (1998) argues that the question of recovered memory needs to be set in the context provided by the relative successes of the women's and children's rights movements in raising domestic and sexual violence as social issues in the US and Western Europe from the 1950s onwards. For Haaken, what matters about recovered memory is not solely whether the events recounted are literally 'true' or not, but rather the ways in which women are able to articulate multiple and at times ambiguous meanings in relation to sexuality, embodiment and emotional distress – 'in a sense, the memory controversy is more about emotion, distress and bodily arousal than it is about memory per se' (Haaken, 1998: 15). Similarly, Sue Campbell (2003) takes issue with the phrase 'memory wars' since it suggests a clearly mapped out set of positions on the 'reality' or 'falsehood' of women's recollections of prior childhood sexual abuse. This framing of the controversy fosters an atmosphere of pervasive suspicion of women's testimony that distracts from proper discussion of abuse and the complex social conditions that surround it. Campbell proposes that what is required is 'accounts of the social resources needed for successful remembering, attention to the vulnerability of specific groups of rememberers, and specific, detailed analyses of how individual and group memories are undermined and pathologized' (Campbell, 2003: 8). Although Haaken and Campbell adopt very different strategies and positions in their analyses of the recovered memory debates, both bring into focus the ways in which women's recollections can be rendered meaningful and credible against the backdrop of scientific and cultural wrangling over the 'subject' of memory (i.e. determining the psychological attributes that accompany accurate and veridical recollection).

In a series of studies, we also have explored this link between testimony and contesting accounts of what counts as 'good' recollection in the 'memory wars' (Ashmore et al., 2004, 2005; Ashmore and Brown, under submission). Our analysis has been concerned with the sets of claims about the nature of memory which are made by rival parties. Like Haaken and Campbell, we have been concerned to avoid taking sides in the debates concerning questions of reality and falsehood. Instead, we have attempted to provide detailed discursive analyses of the rhetorical procedures used in specific settings for building up or undermining the testimony of rememberers. For example, we have examined how competing accounts of the trial of a controversial therapist differed in the assumptions they made about the nature of a past event and what could be reliably heard on an audio tape recording of a therapy session played in court (see Ashmore et al., 2004). The pro-FMSF account was that the tapes clearly demonstrated the therapist manipulating and steering the testimony of a client during therapy. Under this description, the tape was direct confirmation of the FMSF position that recovered memory is an artefact of suggestions made to vulnerable clients by therapists. However, the anti-FMSF reporting emphasised instead the audible and severe emotional distress of the client and the therapeutic working-through needed to manage psychic pain. Our analysis develops the idea that whilst these accounts are ostensibly completely opposed, they draw on a similar notion of the past as events that may be captured in an audio tape recording. This capturing renders the past as to some degree transparent and potentially interpretable by a listener who is sufficiently well versed at listening to such materials; that is, someone who possesses the competence we dub 'professional hearing'. In other words while both sides disagree virulently about what is happening in this particular therapist's consultations, they are united in their commitment that it is possible, on the basis of a hearing of such audio tapes, to establish a veridical account of what happened; both sides are 'tape fetishists'.

Our approach has then been to avoid reifying the positions in the 'memory wars', and to explore the interrelationships between particular claims about memory and the settings in which they are made (e.g. courts of law, therapy sessions, academic articles). We are particularly interested in the rhetorical organisation and pragmatic dimensions of these claims. We consider that matters relating to the accuracy or truthfulness of particular recollections, their experiential validity, their capacity for implantation and distortion, indeed their status *as* memories, depend on a range of social, discursive procedures. These procedures are rooted in the commonsense ways in which people make and dispute factual claims, construct arguments, handle contradiction and disagreement, build convincing narratives, and discount alternative accounts. Our analytical approach avoids aligning with or criticising the accounts, but rather, analyses them *as accounts*, in terms of how they work rhetorically, as factual narrative, as discourse. The task is to examine through a detailed study of discourse practices how the matters at issue are defined and managed by the participants themselves.

A risk entailed by such an approach is that it can be taken to be suggesting that the credibility of a specific account depends purely on the rhetorical skill of the speaker. This is most certainly not the case. We take it as a given that the testimony of women, in particular women who speak of sexual violence, and especially women who speak of childhood sexual abuse, is subject to significant levels of scrutiny and interrogation. Part of the problem here is that memories of abuse are threaded into past and ongoing relationships. To speak of abuse is to open these significant relationships up for moral questioning, including the many ambiguities women may feel about their involvement in the relationships and the implications this has for their current sense of agency (see Reavey, 2003; Reavey and Brown, 2006). The models of remembering inherited from the 'sciences of memory' which are culturally available for understanding the recovery of memory are typically mute about such moral dilemmas. They seek to reduce relationships to the status of 'stimuli' or the 'context' through which psychological operations are activated. When relationships are taken to be external to the proper business of remembering, credibility in recollection is built up when the speaker can demonstrate that their memories do not depend upon the presence or contribution of others. The alternative – to see remembering as constituted in and through relationships (see Haaken, 1998; Campbell, 2003; Middleton and Brown, 2005; Reavey and Brown, 2006) – has nothing like the same level of cultural prominence, and certainly is not a strong part of the professional doxa around recovered memory.

We have attempted in our work to excavate the effects of a non-relational approach to memory when it passes for cultural commonsense. For example, the 'Lost in the Mall' study, undertaken and publicised by Elizabeth Loftus, is often taken as a powerful illustration of suggestibility and the ease of production of false memory (see Loftus and Ketcham, 1994: 93–6). In brief, this is an experimental procedure which involves participants who know one another (originally a pair of brothers). One covertly served as a research confederate and set about persuading the other, on the instructions of the researcher, that he has a childhood memory of getting lost in a shopping mall ('Do you remember that time when you got lost in that shopping mall?'). If the confederate persuades the other participant to agree to or to elaborate this memory then this is taken as evidence of the 'implantation' of a 'false memory' (see Loftus and Pickrell, 1995). Loftus suggests that whilst this phenomenon can be experimentally confirmed in laboratory settings, it can also be performed in classroom exercises or even at parties (Loftus and Ketcham, 1994: 94). We argue that with this joint claim for scientific replicability and commonsense confirmability, Loftus achieves a rhetorical separation of the researcher from the research which powerfully adds to the credibility of 'false memory' (Ashmore *et al.*, 2005). By contrast, advocates of recovered memory are not able to accomplish this separation, since by their very nature the storied accounts of the past which emerge in therapy necessarily involve the therapist in the telling. Recovered memories have a different relationship to both setting and the recipient of the account, with the upshot that therapists cannot achieve the rhetorical performance of neutrality.

In this chapter our focus is on one particular kind of testimony – 'retraction'. This is a form of testimony provided by persons who have previously identified as 'survivors' of repressed sexual abuse. They are also typically ex-accusers who now assert the falsity of their previous knowledge that they were victims of child sexual abuse (sometimes to the extent of suing their ex-therapists) along with the truth of their current realisation that they are victims of false memory syndrome. In the US, some retractors have become minor celebrities with published articles, websites, video and audio tapes to their name.[1] They have been courted by the FMSF and used by this most successful of the anti-recovered memory organisations as 'embodied evidence' for its version of events. As Ost and Nunkoosing (this volume) astutely note, this claim involves taking retraction at face value as clear evidence of prior 'remembering gone wrong'. However, retraction can also be seen as evidence of further inconsistency on the part of the rememberer. If they have changed their minds once about past events, then changing one's mind a second time might be taken to be evidence of a general ambiguity about what is being recalled.

In line with our previous analyses, we are not addressing here questions of the reality or otherwise of retraction, but instead showing how accounts of retraction, provided by both 'retractors' themselves and their families, are rhetorically organised.[2] Our focus will be on how retraction is accomplished as a social activity. We identify the discursive procedures and some of the social resources utilised in constructing retraction accounts. In particular we concentrate on how dilemmas around credibility are managed. We then show how retraction accounts function as moral accounts – how they attend to the obligations and implications of ongoing relationships. We conclude with some thoughts on the lessons retraction might provide for a social approach to remembering.

Retraction discourse

The materials that we have used in our studies consist of publicly available audio and video recordings and transcripts of interviews, court trials, therapy sessions and public lectures along with interviews we have personally conducted. The interviews include accounts provided by retractors themselves and by their families. Some of this material is 'naturalistic data' (cf. Speer, 2002; Potter, 2002), which enables the analysis of 'real-time' interactions, where participants are drawing upon a range of discursive resources to jointly construct meaning. Other materials – such as the interviews published in Pendergrast (1996), the first-person accounts in Goldstein and Farmer (1993) and the 'retractors' stories' regularly featured in the *FMS Foundation Newsletter* (1994–2006) – are more opaque, insofar as they are already edited and presented with reference to the established position of the texts within which they occur.

In this analysis we draw upon a transcript of a video recording made by and on behalf of the FMSF featuring retractor Beth Rutherford and members of her family and from an interview with the mother of a UK retractor. Our analysis is guided by principles of Discursive and Conversation Analysis (see Edwards, 1997; Potter, 1996; Wooffitt, 2005). We are specifically interested in analysing the rhetoric involved in the production and support of retraction accounts. This includes, crucially, the various ways of accounting for the inconsistency between pre- and post-retraction stories and beliefs. How is the gap reduced, or otherwise accounted for, between what you said or believed *then*, and what you say or believe *now*?

In Table 2.1 we have listed six different discursive procedures which we have identified in the accounts of retraction we have studied. We have organised these in terms of two overall 'storylines', prefaced with letters. These encompass the two main ways of formulating the difference between past and present beliefs. The 'plots' then correspond to six ways in which changing one's mind is rationalised (prefaced with numbers). In our data, storyline A is always accompanied with plots drawn from 1 to 3 (i.e. A1–A3). However, storyline B can additionally be rationalised by plots 4–6 (i.e. B1–B6). The last column lists a set of 'devices' associated with each plot. Although we used technical terms in Table 2.1, each device is actually a recognisable piece of mundane reasoning (Pollner, 1987), a small cultural resource which is used to organise the retraction account.

We start then with perhaps the most basic 'choice' to be made in telling retraction stories: how to articulate the size and quality of the gap between 'then' and 'now'. Given that retractors, almost by definition, articulate their

Table 2.1 Discursive procedures in retraction stories

Storylines	Plots	Devices
(A) Partial prior involvement	1– Prior belief as having been situationally driven	Actor-observer effect
	2– Therapy as productive of erroneous prior beliefs	Suggestibility
	3– Current understanding having been actually true all along	Ontological gerrymandering
(B) Thorough and total prior involvement	4– Managing prior stakes of prior involvement	Stake inoculation
	5– Complete denunciation of involvement	Conversion stories
	6– Retraction as necessity for survival	Therapy as abuse

unproblematic commitment to 'now', we found only two overall storylines at this level:

- **A** – treating one's involvement in the pre-retraction, 'survivor,' phase as partial in some way: as articulated inconsistently or as less than wholeheartedly held. This has the rhetorical virtue of reducing the accountable gap between prior claims and current ones. However, it does entail the implication of a general weakness of conviction or commitment which can impact on the credibility of current claims.
- **B** – treating one's involvement in the pre-retraction, 'survivor,' phase as thorough and total. This avoids the rhetorical problem for variant A, that a reduced gap implies you were never a proper claimant or victim in the first place, and so cannot *now* be a proper, bona fide retractor.

A range of supporting plots can be used to elaborate storyline A, including:

- **A1** – accounting for the prior belief as situationally driven, or in-situation, rather than in-person (true of me) or in-fact (true of the world). When therapy is the situation in question, account A1 can be strongly linked to A2. The social phenomenon of accounting for one's own actions as situationally driven, while finding the actions of others causally attributable to some personal characteristic or motivation, is traditionally known as the 'actor-observer error' by social psychologists (Jones and Nisbett, 1971).
- **A2** – describing recovered memory therapy as systematically productive of error, whether through accident ('my therapist was incompetent') or design ('my therapist was evil'). Describing therapy as an error-producing, fantasy-producing process or procedure, of which the current retractor was previously an unwitting victim or dupe, is a strong way of building the credibility of retraction, and is perhaps the most consistent feature of the retractor stories we have examined. It is also useful in accounting for specific inconsistencies between the pre- and post-retraction stories. This appeals to the longstanding cultural concern with 'suggestibility' which has surrounded psychological therapies and counselling in the West for well over two hundred years (see Chertok and Stengers, 1992; Motzkau, 2006).
- **A3** – producing one's current understanding as having been true all along, rather than being fashioned here and now. This is the process of rewriting history which follows consequential changes in cultural or personal cognition; such as a Kuhnian scientific revolution, the discovery of an art forgery, or the cases of retraction we are looking at here. Woolgar and Pawluch (1985) coined the phrase 'ontological gerrymandering' to describe this phenomenon of revising history to fit with current understandings. We might also see links here to the Freudian notion of 'kettle

logic' where inconsistency is created by its very denial ('I never took your kettle in the first place').

Storyline B produces greater rhetorical complexity than does storyline A. This does not mean it affords 'better' or more convincing accounts of retraction. It does, however, set up a stronger contrast between prior involvement and current understanding. As a consequence there is more discursive 'work' to be done to rationalise retraction. All three kinds of plot, as above (relabelled B1, B2, B3) can be and are used by both retractors and their families in accounting for the change of mind. In addition, we have noted the following plots being used for elaboration:

- **B4** – using strategies of stake management and 'stake inoculation' (see Potter, 1996). This term covers the range of ways in which potential accusations of having an 'interest' or 'something at stake' in accounting for one's actions in a particular way are anticipated within the account itself. For example, a retraction account is vulnerable to the potential accusation that it is an expectable phenomenon explicable through family and other social pressures, as is stated regularly by proponents of recovered memory (e.g. Herman and Harvey, 1993). A strategy to ward off this potential accusation is to emphasise that rather than retraction being the soft option, you were afraid of retracting and had a lot to lose by doing it; you risked losing the support of the victims' group before being back with the family, which was not guaranteed to happen; you were afraid of looking crazy or inconsistent; you delayed retracting long after realising you had been mistaken.
- **B5** – the telling of conversion stories, which can be mundane (**B5a**) or miraculous (**B5b**). Conversion implies that commitment to previous belief in recovered memory be seen as complete rather than partial. The shift to the new set of beliefs (i.e. retraction) must be equally complete and total. The focus of this plot is on a pivotal moment where previous beliefs are challenged to such an extent that complete reversal in perspective becomes the only rational way forward.
- **B6** – treating retraction as a necessity; for example, as the only means of saving one's life. This links with and intensifies the negative descriptions of recovered memory therapy found in account B2 to the point where the effect of the therapeutic regime is actually life-threatening. So here retraction is portrayed as the only means of escape from an intolerable situation. This draws upon a longstanding cultural suspicion of therapies that appear to have worse effects than the symptoms they purport to treat. In the case of recovered memories, this constructs therapy as in itself constituting a form of abuse.

In the materials we have reviewed we have identified instances which seem to us to exemplify each of these strategies (A1 to A3 and B1 to B6). Although for the sake of initial clarity we have separated these storylines and plots, they are often mixed together in the arguments and narratives that comprise our data, as we hope to show as we proceed. We will now look in detail at an example of storyline A, showing how the supporting plots we have identified work to bolster the general story. Then we will use two examples of storyline B, and describe the function of some of the supporting plots and devices we have mentioned.

Minding the gap between past and present accounts

Extract 1 is taken from an interview with GH, the mother of a retractor, conducted by Katie MacMillan (KM), a co-researcher on our overall project. The daughter in question (Janie) had made and then subsequently withdrawn allegations of child sexual abuse. At this point in the interview the discussion has turned to the time when the retractions were made. GH describes her daughter's previous memories of abuse as inconsistent and never completely believed at the time. This has the effect of treating the subsequent accusations as having always had the status of being partial *even then*. The former accusations are then rendered as insecure, forced, or said inconsistently. That is to say that the accusations are regarded not as stand-alone statements whose truth or falsehood might be independently inspected, but rather as occasioned – asserted only in specific and special contexts but not in others.

Extract 1 (ABex3. GH/KM. t1A. 611–641)

```
1   KM:   Wh- at what point did Janie say 'well hang on'
2         y'know 'this this is- this is not true' (.) because
3         that would- [that's a difficult
4   GH:              [she (would) do it all the time (.)
5         she did it all the time
6   KM:   what she'd say it's true it's [not true
7   GH:                                 [one to one thing and
8         yes not to another (.)
```

What we see in this small extract is evidence of some of the dilemmas that retraction poses to families. Retraction is, of course, something we might expect a family to welcome, since it involves the withdrawal of prior accusations. But it also creates further difficulties that have to be managed by the account of the events leading up to retraction. In this extract GH uses a version of what we have called storyline A to describe the difference between her daughter's prior and now current beliefs in her previously recovered memories. More specifically, variant A1 is offered – which emphasises that prior beliefs were situationally driven and indexed to a particular set of prior interactional contexts (hence there was variation at the time, as the soon-to-be retractor moved between different contexts). What does GH manage to accomplish here? In line 3 KM suggests that retraction is a difficult position to adopt. In response, GH states that Janie appeared to continuously question her own beliefs in her recovered memories. This is formulated definitively ('all the time') and reiterated ('she did it all the time'). This kind of 'extreme case formulation' (Pomerantz, 1986; Edwards, 2000) is typically used to bootstrap or strengthen an account against expression of disbelief. It provides 'epistemic help' – that is, the appearance of certainty or clear knowledge in the face of possible doubts.

The need for this kind of epistemic help is most visible in British courts of law, during the process of cross-examination. The legal system in the UK is based on an 'adversarial' process, where claims and counter-claims are made prior to their adjudication by either a magistrate or judge and jury. Cross-examination is that part of a legal trial where the legal representative (i.e. barrister) of the opposing party examines the testimony given by a witness. During this examination, the retraction of a prior statement is a significant event. It may be exploited by the barrister as evidence of mere inconsistency, and a sign of the speaker's unreliability as a witness. What holds during formal cross-examination holds also, to some extent, in informal, everyday settings where changing your mind, especially about something that is hugely important and consequential, is socially, discursively, accountable (see Drew and Heritage, 1992).

So in this case, GH's account needs help in warding off the potential accusation of the unreliability of Janie's belief stemming from her change of mind. What is interesting is that GH does this not by minimising Janie's variability, but instead by emphasising it and making it definitive. Janie, GH suggests, was not simply inconsistent, but *consistently inconsistent*. Consider that GH is in the position of having been previously accused of being complicit in the abuse of her daughter. Although the accusations have now been withdrawn, GH must anticipate that there might remain a lingering doubt either about why the accusations were withdrawn or why they were made in the first place – idiomatically, that there is 'no smoke without fire'. By describing Janie as consistently inconsistent in her beliefs, as *never* simply convinced about the abuse, and then further (in lines 7–8) as varying in her accusations according to who she was talking to, GH minimises the gap between Janie's past and present beliefs. Her retraction never had far to go – she never fully believed from the start.

The rhetorical dilemma lies in how to render the current version of events as true, and prior versions as false, when the very act of doing so can imply inconsistency. We see a further attempt at managing this dilemma in the interview with GH. The following extract 2 continues immediately from the prior extract 1:

Extract 2 (ABex3. GH/KM. t1A. 611–641)

```
 9  KM:  s [o
10  GH:   [she always told us it wasn't true (.) interestingly
11        enough always to (.) um ((indistinguishable whisper))
12        always the family GPs (   ) (.) anybody who (.)
13        it (would) really depend entirely upon the orientation
14        of the person [what she said]
15  KM:                 [    yeah.   ] So within therapy,
16        the therapy se-situation it could appear that eh these
17        were (.) true, that (.) these (.) experiences were true
18  GH:   mm
19  KM:   .hhh em whereas when she's back with her family (.)
20        in an in- a different environment then (.) she realises
21        (.) they're not true
22  GH:   yes I mean I think as it goes on increasingly her world
23        became extremely blurred (.) because the psychiatric
24        world is- the wards are very enclosed. (.) Different
25        ward anyway- world isn't it
26  KM:   mm
27  GH:   I mean .hhh just being with (violent) people must be
28        very disturbing (.) (rather horrifying) but I think she-
29        I think (.) she kept coming home (where things)
30        seemed normal
```

In this extract GH goes on to describe how Janie would make different claims relative to the setting which she was currently occupying. The interviewer KM produces some telling uptakes here, that GH goes along with and elaborates. It is not *just* a situational inconsistency, with Janie's stories varying according to whom she was telling them to. That would leave us not knowing which version to accept, and with a picture of Janie as merely confused, inconsistent, unreliable. So in addition to variability, we have 'within the therapy situation' as an environment where '*it could appear*' (line 16) that the abuse stories were true, whereas back home '*she realises*' (line 20) that those stories are false.

The speakers here are orienting to an instance of the 'appearance–reality' rhetorical device. Drawing a distinction between appearance and reality has a long and venerable history in philosophy, including Plato's separation of the given, perceivable world experienced by humans from the essential ideal forms of things, a reality which can only be uncovered through the power of rational thought and argumentation. In social science, studies of scientific argumentation (Gilbert and Mulkay, 1984) and of everyday commonsense reasoning (Pollner, 1987) have treated the appearance–reality device as a cultural resource whereby experiential evidence can be discounted as mere appearance, masking rather than revealing what is really the case. As Edwards (1991) put it:

In conversation, people sometimes warrant accounts, or pursue rhetorical aims, via positing a distinction between superficial appearance, and an underlying reality which represents the true situation, or a preferred version. 'Appearance' will often be couched as a perceptual metacognition: what things look, sound or seem like. The appearance-reality distinction is rhetorically effective in that it recognizes the obviousness of appearances, and so acknowledges the basis for one's own or the other person's (possible) understanding – that it is accountable in terms of appearance. At the same time, it subverts that version in favour of a purportedly more insightful and adequate analysis.

(Edwards, 1991: 532)

Edwards points to the way that the appearance–reality device can be used to unpick what appears to be the given evidence whilst simultaneously acknowledging the power of appearances. In extract 2 we see that GH goes along with KM's uptakes (lines 18, 22), and provides further contrasts between the unreliable things Janie would say in the strange, enclosed, violent, disturbing world of the psychiatric ward, and another thing *consistently-in-that-context* to the folks at home and the family GP ('general practitioner'; a professional who provides some nice corroboration), a more familiar, less strange environment 'where things seemed normal' (lines 29–30) to her. So these contrasts, between the therapeutic environment and home, between appearance and reality, provide ways of *managing* the rhetorical dangers of inconsistency (using a combination of accounts A1 and A2), and working to preserve one side of the story as having been true all along (A3).

In the interview with GH, we have seen one way in which retraction is handled, by minimising the apparent gap between past accusations and present retraction through pointing to doubts and inconsistencies which it is claimed existed at the time. We have also seen that this raises a secondary problem about the credibility of inconsistent reports which is managed through appeals to context and the use of the appearance–reality device. We are not suggesting that this is the only means by which retraction can be discursively managed (we will turn to an alternative example in the following section). What we are claiming is that doing retraction, in whatever way it is done, entails a set of rhetorical and epistemic uses and difficulties that have to be managed and that there is a set of commonsense ways of managing them. Further, we are suggesting that rather than see retraction as an extraordinary psychological phenomenon, possessing critical import for establishing the validity of the concepts of either false or recovered memory, we may instead see retraction as a situated social activity involving very general and pervasive features of factual discourse, which can be managed by families, retractors and their critics alike through the use of well-established social/discursive resources.

Making the break between past and present accounts

We will now turn to two instances of story type B. These come from the recorded, publicly available testimony of various members of the Rutherford family, including the accused father, Tom, and the retracting daughter, Beth. Textual (Rutherford, 1998a) and videotaped ('When Memories Lie', 1997) sources are available for these materials from the False Memory Syndrome Foundation, on whose behalf they are offered as valid and persuasive testimony. We take no position on whether or not that is the case. However, we would argue that such material, although clearly 'sided', still provides insight into the discursive procedures and cultural resources utilised in retraction accounts. In particular it offers insight into the particular appeal of type B accounts, and the way in which they are rendered compatible with the FMSF position on therapy.

In cases of accusations of sexual abuse there is an enormous amount at stake not only for the accuser-turned-retractor, but for the whole family. In the Rutherfords' case Tom (the accused father) lost his job as a minister of their church and was threatened with prosecution. As a consequence the family was split. Beth and her sisters (in support of Beth) left the family home and severed all contact with their parents (Rutherford 1998a, 1998b; 'When Memories Lie', 1997). Prior to the following extract 3 the father, Tom, has described the impact that his daughter's therapy and subsequent accusation of repressed sexual abuse had on himself and his wife. Throughout the family's recorded testimony, bad therapy (Beth's 'two and a half years ((of)) the most horrible counselling' ['When Memories Lie' (1997) transcript, 081, p. 2]) is treated as the only accountable reason for Beth's false accusations against her father.

Extract 3 ('When Memories Lie' [1997] transcript, 302, p. 5, edited)

```
1   Tom:   So regardless of what has brought the person
2          to therapy, if it's depression, an eating disorder,
3          school difficulties, perhaps job stress, there are
4          some underpinnings on the part of the therapist
5          and what they hold to and believe in their thinking
6          the underlying cause of all problems [. . .]
7          it's abuse [. . .] sexual abuse.
```

Tom's way of undermining the claims of therapists, and of his daughter herself prior to retraction, is to produce those claims as being in various ways irrational. They are the product of therapists' prejudices and dispositions, rather than the product of sound observation and judgement. They stem from how therapists think, prior to (i.e. prejudicial to) dealing with any particular case, from a *disposition* to find a hidden history of sexual abuse.

So, rather than a set of well-founded therapeutic findings, these are 'underpinnings' that the therapist will 'hold to' (lines 4–5). The irrationality of that dispositional belief is argued not only by formulating it is *as* a disposition or prejudice, believed in advance and held to, but by listing a series of unrelated, everyday kinds of problems (lines 2–3) that clients might come to therapy for, only to find their lives being taken apart in pursuit of sexual abuse. The therapist knows in advance what the problem is, and how to go about finding it, no matter what problems the client actually presents with. The therapist finds sexual abuse 'regardless' (line 1), where 'regardless' is about as succinct a formulation of non-empiricist prejudice as commonsense language provides.

Extract 4 (continued) ('When Memories Lie' [1997] transcript, 302, p. 5, edited)

```
8   Tom:   And the only way of recovery or healing, we
9          must go back to your past, dig up the past,
10         identify those perpetrators, and then
11         confront the perpetrators. If the abuser
12         doesn't acknowledge his vile acts then they
13         and all who stand with him or her are in denial
14         and we must separate ourselves from them
15         or we'll never get better. One of the under-
16         pinnings of their tenets ((is there's)) no need
17         for collaboration, or external verification, little
18         consideration whatsoever, for fact or logic.
```

Tom continues in extract 4 by accounting for how such a therapeutic process can be sustained in the face of counter testimony, experience, and evidence from accused family members, and even, at least initially, from the client herself. Therapists deploy various ways of discounting and avoiding such counter-evidence. Clients and accused family members are part of the problem, part of the pathology. Rather than any kind of independent voice, they are said to be 'in denial'. And separating oneself from those dissenting voices is part of the solution, an essential part of how to 'get better' (line 15). So therapists are depicted as having built a self-contained world of beliefs and practices that sustains their irrationality, their immunity from counter-evidence, and one that is capable of recruiting unwitting clients to their cause. What we see Tom building towards here is variant B5 – Beth's retraction will come as a result of her realisation that her claims lack any grounding in 'fact or logic' (line 18).

In the following extract the speaker is Beth, Tom's retracting daughter, who describes what happened to her in therapy using the acronym 'PROCESS', with each letter of the word prompting a description of how she moved from believing she had a happy childhood to recovering memories of being sexually abused by her father between the ages of 7 and 14.

Extract 5 (Rutherford, 1998a)

P- Putting doubts in my mind about my family, our relationships, my childhood, and my own memory.
R- Remembering my childhood.
O- Omitting the good and focusing on the perceived bad.
C- Commitment that dreams and ideas are 'true memories' and flashbacks of reality.
E- Emotionalizing the memories and establishing loyalties to my therapist.
S- Separating from my parents and from all those who did not believe me.
Then taking..
S- Steps of accusation and confrontation.

The 'process' tells the story of how therapy plays around with the mind, implanting suggestions, providing an interpretative frame for experiences and dreams, and diagnosing illness as the result of repressed memories, with the prescribed cure requiring that memories of abuse are brought to conscious awareness. The use of this mnemonic is interesting for several reasons. First, it implies that therapy systematically seeks to recruit the belief of clients and has a worked-out set of procedures for doing so. Second, it constructs Beth as someone who has gained insight into the supposed machinations of therapy, and is therefore a credible expert on her own previous behaviour. Third, it accounts for the difference between Beth's previous accusations and the prior and once-again current beliefs that she experienced 'a wonderful family and childhood' (Rutherford, 1998a). The accusations are now separated from and book-ended between what Beth constitutes as the 'reality' of her solid family relations.

In the following extract 6, Beth goes on to describe her progress through these stages.

Extract 6 ('When Memories Lie' [1997] transcript, 424, p. 9, edited)

```
1   Beth:   Ahm, the next phase then that kinda occurred
2           was the 'C' there, the commitment that dreams
3           ((and ideas)) are really true memories and
4           flashbacks. Um, at this a-point, um I was given
5           a lot of books to read about sexual abuse children,
6           about their stories, about what happened to them.
7           We spent a lot of time talking about that kind of
8           thing 'cause at that point I still wasn't remembering
9           (.) anything having happened to me s-by way of a
10          sexual abuse event, ahm, but spending that much
11          time and focus on that kind of a subject and
```

12	taking home books and reading it that kinda
13	thing. I dream a lot ((*laughs*)) >I had two dreams
14	I was just telling my mum and dad about this
15	morning last night I just dream a lot< and ahm
16	consequently spending that much time on that
17	kinda content I began to dream about being, ah
18	raped, or sexually abused, and that kinda thing.
19	And I was told you know one of the big things
20	was to come into therapy and tell what kind of
21	dreams you had had that week, and I was told
22	'no, those are not dreams they are really
23	flashbacks, they are really times in your mind
24	that- that's trying to come out, a memory's trying
25	to come out' and that she would help me get
26	these horrible things out of my- my memory

This is an account of the therapeutic process after the event which is designed to render Beth's retractions explicable and understandable. Beth's descriptions of her experiences of therapy attend in various ways to how it could be that she is now retracting a series of extremely damaging accusations that she had previously made against her father. She uses a range of identifiable rhetorical and narrative devices. Her prior beliefs are *externally accounted for*, as the result of what therapy imposed upon her, systematically and over a sustained period of time.

For example, her 'Commitment' is described as a required part of the therapy (as summarised in the PROCESS acronym). This undermines its status as something Beth herself previously thought, or concluded, or asserted, independently, or on the basis of what she may have experienced and remembered. One way of accounting for having changed your mind is to separate 'self' from the making of statements which are seen as directly controlled by the demands of the therapeutic process: 'it wasn't really me that was saying those things'. Indeed, the very requirement for 'Commitment' stemmed from the fact that, just at the point when the PROCESS called for it, 'I still wasn't remembering (.) anything . . .' (lines 8–9). Remembering is not then treated as a natural, spontaneous recollection of past events, but rather as the systematic conversion of Beth's dreams (themselves conditioned by the required reading of 'a lot of books' [line 5] about childhood sexual abuse) into flashbacks at the behest of her therapist.

So, rather than *reducing the gap* as in storyline A, between time 1 (accusation) and time 2 (retraction), the work done here in support of storyline B is to *decouple* those two times, and provide each with a different, contrasting epistemic basis. According to the account Beth provides, the epistemic basis of the prior accusations at time 1 is explicable in terms of several factors. The therapist applied external pressure and influence to produce recollections of abuse, through 'giving' Beth books on recovered memory, with the implication here being that these came to serve as templates for interpreting what had happened to her. The therapeutic process is also described in terms of the amount of time and effort spent discussing childhood sexual abuse (lines 7, 10–11, 16). Note that ordinarily spending 'a lot of time' (line 7) talking about a particular issue in therapy would be taken as evidence that therapy was proceeding systematically and appropriately, and may even be used as a sign that 'progress' is being made.[3] But in this account repetition implies a deliberate and concerted effort on the part of the therapist to achieve the goals ascribed to the PROCESS. Finally, the discussion of dreaming and what the therapist did with it is designed to accomplish the notion that the PROCESS directly influences the sexual content of her dreams (lines 15–18). This leads to a direct causal inference that this manipulation of her dreams made the production of memories she now regards as 'false' appear meaningful at the time. There is an interesting apparently incidental feature here. Beth ordinarily happens to 'just dream a lot' (lines 13, 15). The 'just' is a nice detail here, specifying dreaming as nothing of any special significance or causal consequence, thereby minimising the implication that the occurrence of the dreams themselves may actually, despite her description of the PROCESS, be taken as evidence of abuse, again using a 'no smoke without fire' form of commonsense reasoning.

What we see in the above extracts is the way in which a gap between present and past is emphasised in B-type retraction accounts. Past accusations are now deemed in error. However, the fervour and commitment with which the retractor previously held to the veracity of their accusations of past abuse are not denied, but instead used as evidence of just how deeply embedded the retractor previously was in the systematic and (now-seen-as) misdirected mechanics of therapy. But there remains a rhetorical 'blindspot'. If past accusations were under the control of therapists rather than the agency of the retractor, then it follows that the same might potentially be said of their present retraction account. That is, the claims they are now making are once again not really the product of their own rational self-insights but are the product of external influences and manipulation – in this case those of organisations such as the FMSF and the formerly accused parents.

We see this as a practical instance of what is sometimes known in philosophy as the 'black swan' argument. Classically, this is an argument levelled against inductively derived claims that notes the logical possibility that *one day* there may be an observation which contradicts the overall claim ('You say that, based on your evidence, all swans are white. But is it not possible that one day you will encounter a swan which is black? Where will that leave your claim?'). Here the argument would run that despite the best efforts of the retractor and their family it is still a logical possibility that they will change their mind again. And indeed, this remains a logical possibility irrespective of the strength of claims made for current retraction, even to the extent that efforts to completely discount past beliefs may perversely be seen as affirming the strength of the black swan objection ('But is it not still logically possible that they might change their mind again at some point in the future?'). The black swan argument forces us to entertain the possibility of something like 'second-order retraction', where there is a return to the original claims on the basis that the retraction was itself made in error under the influence of external forces. However, from our perspective we would see this as entirely explicable and in some sense predictable given the nature of the rhetorical and discursive resources which are in play around retraction – storyline B accounts, no less than storyline A accounts, are already organised around and anticipate potential disbelief.

Retraction as moral accounting

If we understand memory primarily with reference to the exercise of cognitive capacities to recall the past, then it follows that the central question to be asked is about the nature and quality of these capacities and the degree of accuracy involved in any particular instance of recollection. Seen against this backdrop, the memory wars may be ended by establishing whether recovered memory or false memory is the appropriate model for understanding claims of hitherto unrecognised childhood sexual abuse made later in life. Retraction then matters because it offers a kind of 'natural laboratory' experiment where persons change their minds about their own past not just once, but twice. Retraction must then be considered an extraordinary phenomenon which holds the key to unlocking the recovered/false memory dispute.

Our argument is that retraction ought not to be considered extraordinary at all. As a situated social activity, it involves the use of recognisable discursive resources to attend to the problem of factual accounting in testimony. We have identified two major groupings of these resources and indicated through examples how they may be used in practice. From this perspective, the retraction of prior claims of sexual abuse does not involve an epistemic difference in kind from other social activities which involve the defence of testimony against suspicion and disbelief (e.g. in courts of law; in public accounts; in autobiographical storytelling). All of these practices draw upon similar sets of social-discursive resources in the construction and defence of versions of the past. Campbell (2003) suggests that analysis of such resources can assist in identifying ways of supporting women's testimony. On this basis we would observe that storyline A accounts are vulnerable to the 'no smoke without fire' accusation, since they do not seek to deny past variability, but rather make it the basis for understanding the current 'change of mind' (as in GH's claim that Janie switched stories 'all the time' even *at the time*). Conversely, since storyline B accounts make such a clear opposition between past and prior beliefs they are vulnerable to 'black swan' type arguments, where the rejection of further changes of mind may be taken to strengthen the logical argument in favour of just such a possibility. Neither type of account could be said to be necessarily more rhetorically effective, but it is possible to anticipate the likely form that challenges to women's testimony may take given the particular variant offered in a given instance of retraction.

We are not suggesting that the making of claims of childhood sexual abuse or instances of their retraction is a routine occurrence, nor that this pragmatic consideration of rhetorical organisation of accounts is the sole way in which memories of abuse come to matter. Clearly such claims are vastly significant, complex and traumatic matters. Following Haaken (and Bartlett), we adopt the position that questions of absolute accuracy are not what is primarily at stake. Accounts of traumatic events may interweave multiple layers of explanation. As Reavey and Brown (2006) put it:

> Such 'layers' may hold within them both testimonies of pleasure and rebellion, as well as pain, feelings of love and hate towards an abuser and other such ambivalent emotions and destructive forces. In this way adult survivors may be seen to actively construct meaning from their past experience in order to make sense of their present identity.
>
> (2006: 180)

The construction of meaning through testimony about the past is a form of moral accounting. Such moral accounting is classically considered as central to the act of remembering. To speak of the past is to engage with contradictions and ambivalences, with multiple versions of what happened, but to nevertheless be placed under the obligation to establish its significance for present and future courses of action. Retraction accounts may then be seen, along with accounts of abuse, as exploring what Harré (1979) once referred to as a 'local moral universe', that is a nexus of rights, obligations and responsibilities between persons that is practically worked out in social relationships. The central question of such a moral account is not then of the literal accuracy of what is recalled, but rather of what follows, what rights have been violated, what responsibilities abnegated, and what is to be done as a consequence.

We have treated the extracts we have reviewed here as rhetorically organised accounts, but they are also moral explorations. They are attempts to set up a local moral universe which can hold the past in the present in such a way that it sketches out possible futures. In this sense our concern with rhetoric may appear to have rather missed the point of these accounts. This is simply not the case. In the wake of the science of memory, the idea that the public performance of recollection is a window (and often an opaque one) onto the truth of memory gained currency. Classical philosophy makes no such distinction; truth is a public matter which is to be established by debate and argument. The conduct of such a debate requires the application of 'arts', amongst which is counted *ars-rhetorica*. The diversity and potency of this range of arts for recollection and the exercise of judgement has been occluded by the sciences of memory. The lesson to be drawn for the study of remembering, from both retraction and the memory wars more generally, is that a return to a pluralist conception of the relationships between recollection, truth, procedure and judgement (to, that is, a setting-specific notion of what ought to count as 'good memory'; see Reavey and Brown, 2006) increases our ability to both inspect and respect remembering as a properly situated social activity.

Acknowledgements

Katie MacMillan and Derek Edwards contributed substantially to early presentations of this work. We thank them for their analytic insights and enthusiasm.

Transcription conventions

[[	start of overlapping speech
]]	end of overlapping speech
(.)	micro pause (less than tenth of a second)
( )	unheard
(word)	unsure hearing, best guess
(( ))	transcriber's comment
.hhh	inbreath
→	side arrows are not transcription features, but indicate the drawing of analytic attention to specific features

Notes

1 See Goldstein and Farmer (1993), which features ten retractor stories including those of Lynn Gondolf, Melody Gavigan and Laura Pasley, whose pictures grace the front cover and whose CVs printed on page v include references to nine television appearances, and fifteen publications between them. Pasley's story also appears in Pendergrast's *Victims of Memory* (1996), which includes nine further retractor accounts. In the 1990s both Gavigan and Pasley published now defunct print and internet newsletters for and about retractors. One retractor heavily promoted by the FMSF was Beth Rutherford, whose videotaped story forms some of the data for this chapter. Stories of retractors were a regular feature in issues of the *FMS Foundation Newsletter* and retractors appeared frequently as 'star turns' at FMSF conferences. These are only the most prominent. As Davis (2005: 220) notes, 'There are now several hundred retractors' whose effectivity, especially in the context of retractor-initiated law suits, against therapists is notable: by the mid 1990s retractors had become the anti-recovered memory 'countermovement's most potent weapon' (Davis, 2005: 221).
2 Work on retractors which does seek to address questions of veridicality includes De Riviera (1997), Lief and Fetkewicz (1995), Nelson and Simpson (1994), and Ost *et al.* (2001, 2002). Work, like ours, which is more interested in the accounts themselves, is rarer (e.g. Davis, 2000).

3 In other work (Ashmore and Brown, forthcoming a and b) we have considered how signs of progress are rhetorically organised in therapeutic work which involves not only recovered memories but also 'multiple personalities'. Repetition can be a contested sign. For therapists it may be used as evidence that progress is being made despite the unconscious defensive responses of the client (and in multiple personality disorder therapy this includes 'alter' personalities). For outside agencies, such as insurance providers who are footing the bill, it may be evidence of a lack of progress and serve as the basis for accusations of inappropriate therapeutic progress.

References

Ashmore, M. and Brown, S. D. (forthcoming, a) 'Counting in parts: progress and process in therapy for multiple personality disorder'. Under submission

Ashmore, M. and Brown, S. D. (forthcoming, b) 'Speaking in parts: agency and agony in therapy for multiple personality disorder'. Under submission

Ashmore, M., Brown, S. D. and MacMillan, K. (2005) 'Lost in the mall with Mesmer and Wundt: demonstrations and demarcations in the psychologies', *Science, Technology, and Human Values* 30(1): 76–110.

Ashmore, M., MacMillan, K. and Brown, S. D. (2004) 'It's a scream: professional hearing and tape fetishism', *Journal of Pragmatics* 36: 349–74.

Bartlett, F. C. (1932) *Remembering: An Experimental and Social Study*. Cambridge: Cambridge University Press.

Broca, P. (1861) 'Perte de la parole, ramollissement chronique et destruction partielle du lobe antérieur gauche de cerveau', *Bulletin de la Société Anthropologique* 2: 235–8.

Campbell, S. (2003) *Relational Remembering: Rethinking the Memory Wars*. Lanham, MD: Rowman and Littlefield.

Chertok, L. and Stengers, I. (1992) *A Critique of Psychoanalytic Reason: Hypnosis as a Scientific Problem from Lavoisier to Lacan*. Stanford, CA: Stanford University Press.

Davis, J. E. (2000) 'Accounts of false memory syndrome: parents, "retractors", and the role of institutions in account making', *Qualitative Sociology* 23(1): 29–54.

Davis, J. E. (2005) *Accounts of Innocence: Sexual Abuse, Trauma, and the Self*. Chicago: The University of Chicago Press.

De Rivera, J. (1997) 'The construction of false memory syndrome: the experience of retractors', *Psychological Inquiry* 8(4): 271–92.

Drew, P. and Heritage, J. (eds) (1992) *Talk at Work: Interaction in Institutional Settings*. Cambridge: Cambridge University Press.

Ebbinghaus, H. (1885) *Memory: A Contribution to Experimental Psychology*. New York: Teachers College.

Edwards, D. (1991) 'Categories are for talking: on the cognitive and discursive bases of categorization', *Theory and Psychology* 1(4): 515–42.

Edwards, D. (1997) *Discourse and Cognition*. London: Sage.

Edwards, D. (2000) 'Extreme case formulations: softeners, investment, and doing non-literal', *Research on Language and Social Interaction* 33(4): 347–73.

Gilbert, G. N. and Mulkay, M. (1984) *Opening Pandora's Box: A Sociological Analysis of Scientists' Discourse*. Cambridge: Cambridge University Press.

Goldstein, E. and Farmer, K. (1993) *True Stories of False Memories*. New York: Sirs.

Haaken, J. (1998) *Pillar of Salt: Gender, Memory and the Perils of Looking Back*. London: Free Association Books.

Hacking, I. (1995) *Rewriting the Soul: Multiple Personality and the Sciences of Memory*. Princeton: Princeton University Press.

Harré, R. (1979) *Social Being*. Oxford: Blackwell.

Herman, J. L. and Harvey, M. R. (1993) 'The false memory debate: social science or social backlash?' *The Harvard Mental Health Letter* 9(10), April.

Holmes, D. S. (1990) 'The evidence for repression: an examination of sixty years of research', in Singer, J. L. (ed.) *Repression and Dissociation: Implications for Personality Theory, Psychopathology and Health*. Chicago, IL: The University of Chicago Press, pp. 85–102.

Jones, E. E. and Nisbett, R. E. (1971) *The Actor and Observer: Divergent Perceptions of the Causes of Behavior*. New York: General Learning Press.

Krell, D. F. (1990) *Of Memory, Reminiscence and Writing: On the Verge*. Bloomington: Indiana University Press.

Lief, H. I. and Fetkewicz, J. (1995) 'Retractors of false memories: the evolution of pseudomemories', *Journal of Psychiatry and Law* Fall: 411–35.

Loftus, E. F. and Ketcham, K. (1994) *The Myth of Repressed Memory*. New York: St Martins.

Loftus, E. F. and Pickrell, J. E. (1995) 'The formation of false memories', *Psychiatric Annals* 25: 720–5.

Margalit, A. (2002) *The Ethics of Memory*. Cambridge, MA: Harvard University Press.

Matsuda, M. K. (1996) *The Memory of the Modern*. New York: Oxford University Press.

Middleton, D. and Brown, S. D. (2005) *The Social Psychology of Experience: Studies in Remembering and Forgetting*. London: Sage.

Motzkau, J. F. (2006) Cross-Examining Suggestibility: Memory, Childhood, Expertise. Unpublished PhD dissertation, Loughborough University.

Nelson, E. L. and Simpson, P. (1994) 'First glimpse: an initial examination of subjects who have rejected their recovered visualizations as false memories', *Issues in Child Abuse Accusations* 6: 123–33.

Ost, J., Costall, A. and Bull, R. (2001) 'False confessions and false memories? A model for understanding retractors' experiences?' *The Journal of Forensic Psychiatry* 12: 549–79.

Ost, J., Costall, A. and Bull, R. (2002) 'A perfect symmetry? A study of retractors' experiences of making and repudiating claims of childhood sexual abuse', *Psychology, Crime and Law* 8: 155–81.

Pendergrast, M. (1996) *Victims of Memory: Sex Abuse Accusations and Shattered Lives*, 2nd edn. New York: Upper Access Books.

Pollner, M. (1987) *Mundane Reason: Reality in Everyday and Sociological Discourse*. Cambridge: Cambridge University Press.

Pomerantz, A. M. (1986) 'Extreme case formulations: a way of legitimizing claims', *Human Studies* 9(2/3): 219–29.

Potter, J. (1996) *Representing Reality: Discourse, Rhetoric and Social Construction*. London: Sage.

Potter, J. (2002) 'Two kinds of natural', *Discourse Studies* 4(4): 539–42.

Reavey, P. (2003) 'When past meets present to produce a sexual "other": examining professional and everyday narratives of child sexual abuse and sexuality', in

P. Reavey and S. Warner (eds) *New Feminist Stories of Child Sexual Abuse: Sexual Scripts and Dangerous Dialogues*. London: Routledge.

Reavey, P. and Brown, S. D. (2006) 'Transforming agency and action in the past, into present time: adult memories and child sexual abuse', *Theory and Psychology* 16(2): 179–202.

Rutherford, B. (1998a) 'A retractor speaks, Part 1', *False Memory Syndrome Foundation Newsletter* 7(1) Jan/Feb 1998 (e-mail edition).

Rutherford, B. (1998b) 'A retractor speaks, Part 2', *False Memory Syndrome Foundation Newsletter* 7(3) April 1998 (e-mail edition).

Schacter, D. L. (1996) *Searching for Memory: The Brain, the Mind and the Past*. New York: Basic Books.

Speer, S. A. (2002) ' "Natural" and "contrived" data: a sustainable distinction?' *Discourse Studies* 4(4): 511–25.

Sutton, J. (1998) *Philosophy and Memory Traces: Descartes to Connectionism*. Cambridge: Cambridge University Press.

Terr, L. (1994) *Unchained Memories: True Stories of Traumatic Memories, Lost and Found*. New York: Basic Books.

Van der Kolk, B. A. (1995) 'The body, memory and the psychobiology of trauma', in J. L. Alpert (ed.) *Sexual Abuse Recalled: Treating Trauma in the Era of the Recovered Memory Debate*. London, NJ: Aronson, pp. 29–60.

Winograd, E. and Neisser, U. (1988) *Remembering Reconsidered: Ecological and Traditional Approaches to the Study of Memory*. New York: Cambridge University Press.

'When Memories Lie – The Rutherfords speak to families', 1997, video tape, available from the False Memory Syndrome Foundation, Philadelphia.

Wooffitt, R. (2005) *Conversation Analysis and Discourse Analysis: A Comparative and Critical Introduction*. London, Newbury Park, CA, and New Delhi: Sage.

Woolgar, S. and Pawluch, D. (1985) 'Ontological gerry-mandering: the anatomy of social problems explanations', *Social Problems* 32: 214–27.

Yates, F. (1992) *The Art of Memory*, new edn. London: Pimlico.

3 Reconstructing Bartlett and revisiting retractions of contested claims of abuse

James Ost and Karl Nunkoosing

> Life is a continuous play of adaptation between changing response and varying environment ... Remembering is a function of daily life, and must have developed so as to meet the demands of daily life.
>
> (Bartlett, 1932: 16)

It was known as the 'recovered/false memory controversy' and started in North America in the mid-1980s and made its way across the Atlantic to the United Kingdom. The controversy surrounded alleged episodes of childhood sexual abuse that were remembered by adults. Sometimes these claims were made after a period of therapy during which the individual 'recovered' memories of such abuse. In most cases, the individuals claimed to have had a significant period of non-awareness of the occurrence of the abuse (the argument was that the trauma of the abuse had led the individual to 'repress' or 'dissociate' all memory of it happening). As one might expect the accused (often the individual's parents) strenuously denied any wrongdoing. In some cases the accused was the subject of both civil and criminal proceedings. Professionals were divided over whether these claims of abuse were based on genuine repressed memories that had been recovered by careful therapeutic intervention, or whether they were false memories induced, in part, by suggestive and inappropriate therapeutic techniques. Partly due to the paucity of direct evidence at the time, psychologists became engaged in something of a turf war concerning the status of these contested abuse claims (see Brainerd and Reyna, 2005; McNally, 2003; Ost, 2006).

As a result of this controversy, the last 15–20 years have witnessed an explosion of research into contested claims of childhood sexual abuse (Brainerd and Reyna, 2005; Wright *et al.*, 2006). We now understand more about the nature of human memory for traumatic events – for example, that what might appear to be an inability to *remember* a traumatic event may, in fact, be more parsimoniously explained in terms of an unwillingness to *report* a traumatic event (McNally, 2003). Whilst a great deal has been accomplished, there are many unresolved issues. For example, in the clinical literature, the notion of what constitutes a 'traumatic stressor' has shifted considerably. In DSM-III, a traumatic stressor was defined as an event that would evoke significant symptoms of distress in almost everyone and was outside the usual range of human experience (e.g. combat exposure, witnessing death). Yet conceptual bracket creep has led to the situation where overhearing sexist jokes in the workplace is considered a criterion A traumatic stressor, capable of triggering post-traumatic stress disorder (PTSD) (see McNally, 2003, 2006). Likewise, a recent exchange in the journal *Memory and Cognition* raised the issue of whether the growing body of research on 'false memory' actually examines 'memory' at all. In their article Pezdek and Lam (2007) argue that, as the majority of published studies purporting to demonstrate 'false memory' use lists of words as stimuli, rather than entire autobiographical events, the findings of such studies should be referred to by another name (e.g. 'memory flaws'; see the reply by Wade *et al.*, 2007).

What these recent disagreements about terminology highlight is that psychological 'objects' have 'biographies' (Danziger, 2003). Ideas, concepts, events, people, experiences and so on become the object of psychological investigations and in the course of these investigations these 'psychological objects' change, are given new meaning, get neglected, or acquire new identities. Scientific or psychological objects are also given new meanings or take on new meanings as a consequence of changing social, cultural, historical and political conditions (see Bruce and Winograd, 1998; Danziger, 2003; Pezdek and Lam, 2007). As the exchange in *Memory and Cognition* highlights, notions of memory and remembering are no exception to this. In this chapter we explore two biographies of Sir Frederic Bartlett's theory of reconstructive remembering. We show how adopting his relatively neglected social approach to remembering allows a more nuanced understanding of contested claims of abuse by applying this theory to the story of a woman who has made, and subsequently retracted, claims of childhood sexual abuse. As we will show, the status of any particular claim to remember can also shift according to the context of remembering. This is important because it demonstrates that legal considerations about the truth or falsity of any particular memory claim are likely to be too simplistic.

(Mis)Remembering Bartlett

Bartlett's work has been invoked in work on the development of script and schema theory in cognitive psychology (Alba and Hasher, 1983; Brewer, 2000), parallel distributed processing (Costall, 1991; Rumelhart *et al.*, 1986), cultural psychology (Cole and Cole, 2000), and theories of social remembering (Edwards and Middleton, 1987; Middleton and Brown, 2005). His work has also been cited in applied areas, such as the transmission of rumours during wartime (Allport and Postman, 1947), eyewitness testimony (Loftus, 1979; Tuckey and Brewer, 2003) and, more recently, in debates concerning contested memories of childhood abuse (Brainerd and Reyna, 2005; Ost,

2003; Ost *et al.*, 2000). Bartlett's theory also has had a significant impact on other disciplines, such as anthropology (Klapproth, 2004; Saito, 2000) and English literature (Spivey, 1997).

Two distinct 'biographies' (or trajectories) of Bartlett's (1932) ideas about memory have developed in the psychological literature. The first (which we call the 'cognitivist' biography) is dominant in mainstream psychology, and the literature on contested claims of childhood abuse. According to this cognitivist biography, memory is an internal, schema-driven process of reconstruction. False memories, in the sense of the correspondence between the schema and external events, are likely because memory and remembering are inherently reconstructive and unreliable (Brainerd and Reyna, 2005). In many textbooks, as well as more specialist literature, one can find the assertion, attributed to Bartlett, that *memory is reconstructive and inherently unreliable* (see Ost and Costall, 2002, for examples).

Yet attributing to Bartlett, and particularly his 1932 text, the idea that *memory is inherently reconstructive and unreliable* is misleading for a number of reasons. First, although he made these claims in some sections of *Remembering*, neither his own experiments, nor the logic of his schema theory permitted him to draw such general conclusions. There is evidence that Bartlett, at least in some sections of his book, may have reconstructively remembered his own theory (Ost and Costall, 2002).[1] Second, Bartlett gave many examples of detailed and accurate recall (e.g. Sonia Kovalevsky; the 'wonderful' memory of the Bantu; Bartlett, 1932: 230 and 250–1). Although he states in the introduction that his aim was to challenge Freud's notion of memory as a 'static mass', he accepted the idea that, under certain circumstances, remembering could be accurate.[2]

In fact, Bartlett's position on remembering is more subtle and nuanced than is generally acknowledged. We refer to this as the 'social' biography and it has been adopted by researchers in a number of fields (Ost and Costall, 2002). According to the social biography of Bartlett, remember*ing* is a process of meaning-making, dependent upon the context in which it takes place (e.g. 'occasioned phenomena', Edwards, 1997). Put another way – rather than being an internal process of reconstruction – remembering is a dynamic, narrative, social and context-dependent activity that occurs between people as they attempt to understand and make sense of the past *in the context of the present* (Middleton and Brown, 2005; Middleton and Edwards, 1990; Reavey and Brown, 2006; see also Conway, 2005). For Bartlett, remembering is not about accurately (or inaccurately) recalling 'traces' of past events – it is a process of *effort after meaning*:

> An organism ... might be able, not exactly to analyse the settings, for the individual details that have built them up have disappeared, but somehow to construct or to infer from what is present the probable constituents and their order which went to build them up. It would then be the case that the organism would say, if it were able to express itself: *This and*

> this and this must have occurred, in order that my present state should be what it is.
>
> (Bartlett, 1932: 202, italics added)

What are the implications of thinking of remembering as a process of inference? This theory of remembering reverses the traditional logic that 'a "chain of successive memories" creates a sense of continuity and stability in the self' (Reavey and Brown, 2006: 179). It suggests that remembering is a process of reasoning and making sense of the past *in light of the present* (Conway, 2005). In other words, remembering involves working backwards from what is known and inferring what must have happened in the past. So the depressed patient in psychotherapy who is told that she/he displays all the indicators of an abuse survivor might reason 'I am currently depressed and therefore *must have been abused* for me to be in this state' (see Blume, 1990, for a list of such indicators). Similarly, a participant in a psychological study on false memory who is asked to give an account of a doctored photograph of herself might reason, 'The experimenter has just presented me with a photograph of myself in a hot air balloon therefore it *must have happened*' (see Wade *et al.*, 2002). Haaken (1998) points to another element of the present that might influence current narratives of abuse. Particular narratives of childhood sexual abuse gain currency due to their fit with culturally resonant ideas regarding femininity and powerlessness. In these contexts, then, remembering is a process of weaving together a coherent, meaningful narrative about the past, based on information in the *present*. As we will show in the final section of this chapter, taking this approach to remembering can shed light on why people might come to make, and subsequently retract, claims of abuse. Before doing so, we review available research on individuals who repudiate claims of childhood sexual abuse.

Retractors and contested claims of abuse

Some adults who make claims of having been sexually abused as children repudiate those claims. These individuals have been referred to in the literature as 'retractors', or 'returners'.[3] Studies of 'retractors' have employed case studies (e.g. Pendergrast, 1996; Goldstein and Farmer, 1993), surveys (Lief and Fetkewicz, 1995; Nelson and Simpson, 1994; Ost *et al.*, 2002) or more formal interview techniques (de Rivera, 1997) to investigate the dynamics involved in coming to make such claims.

One inevitable problem with the study of the processes of recovery or retraction concerns the corroboration of the events (Coons, 1997). Retractors might seem at first to provide the ideal solution to the study of the development of 'false' abuse claims since they now distance themselves from their earlier reports. The authors of many studies of retractors appear disposed to take the retractors at their word and to accept that their claims of abuse were false. For example, Schacter *et al.* (1997), while acknowledging the inherent limitations of relying on retractors' self-reports of their experiences, nevertheless argue that retractions should generally be taken 'at face value' (p. 78).

Other researchers suggest that retractors' retractions are no more – and perhaps less – reliable than their initial claims of abuse. Singer (1997) argues that 'retractors are unlikely to be reliable informants [because] they have produced two dramatically divergent accounts of significant events in their lives and at different times held adamantly to the truth of each contradictory account' (p. 328). Likewise Kassin (1997) also cautions that retractors are individuals 'with a prior record of deception and with self-justification motives that might systematically have corrupted their self-reports' (p. 300). Others argue that this vacillation might be due to the fact that 'retractors' are in fact highly suggestible individuals who have been 'talked' into believing that they were not abused (Blume, 1995; but see Gudjonsson, 1997: 297; Ost *et al.*, 2001, 2002).

A further source of concern is that many individuals who make public retractions are associated with advocacy groups (e.g. the British False Memory Society or the False Memory Syndrome Foundation). Such affiliations raise concerns about biases that these individuals may have in presenting events in a particular light. While such concerns are justified, they need not extend to dismissing their accounts. As Schooler, Bendiksen and Ambadar state:

> There is simply no principled reason why we should believe individuals when they recover memories but then disbelieve them when they retract them. Nor, for that matter, can we disbelieve recoveries and use retractions as evidence of memory fabrication. Ultimately, the fact that individuals can shift between believing and disbelieving illustrates the fundamental uncertainty that surrounds such memories.
> (Schooler *et al.*, 1997: 258)

Part of the problem concerns the evidential function of retractor stories in the false memory debate. For one group of researchers, retractors provide clear evidence of *remembering gone wrong*. For another group of researchers, the accounts serve as evidence that abused individuals can *re-repress* (or re-deny) memories of their abuse. Yet both of these positions take retractors' stories as if they were a unified whole – as if, on some meta-level, the stories were the same and served the same function for the individuals concerned. Even the more nuanced position taken by Schooler and colleagues does not really advance beyond this stage. Although these researchers point out the 'fundamental uncertainty' that remains, this position does not really help us understand the nature of that uncertainty. What is important, psychologically at least, is to understand how people make sense of such uncertainties (*effort after meaning*) and come to accept one theory about their past over another.

In working through this dilemma, Bartlett's notion of remembering as a social *process* can shed light on retractors' experiences. Such an approach emphasises that both the initial story of abuse, as well as its retraction, were ongoing attempts at *effort after meaning*, rather than the recall of memories that are either 'true' or 'false'.[4] This allows us to investigate more closely some of the reasons for this 'fundamental uncertainty' and the vacillation between belief and disbelief. It also allows us to question (again) whether 'memories' (at least as traditionally defined) should be the focus of current concerns about contested claims of abuse.

Researching retraction

Early research on retractors' experiences took the form of anecdotal, first hand accounts and single case studies (e.g. Goldstein and Farmer, 1993; Pendergrast, 1996, 2000) and was therefore open to criticisms concerning the objectivity of the findings (e.g. Conte, 1999). Some researchers have used grounded theory (de Rivera, 1997) or a survey approach (Lief and Fetkewicz, 1995; Ost *et al.*, 2001, 2002) to explore the dynamics surrounding the making and retracting of such claims. Both methodologies are limited in the sense that they necessarily make assumptions about what the participants' version of events will be before any data are gathered, rather than allowing participants to tell their own stories (see de Rivera, 1997; Lief and Fetkewicz, 1995; Ost *et al.*, 2001, 2002).

Typically, psychologists have seen language as a resource for providing clues about what might be going on inside people's minds. The social constructionist perspective of our present analysis acknowledges that meanings change according to social, cultural, political and historical contexts. Our analysis is guided by both narrative psychology (Sarbin, 1986; Crossley, 2000; McAdams *et al.*, 2006) and discursive psychology (Harré and Gillett, 1994; Edwards, 1997). Discourse analysis takes language itself as the locus for examining how people construct versions of events. Such linguistic versions of objects, people, ideas or events are referred to as discourses. Participants are positioned by their knowledge and social location (Davies and Harré, 1990), and from their cultural and historical location (Haaken, 1998), which can be revealed by examining the discourses used to describe their experiences (in this context, in making and retracting claims of childhood sexual abuse). As Billig (1997: 42) argues, the emphasis in discourse analysis is on 'examining what people are doing when they make memory *claims* and how, in the course of conversations, people can, through their joint talk construct stories about past events' (italics added).

In the remainder of this chapter we present a discourse analysis of an interview we conducted with a retractor with the pseudonym Nicola. She made contact with the first author (JO) through the British False Memory Society (BFMS) whom she had contacted in order to further understand her growing doubt concerning her belief that she had been sexually abused as a child. The BFMS referred her to the first author as someone who might be able to tell her more about the memory literature in order to help her make sense of what she had experienced. When she contacted the first author she was having doubts about the veracity of her belief that she had been abused as a child. The first author met her to discuss her experiences in late 2001. He discussed with her why she was having doubts, and recommended some reading that she might find helpful. Throughout the discussion, which lasted roughly 90 minutes, the first author was careful to stress on several occasions that he could not, and would not, offer an opinion concerning the truth of her beliefs. He emphasised that any decision had to be hers. Once this discussion was concluded, Nicola agreed that she would be willing to be contacted to participate in further research if such an opportunity were to arise. Thus, the second author (KN) subsequently interviewed Nicola in late 2002. The inductive interview covered a wide range of subjects with the interviewer taking the role of facilitating Nicola to tell her story from the current perspective of someone who has claimed to have been sexually abused by her father and has subsequently withdrawn the claim. The interview was transcribed verbatim.

In our discursive analysis of the interview, our intention here is not to provide a forensic or legal assessment of the likely truth or falsity of her claims. Rather, it is to show how the explanatory power of any narrative (or claim to 'remember') is transient and context dependent. We demonstrate how the 'biography' of Nicola's story develops. From an initial feeling or sense that she has been abused she begins to vividly recall images of abuse. She comes to understand these experiences as being a consequence or part of her fragile mental health. Finally, Nicola comes to an understanding that she has not been abused. There are many actors in the story that Nicola tells and they will figure as the analysis develops. The actors include: Nicola herself, her father, her mother, the churchman she confided in, her childhood friend, various psychiatrists and other physicians, the child sexual abuse community/ the British False Memory Society, her past husband, her children and her current husband/partner. For the most part we prefer to let Nicola's own words speak for themselves but where we feel that the interviewer's questions were particularly important, we have included them.

Nicola begins her story with her depression after the birth of her third child and the breakdown of her marriage.

Karl: Alright. Well, let's, let's start saying 'what is your story?'
Nicola: Well I think . . . it started as I started to get ill . . . I think it began a year after I had my third child . . . I started getting very, very depressed.

(page 4: lines 1–6)[5]

Her marriage had 'split up' for about a year when she sought the support of the vicar in her local church. She went to talk about how she felt about her 'marriage breaking up'. Her father was also a vicar in the local church. In these initial sessions, Nicola talked about a vague remembrance of 'some sort of sexual incident,' but she did not recall that this incident involved her father.

And I do remember at that time having some sort of belief about some sort of sexual incident but I was, I remember being very vague about it at first, and it certainly wasn't my father. It definitely was not my father. And I'd made that very clear. And I do remember, he kept – I think because he knew my father as a colleague . . . he did, sort of keep saying: 'look, I do need to be really sure that it wasn't your father, because he is a vicar and I would need to report it'. And I-I kept saying 'no-no it isn't my father'. And to be honest with you, I haven't got really strong memories of what ever about that section, so I don't even think I [was?] saying it was childhood abuse, it was an isolated incident, I don't think it as anything more than a one-off incident . . .

(page 4: lines 16–23; page 5: lines 1–15)

In the excerpt below a new meaning is added to what was a vague memory, as it becomes constructed as one of sexual abuse. When asked about the problems in her marriage, she disclosed to the vicar that 'sex was the big problem and that I didn't enjoy it'. It is in this context that her 'belief about some sort of sexual incident' gets elaborated.

And he's asked what the problems were in the marriage, and I'd said, you know, sex was the-the big problem and that I didn't enjoy it, and that I couldn't relax, and he's started to probe from there. And I think all I'd really said was, I had some sort of memory that sometime, and I think I'd that I . . . when I was about sixteen and something had happened to me and I couldn't be more clear than that. He, I think he kept probing away, and he did give me books to read about sexual abuse and things like that . . . And it got to the point that he really started pushing, saying 'I will have to say that what you've told me in confidence can't be kept confidential, if I decide I think your father's involved in it'.

(page 6: lines 5–23; page 7: lines 1–4)

In this excerpt, Nicola offers a theory of the vicar's rationale for probing about the father's possible involvement. It is possible that the book given to Nicola to read was also the source for this man's theory about the involvement of the father as the perpetrator of Nicola's abuse.

Nicola is upset about the end/break-up of her marriage – an ordinary enough story of everyday life. She identifies that one of the 'causes' of this break-up was her inability to relax and find enjoyment in sex with her husband. Nicola also describes vague memories of something sexual happening to her (or involving her) around the age of 16. This element became woven into her story as a causal event – it was the reason for her low libido that eventually led to the marriage breaking up. Despite the fact that it is a vague memory with no actors or location, this recollection nevertheless has the power to be theorised and made meaningful by the vicar as the cause of her distress. Furthermore, if there was a sexual incident by definition there also was a perpetrator. The horror of this story is increased if the actor/perpetrator is the adolescent's father. This is but one way that this story can be told – admittedly it is probably the most dramatic version. However, our point here is that the story *could* have been elaborated through an alternative discourse – that of resistance to a demanding and unhelpful husband for whom sex was a 'marital right'. The point here is that, as we will see later, psychiatry appears to privilege the abuse story over Nicola's story of resistance.

Karl: So now that, that you know what you know, why do you think you kind of, you didn't enjoy sex with your first husband?

Nicola: I think, probably, and partly because we had a lot of problems in our relationship, you know, he was a, quite a, I suppose very old fashion bit of a bully; I would have to stay at home, look after the children, he, you know, and he didn't help with the children. I had three children under three, and no it just didn't work, and we split up obviously because we weren't happy. And I think it really was as simple as that really. Yes I don't think there were- you know, I've never had a problem in another relationship. So I don't think there were psychological reasons other than that, that you know. I was completely exhausted, and he didn't help. And he was very unsympathetic to it, you know. He saw sex as his marital right and he was very, he used to get very angry about. And yes . . . And he I'm not saying – he certainly didn't force me to do anything, but he'd get very angry that I wouldn't.

(pages 27 and 28: lines 12–23 and 1–19)

The story told here, as with any other human story, is made up of events and plots. The plot is a way of making sense of events and these can be assembled into different narratives (Sarbin, 1986). Each narrative can serve different purposes. Storied forms of remembering can also serve different theoretical purposes for the rememberer. If one starts with the theory that Nicola's resistance or incapacity to respond to her husband's sexual needs was caused by 'childhood' sexual abuse, it is relatively easy to incorporate these events (some with little or no evidence) into a story of childhood sexual abuse by her father. The question then becomes what makes this story (instead of others) believable?

I think, I thought 'this is, you know, this is, I don't know, almost getting out of control here' I'm almost, perhaps being forced to think something that I wasn't even saying in the first place. I think he was getting very panicky about the fact that my dad worked with children and everything. And that's all I really remember about that stage with the vicar, because he left our parish after that. . . . But he then did, I did remember he did write to my father and tell him, the things I'd been saying, which I was very angry about.

(page 8: lines 1–20)

In the letter to Nicola's father, the vicar said:

It's (the allegations) a complete load of nonsense, she's made it up for attention.

(page 9: lines 21–2)

In conversation with Nicola the vicar said:

If it is – if I decide it is your father you're talking about, you know, this person you're talking about is your father, I will have to take it further.

(page 9: lines 17–19)

Note that the vicar has not yet established that Nicola is speaking about her father, although in the vicar's mind, the absent person in this vague memory is indeed the father. Constructing the story with the unnamed and absent perpetrator as Nicola's father fits with the prevailing theory that her sexual troubles, which led to the failure of her marriage, were caused by childhood sexual abuse.[6] Although the vicar did inform Nicola's father of the 'allegation', the story leads to another interpretation – one where Nicola is cast as attention seeking and her story as 'a load of nonsense'. Her vague memory of these same events leads to yet another interpretation. In this new interpretation, the father is not accused but, rather, is made aware that his daughter has been telling vague stories of sexual abuse.

But he did contact my father. But when I went into hospital, I was very, very withdrawn, very quiet and they sort of started getting me into counselling . . .

(page 11: lines 13–16)

Around that time, Nicola's mental health deteriorated and she was hospitalised.

And I think what's unfortunate, is, looking back at it now, I-I think I had postnatal depression. I don't think they knew as much about it, you know, back then as they do now. Because it really was very shortly after <name> was born that (it) started happening. And <name> was a twin birth and the twin had died. So it was a very traumatic time, my marr- you know, my marriage had broken up as well . . .

(pages 10 and 11: lines 22–3 and 2–10)

She was persuaded to seek medical help by the vicar.

And then I think it was the vicar that persuaded me to go to my GP . . . and because I'd really got quite poorly by then, I think . . .

(page 12: lines 4–9)

The result of her seeking medical help was a diagnosis of schizophrenia. However, as she now claims, she doubts both this diagnosis and the need for the ECT treatment that she received. She also had counselling sessions with a psychiatrist, which included probing for recollections of sexual abuse.

The diagnosis of schizophrenia, and its association with the causal belief about childhood sexual abuse, exposes an interesting contradiction which also reveals the two competing explanations, each serving the disciplining purpose of the two camps in the repressed and false memory debate. This diagnosis both legitimates and denies claims of childhood sexual abuse: On one hand her madness is caused by the experience of childhood sexual abuse that has been repressed. On the other hand her claims of childhood sexual abuse are not believable because of her madness.

And, I think around that time (treatments with anti psychotic medications and ECT) that's the counselling session started with my psychiatrist. And then I think that's when these beliefs really started to come into place. And I had just very amazingly strong beliefs, that it definitely was my father by then. It was my father and it was other people; it wasn't just my father, he was you know, the main one, but it . . . I remember it all happening in a church and you had, and I was very specific about it all. There was the man next door, who I just know him as 'uncle <*name*>'. And they were horrendous things I remembered really . . .

(pages 13 and 14: lines 11–23 and 1–14)

Here Nicola's narrative takes a new turn. It was now definitely her father and other men who abused her in a church. Is this the truth that was revealed to her through counselling? Before we address this question, it is important to bear in mind that Nicola was also taking antipsychotic medications and undertaking ECT for her depression and she believes that these were the cause of her 'experiences' of abuse whilst in the psychiatric hospital. The other factor to note is that the vivid experiences of abuse she relived in the hospital were different from the vague subject of her talk with the vicar about something that she felt occurred when she was about 16. Another significant point is that these 'rememberings' are described as 'beliefs'. A 'belief' is not a fact. One can believe in God without ever encountering a divine presence, and this belief can be reinforced by the experiences of other believers. Did Nicola think that these were 'beliefs' at the time when the events were recalled in therapy? What does it mean to profess belief that an event took place as opposed to 'knowing' that this same event occurred? (For discussions see Scoboria *et al.*, 2004; Smeets *et al.*, 2005; Tulving, 1989.)

> No, it (the counselling) made me extremely ill . . . I'd say it's much, much worse, talking about it. I think they thought, if you get it all out I suppose, I suppose, you know, it's going to make her better if she talks about it . . . You know there were other sexually abused people in the hospital as well and they very much encouraged us to talk together and sort [of] share our experiences.
>
> (pages 14 and 15: lines 19–23 and 1–8)

> Yeah, I-I think that they do almost dig for there to be a cause really. I mean, this sort of books, self-help books, that you're given to read when you go into hospital and things like that . . . I think, well, they do suggest. And perhaps you even start to think 'well yes, that's . . .' I don't know . . .
>
> (page 26: lines 5–8)

It is possible that these 'encouragements to talk' about experiences of sexual abuse also created a 'culture' of shared experiences and that not to have an experience to share in this circumstance may make it difficult to be part of the culture (Nelson and Simpson, 1994). Furthermore this culture creates the language – forms of talk – that provides means of understanding each other's experiences. To have an experience to share legitimises the person's presence in the place (psychiatric hospital) and amongst the group of persons who have also been abused.

> Now these became things that had happened (in) very early childhood, when I lived at <place>. Which meant I could only (have) been about five, six, seven. I moved from <place> . . . to <place> at nine. And I don't think I talked about things happening after that time . . . But a lot of it, I remember saying, that it happened in the church, and I remember talking about things like my dad shutting me out in the garden in thunderstorms with no clothes on and just, I mean looking back now, really quite bizarre. Bizarre things. And detailed exactly where it happened in the church and everything.
>
> (page 16: lines 4–21)

The events in the church took place when Nicola would have been between 5 and 8 years old and are remembered in some detail (e.g. such as the thunderstorm, her nakedness and the location of the church). So are these the constructions of a mentally fragile woman in the specific psychiatric hospital culture of disclosure and the wider culture where self-help groups are commonplace and personal stories, biographies and diaries are literary commodities and public confession is a television genre? Or is this the recall of events that actually took place but were forgotten and are only now being remembered? How we answer these questions depends upon which of the two theories we espouse. The first theory suggests that these experiences are so damaging to the ego that they have been repressed and have 'leaked out' as mental illness and problems with sex for the adult. The second argues that these memories were themselves part of the vivid 'hallucinatory' experiences of a very troubled 'mind'. Both of these theories rely on the presence of mental illness. According to theory one, the illness is caused by the 'experience' that took place in early childhood and according to theory two, the experiences are lived cognitively and constructed through the therapy and the other events surrounding the 'talking cure' of mental illness.[7]

> And yet now, I-I can hardly even remember you know, even remember the church, but . . . I mean I would sit in my room and scream, it was so vivid, and so real. I became very frightened of men in hospitals, very few men I would interact with. Really, apart from the psychiatrist that, you know, I (had) very good relationship with him, I think I still do . . . And when I was in a psychotic state, I wasn't really aware there was anybody else around me, and I would just relive all these things, and just be sitting there, screaming and crying and yeah, just in a terrible . . . it was horrible, horrible existence, it was yeah, I know and that, you know, went on for years on and on really . . . For the majority of those eight years I was extremely unwell, really really unwell.
>
> (pages 16 and 17: line 23 and lines 1–21)

Nicola's own theory is that the vivid (and horrible) experiences of abuse that she was relating whilst in hospital came from her mental illness at the time. What was being 'relived' or experienced in the above excerpt has an ambiguous status; these 'vivid and real' experiences are either recollections of these events, or reliving of the experiences or flashbacks. If she has not been abused, then one could consider these vivid and distressful experiences as hallucinatory. At the time, with the interpretations of the psychiatrist, Nicola interpreted these experiences as signs of her childhood sexual abuse and at that time in her own words she was really unwell.

However, after adopting the explanation that her suffering was caused by her childhood experiences of abuse, Nicola then retracts that explanation during a period when she was feeling well. As noted, her retraction could be seen as evidence of her coming to terms with the fact that the abuse had not occurred. Alternatively, it could be seen as evidence of her re-repressing (or denying) the reality of abuse she had suffered. Either case can lead to a final resolution for her. But as the next section shows, for Nicola, the issues are far from resolved. There is no clearly demarcated boundary between her 'old' belief and her 'new' belief. Rather, she is engaged in an ongoing process of *effort after meaning*.

> Then I had a period, for about six months, when I was very well, right in the middle of it, I suppose about five years, six years through my illness. I had about six months of being very well. And the beliefs started to go.

I was (off) my antipsychotics, I was back living at home. And I really started at that point to question it, and I started to have a bit of contact with my dad again. I'd started to say to friends at that point 'you know, I don't understand this. Why do I, you know, really believe this, when I'm that ill and on antipsychotics and every thing, and now I'm really starting to question it.' But unfortunately I did get poorly again.

(pages 19 and 20: lines 11–23 and 1–5)

Depending on the theoretical (and ideological) position one takes, it is possible to suggest that Nicola 'got better' as a result of her pharmacological and therapeutic treatments, that she had dealt with the traumatic childhood experiences of sexual abuse, and that these experiences no longer troubled her. However, she is suggesting something else with the above talk. She is questioning the veracity of the events that she experienced during her illness. Note also that 'being very well' did not entirely eradicate the 'belief' or the experience of abuse. One might question if the belief and 'experience' were the product of lived abuse or the product of her mental illness. Again depending on one's position, one could posit that it was the questioning of the lived experience of sexual abuse that contributed to her getting ill again.

One of the friends referred to in the above segment is Nicola's childhood friend and companion. This woman does not believe that Nicola's father sexually abused her:

Some friends, I-I would say my best friend didn't. My best friend has known me since I was nine. And it's funny, because she doesn't actually particularly like my father. She thinks he's quite eccentric old . . . And she doesn't like the way, you know, just silly things, the way he brought us up. But she didn't believe he'd abuse me. She-she's always said that. And she's, you know, she'll say it now. She just thinks she was around far too much, around me, and spent enough time with me, that I would of told her . . . she'd listen but she would never go along with it really. Whereas other friends do.

(pages 20 and 21: lines 6–23 and 1–6)

The childhood friend is brought into the story, at this juncture in the plot, because she has a privileged relationship with Nicola and knowledge of her childhood. Her account is given credence because she did not like Nicola's father and also that since they had spent a lot of time together, the friend would have been told of any abuse that had taken place. However, one could immediately offer a counter-argument that these events of sexual abuse were so traumatic that they were immediately 'locked' away in memory, only to emerge later as psychiatric trouble for Nicola. Yet to accept this theory, one would also have to believe that the 'repression' was so powerful that the events were immediately forgotten and that these did not have any influence or effect on her behaviours and emotion during the time when these abuses occurred.

Karl:	Was he (the father) upset?
Nicola:	Oh, very, both of them devastated, yeah, really devastated, and 'how c-how can you possibly be saying these things about us?'
Karl:	Did you believe these things happened?
Nicola:	Well I did, I honestly did at the time.
Karl:	So how did you react to them telling you 'why do you say these things about us. It did not happen'?
Nicola:	I think I was hurt and angry that, you know, they could at least admit that he had done it. And you know, and try to support and work through it, you know. And I think that's where Doctor (name) was coming from, that he was trying to say 'look, if we, if you can confront this and he will admit that he did it, we will be able to work together'. I don't know, but then when they started to come and see me in hospital . . . the nurse and the doctors decided my, that my condition was hugely deteriorating after I had a visit from them. And they wrote, Dr <*name deleted*> wrote to them and asked them not to come and see me.

(pages 23 and 24: lines 11–23 and 1–12)

Karl:	That letter implied that he was guilty . . .
Nicola:	Yes. Yeah. Yeah. Oh isn't it, I mean, there was no doubt in my mind that Dr <*name deleted*> did believe he was. Yeah. Dr <*name deleted*> did believe it happened.

(pages 24 and 25: line 23 and lines 1–2)

Karl:	Looking back at your childhood . . .
Nicola:	I remember, yeah, sort of patchy bits and that was the strange thing when I started to get better. That really when I was ill, I couldn't remember any good bits. No I didn't remember all the good bits that I can remember now. No.

(page 26: lines 15–19)

There was no way, until I got ill, I had any beliefs at all about my dad abusing me. My husband was afraid that he, for some reason my ex-husband is convinced now that my dad did abuse me, but he'd have to admit that until I got ill, I'd never said anything to him or to anybody else, not to anybody. I had no beliefs at all until I'd got ill that I'd been abused.

(page 29: lines 5–17)

It may be that casting 'abuse' as the cause of Nicola's resistance to the sexual demands of her husband serves the purpose of the husband. Another aspect of this account is Nicola's association of her 'belief' about being abused with her illness. The tension here is between either (a) her illness being caused by childhood sexual abuse or (b) her recollection of sexual abuse being a by-product of her illness and the psychotropic medication that she was taking at the time. For Nicola, the latter theory has more credibility, although she had started off by believing the former version. Her understanding of how her mental illness, its treatment and the culture of disclosure of the psychiatric hospital contributed to her belief about her childhood sexual abuse led to her doubt about the abuse itself. Now that she is no longer ill, no longer in a sexually demanding relationship, she has no need for the story of abuse as the cause of her troubles.

Nicola: ... the psychiatrist who works for me now, we're both absolutely adamant 'leave well alone, just get on with ... you're really well now, and you are lucky to be this well. Don't go down that road, digging it all back up again and risk getting ill, just move on with your life and be happy.'

Karl: How did you interpret that? I mean what he said ...

Nicola: I've spent eight years of absolute ... it's been absolutely a nightmare of an existence. And that's all it was, it was an existence. It wasn't living. And I was very frightened, very frightened to risk ending up in hospital again, by going down that road. . You know I-d, I thought 'no, I am going to have to go on with their advice really' ... And I really cried and I said to my husband 'no I've got to do it, I've got to know, partly for my dad's sake, but also for my own sake, I've got to know whether it happened or whether it didn't happen.' I must admit, at the time my husband was saying 'look, you've been told by everybody not to do it. You know, just listened to them, you must take their advice.' But I just couldn't, I had, I had to find out ... so I went back to Dr <*name deleted*> who's the psychiatrist that I see now and I said 'I am sorry, I do need t-to take this further, I need to find out, even if I just start reading books or something ... I am going to say to my father that, you know I am going to do something, and I wrote to dad and I said 'no, I-I owe it to you and to our relationship that we at least explore this a bit further now. ... and he said 'well I know somebody that might be able to help us'.

(page 30: lines 21–2; page 31: lines 1–23; page 32: lines 1–23; page 33: lines 1–7 and 12–23; page 34: lines 1–2 and 23)

It is difficult to be certain whether Nicola's doubts about the abuse preceded her belief that the recollections of abuse were the result of her experiences in hospital (i.e. as opposed to genuine recollections of lived abuse). Regardless of which came first, Nicola's account takes a new turn – that of seeking confirmation from the father that he did not abuse her. The absence of visits from her parents after the birth of her child seemed to be a pivotal moment in her determination to meet with her father. This meeting was not to establish her father's role in her childhood sexual abuse. Rather, the meeting grew out of her desire for reconciliation. The absence of her parents in her life and her children's needs of their grandparents are more important than maintaining the belief that she had been abused as is her need to resolve the cognitive dissonance between two different versions of her remembered childhood.

> And we came together to see <*name deleted*>. And I think it was just at that stage that I, you know, I was prepared, I was prepared to delve a bit deeper really and more objectively and I think I'm going to, you know just, think for myself, lets not, this time, and not listen to what everybody's telling professionally is right, and-and I did a lot of reading. <*name deleted*> gave me quite a lot of materials to read. And I started to read other things as well. And other books, and I remember something that <*name deleted*> said to me when I was here, that ermm 'one way, the-the pieces of the jigsaw puzzle will either fit together or they won't'. And I think that's the thing that stayed most in my mind, and they didn't fit. You know, that I had some really good memories of being little that just didn't go with the other memories. They didn't fit together at all. And the memories that I had when I was ill, although I couldn't, I certainly can't remember them anyway. I mean I remember when, when I was ill. I could tell you huge, vivid graphic detail of all this, I wouldn't even be able to do that now. I really wouldn't. And ermm, it was almost like I can see now, it, it's like some sort of story. Some, some different things that happened and it really didn't happen. You know, and I can see that, it, it really- And I could- I think what really made me realise is when I let my dad see the children again, and I had no fear at all about him being round my children. None at all. Now I knew then, if I really believed it had happened, I wouldn't want him anywhere near the kids. I wouldn't. You know, and now he's had them on his own, you know with just my mum, he's taken them out, and I have no fear about that at all. I am totally convinced that it was totally a thing of my illness. And it didn't happen, and I would never, never ever let my children be alone with him if I believed now that it happened.
> (page 34: lines 4–23; page 34: lines 1–23; page 35: lines 1–23; page 36: line 1)

Just as the psychiatrist relied on theory to explain Nicola's 'recovered memories', she too needed knowledge and theory to explain why she could have believed that she was sexually abused when, in her new understanding, events she remembers about her childhood did not fit into the story of abuse. At the time of the interview, Nicola has already decided that the abuse was imagined during her illness. What she is now seeking is an explanation of how she came to believe so vehemently that an event took place that did not in fact occur. In confirming her new belief that her father was not an abuser, she is able to leave her children with their grandfather.

Conclusion

We opened this chapter with a quote where Bartlett asserts that life is a continuous play of adaptation between changing response and varying environment. Given that remembering is a function of everyday life, Bartlett argues that mechanisms of memory must have developed to meet these needs. We then considered in more detail the social nature of Bartlett's theory of remembering – specifically his notion of *effort after meaning*. Finally we introduced Nicola, a woman who at first believed, and then disbelieved, that her father had sexually abused her when she was a child. Nicola's story provides a concrete example of the *effort after meaning* to which Bartlett was referring.

For example, remembering in different contexts at different times served a range of social functions. When she made her claims of abuse, it was in the context of seeking treatment for her illness. One interpretation would be that the abuse caused her illness. However, her claim to remember such abuse cannot be divorced from the environment in which she was 'doing' the remembering. Nicola and those around her were all engaged in a process of *effort after meaning* in order to explain why she was ill. Similarly, when the claims of abuse were retracted, it was in the context of seeking reconciliation with her parents. Again, one interpretation would be that Nicola retracted the claims because she realised they were false. But as she states herself, this was not the case. Rather, she had some doubts that may have been strengthened by her visit to the first author. Thus, the immediate context now supported, and allowed for, an element of doubt. More than that, it provided an alternative theory to explain what had happened to her. Each time different forms of evidence are marshalled in support of her position. It is therefore entirely possible that, should Nicola become ill again, a repressed memory narrative might once again become a useful explanatory device. This retractor could, in fact, retract her retraction.

A related point is that at any given time, there can be competing frames for understanding the same 'memory' (recall that Nicola's initial claim was taken seriously by the vicar, but then dismissed as an 'attention-seeking' ploy). For example, for a lawyer, the initial act of remembering might serve as evidence for childhood abuse whereas the retraction of the veracity of that act would serve as evidence for a claim of professional malpractice. For the psychologist, the initial memory might serve as an example of the effects of trauma, and the retraction might serve as evidence of the malleability of memory. For Nicola, her initial remembering provides evidence that supports an explanation for her distress: the retraction then serves as evidence of her illness.

The availability of multiple interpretations of the same 'remembering' highlights that legal (and experimental) considerations about the 'truth' or 'falsity' of any particular memory claim are likely to be too simplistic. While terms such as *false* memory and *recovered* memory may serve legal functions in adjudicating claims about the past, they do not promote or facilitate clear communication and understanding. As Hyman (2000: 374) puts it:

> For any given individual, interpreting a recovered memory is always an either-or question: the memory is either false or true ... In contrast, the scientific aspect of the recovered memory question need not be posed as an either-or question.

How then should we pose this question scientifically? From a Bartlettian perspective, we also need to ask what *purpose* the remembering served, and what *needs* did it meet at the time? Rather than simply speaking of static and internal concepts like 'true' and 'false' 'memories' of abuse we also need to understand that people are constantly engaged in a process of narrative construction of their lives (Bruner, 2002). Thus any claim to remember needs to be understood, not just as a claim about the past, but also as an attempt at *effort after meaning*. In doing so we may be able to resolve the either–or dichotomy that has dominated this debate and promote a more fruitful dialogue about the status of contested claims of abuse.

Notes

1. Bartlett appears to reconstructively remember his own findings, especially in the chapter summaries of his 1932 book. The logic of his schema theory in fact permits literal (i.e. accurate, reproductive) remembering – thus citing Bartlett's work in support of the claim that remembering is reconstructive is incorrect.
2. As he noted, 'the immediate return of certain detail is common enough and it certainly looks very much like the direct re-excitation of certain traces' (Bartlett, 1932: 209).
3. A distinction is sometimes drawn between people who publicly retract their previous claims of childhood sexual abuse ('retractors') and those who resume contact with their families but do not publicly retract the abuse claims ('returners').
4. Although one can certainly try and establish whether specific events did, or did not, occur in order to satisfy legal requirements (e.g. 'beyond reasonable doubt'), most of us do not engage in this kind of verification when remembering our past.
5. These refer to the page and line numbers in the interview transcript.
6. Was she sexually active at 16? This is a question that no one dared to ask, including us as interviewers. Was this 'experience' a consensual one that she regrets? What is it about that event that a 16-year-old adolescent simply cannot remember?
7. It is worth noting that poorer women may not have these experiences because they are mostly prescribed drugs for their depression.

References

Alba, J. W. and Hasher, L. (1983) 'Is memory schematic?', *Psychological Bulletin* 93: 203–31.

Allport, G. W. and Postman, L. (1947) *The Psychology of Rumor*. New York: Henry Holt.

Bartlett, F. C. (1932) *Remembering: A Study in Experimental and Social Psychology*. Cambridge: Cambridge University Press.

Billig, M. (1997) 'Rhetorical and discursive analysis: how families talk about the royal family' in N. Hayes (ed.) *Doing Qualitative Analysis in Psychology*. London: Psychology Press, pp. 39–54.
Blume, E. (1990) *Secret Survivors: Uncovering Incest and its After Effects in Women*. Canada: John Wiley and Sons.
Blume, E. S. (1995) 'The ownership of truth', *The Journal of Psychohistory* 23: 131–40.
Brainerd, C. J. and Reyna, V. F. (2005) *The Science of False Memory*. New York: Oxford University Press.
Brewer, W. F. (2000) 'Bartlett's concept of the schema and its impact on theories of knowledge representation in contemporary cognitive psychology', in A. Saito (ed.) *Bartlett, Culture and Cognition*. Guildford: Psychology Press, pp. 67–89.
Bruce, D. and Winograd, E. (1998) 'Remembering Deese's 1959 articles: the Zeitgeist, the sociology of science and false memories', *Psychonomic Bulletin and Review* 5: 615–26.
Bruner, J. (2002) *Making Stories: Law, Literature, Life*. Cambridge, MA: Harvard University Press.
Cole, J. and Cole. M. (2000) 'Re-fusing anthropology *and* psychology', in A. Saito (ed.) *Bartlett, Culture and Cognition*. Hove, UK: Psychology Press, pp. 135–54.
Conte, J. R. (1999) 'Memory, research, and the law: future directions', in L. M. Williams and V. L. Banyard (eds) *Trauma and Memory*. Thousand Oaks, CA: Sage Publications, pp. 77–92.
Conway, M. A. (2005) 'Memory and the self', *Journal of Memory and Language* 53: 594–628.
Coons, P. M. (1997) 'Distinguishing between pseudomemories and repression of traumatic events', *Psychological Inquiry* 8: 293–5.
Costall, A. P. (1991) 'Frederic Bartlett and the rise of prehistoric psychology', in A. Still and A. Costall (eds) *Against Cognitivism: Alternative Foundations for Cognitive Psychology*. London: Harvester Wheatsheaf, pp. 39–54.
Crossley, M. (2000) *Introducing Narrative Psychology: Self, Trauma, and the Construction of Meaning*. Buckingham: Open University Press.
Danziger, K. (2003) 'Where history, theory, and philosophy meet: the biography of psychological objects', in M. J. Krall and D. J. Hill (eds) *About Psychology: Essays at the Crossroads of History, Theory, and Philosophy*. New York: State University of New York Press, pp.19–33.
Davies, B. and Harré, R. (1990) 'Positioning: the discursive production of selves', *Journal for the Theory of Social Behaviour* 21: 43–63.
de Rivera, J. (1997) 'The construction of false memory syndrome: the experience of retractors', *Psychological Inquiry* 8: 271–92.
Edwards, D. (1997) *Discourse and Cognition*. London: Sage.
Edwards, D. and Middleton, D. (1987) 'Conversation and remembering: Bartlett revisited', *Applied Cognitive Psychology* 1: 77–92.
Goldstein, E. and Farmer, K. (1993) *True Stories of False Memories*. Florida: Upton Books.
Gudjonsson, G. H. (1997) 'False memory syndrome and the retractors', *Psychological Inquiry* 8: 296–9.
Haaken, J. (1998) *Pillar of Salt: Gender, Memory and the Perils of Looking Back*. New Brunswick: Rutgers University Press.
Harré, R. and Gillett, G. (1994) *The Discursive Mind*. London: Sage.
Hyman, I. E. (2000) 'The memory wars', in U. Neisser and I. E. Hyman (eds)

Memory Observed: Remembering in Natural Contexts, 2nd edn. New York: Worth Publishers, pp. 374–9.
Kassin, S. M. (1997) 'False memories turned against the self', *Psychological Inquiry* 8: 300–2.
Klapproth, D. M. (2004) *Narrative as Social Practice: Anglo-western and Australian Aboriginal Oral Traditions*. New York: Mouton de Gruyter.
Lief, H. and Fetkewicz, J. (1995) 'Retractors of false memories: the evolution of pseudo-memories', *The Journal of Psychiatry and Law* 23: 411–36.
Loftus, E. F. (1979) *Eyewitness Testimony*. Cambridge, MA: Harvard University Press.
McAdams, D. P., Josselson, R. and Lieblich, A. (eds) (2006) *Identity and Story: Creating Self in Narrative*. Washington DC: American Psychological Association.
McNally, R. J. (2003) *Remembering Trauma*. Harvard, MA: Harvard University Press.
McNally, R. J. (2006) 'Cognitive abnormalities in post-traumatic stress disorder', *Trends in Cognitive Sciences* 10: 271–7.
Middleton, D. and Brown, S. D. (2005) *The Social Psychology of Experience: Studies in Remembering and Forgetting*. London: Sage.
Middleton, D. and Edwards, D. (1990) *Collective Remembering*. London: Sage.
Nelson, E. L. and Simpson, P. (1994) 'First glimpse: an initial examination of subjects who have rejected their recovered visualizations as false memories', *Issues in Child Abuse Accusations* 6: 123–33.
Ost, J. (2003) 'Essay review: seeking the middle ground in the "memory wars"', *British Journal of Psychology* 94: 125–39.
Ost, J. (2006) 'Recovered memories', in T. Williamson (ed.) *Investigative Interviewing: Rights, Research, Regulation*. Devon, UK: Willan Publishing, pp. 259–91.
Ost, J. and Costall, A. (2002) 'Misremembering Bartlett: a study in serial reproduction', *British Journal of Psychology* 93: 243–55.
Ost, J., Costall, A. and Bull, R. (2000) 'Bartlett's social theory of remembering and the recovered memory debate', in A. Czerederecka, T. Jaskiewicz-Obydzinska and J. Wojcikiewicz (eds) *Forensic Psychology and Law: Traditional Questions and New Ideas*. Krakow, Poland: Institute of Forensic Research Publishers, pp. 236–9.
Ost, J., Costall, A. and Bull, R. (2001) 'False confessions and false memories? A model for understanding retractors' experiences?', *The Journal of Forensic Psychiatry* 12: 549–79.
Ost, J., Costall, A. and Bull, R. (2002) 'A perfect symmetry? A study of retractors' experiences of making and repudiating claims of early sexual abuse', *Psychology, Crime and Law* 8: 155–81.
Pendergrast, M. (1996) *Victims of Memory: Incest Accusations and Shattered Lives*, 2nd edn. Hinesburg, VT: Upper Access, Inc.
Pendergrast, M. (2000) 'A retractor's story', in U. Neisser and I. E. Hyman (eds) *Memory Observed: Remembering in Natural Contexts*. New York: Worth Publishers.
Pezdek, K. and Lam, S. (2007) 'What research paradigms have cognitive psychologists used to study "false memory," and what are the implications of these choices?', *Consciousness and Cognition* 16: 2–17.
Reavey, P. and Brown, S. D. (2006) 'Transforming agency and action in the past, into the present time: adult memories and child sexual abuse', *Theory and Psychology* 16: 170–202.
Rumelhart, D. E., Smolensky, P., McClelland, J. L. and Hinton, G. E. (1986)

'Schemata and sequential thought processes in PDP models', in J. L. McClelland, D. E. Rumelhart and the PDP Research Group (eds) *Parallel Distributed Processing: Explorations in the Microstructure of Cognition*. Cambridge, MA: MIT, pp. 7–57.

Saito, A. (2000) *Bartlett, Culture and Cognition*. Guildford: Psychology Press.

Sarbin, T. R. (ed.) (1986) *Narrative Psychology: The Storied Nature of Human Conduct*. New York: Prager.

Schacter, D. L., Norman, K. A. and Koutstaal, W. (1997) 'The recovered memories debate: a cognitive neuroscience perspective', in M. A. Conway (ed.) *Recovered Memories and False Memories*. Oxford: Oxford University Press, pp. 63–99.

Schooler, J. W., Bendiksen, M. and Ambadar, Z. (1997) 'Taking the middle line: can we accommodate both fabricated and recovered memories of sexual abuse?', in M. A. Conway (ed.) *Recovered Memories and False Memories*. Oxford: Oxford University Press, pp. 251–92.

Scoboria, A., Mazzoni, G., Kirsch, I. and Relyea, M. (2004) 'Plausibility and belief in autobiographical memory', *Applied Cognitive Psychology* 18: 791–807.

Singer, J. (1997) 'How recovered memory debates reduce the richness of human identity', *Psychological Inquiry* 8: 325–9.

Smeets, T., Merckelbach, H., Horselenberg, R. and Jelicic, M. (2005) 'Trying to recollect past events: confidence, beliefs, and memories', *Clinical Psychology Review* 25: 917–34.

Spivey, N. N. (1997) *The Constructivist Metaphor: Reading, Writing, and the Making of Meaning*. San Diego: Academic Press.

Tuckey, M. R. and Brewer, N. (2003) 'How schemas affect eyewitness memory over repeated retrieval attempts', *Applied Cognitive Psychology* 17: 785–800.

Tulving, E. (1989) 'Memory: performance, knowledge, and experience', *European Journal of Cognitive Psychology* 1: 3–26.

Wade, K. A., Garry, M., Read, J. D. and Lindsay, D. S. (2002) 'A picture is worth a thousand lies: using false photographs to create false childhood memories', *Psychonomic Bulletin and Review* 9: 597–603.

Wade, K. A., Sharman, S. J., Garry, M., Memon, A., Mazzoni G., Merckelbach, H. and Loftus, E. F. (2007) 'False claims about false memory research', *Consciousness and Cognition* 16: 18–28.

Wright, D. B., Ost, J. and French, C. C. (2006) 'Ten years after: what we know now that we didn't know then about recovered and false memories', *The Psychologist* 19: 352–5.

4 Speaking up against justice
Credibility, suggestibility and children's memory on trial

Johanna F. Motzkau

Introduction

Judge: And if you do always tell the truth where will you go when you die?
Girl: Up to heaven sir.
Judge: And what will become of you if you tell lies?
Girl: I shall go down to the naughty place, sir.
Judge: Are you quite sure of that?
Girl: Yes, sir.
Judge: Let her be sworn, it is quite clear that she knows more than I do!
(Mr Justice Maule (1788–1858) examining a young witness on the nature of the oath, quoted in Spencer and Flin, 1993: 51)

Child witnesses have always posed a challenge to legal practice, testing the laws of evidence and necessitating special rules and procedures. The quote above gives an historic example of special procedures introduced for child witnesses. In the mid nineteenth century in England judges had to examine child witnesses on the nature of the oath to establish whether they were competent witnesses, worthy to take the oath. In this brief exchange with the young witness Mr Justice Maule negotiates and establishes what can be termed the 'conditions of credibility'. He is not concerned with the reliability of the girl's memory or her truthfulness, but being of young age she must demonstrate, by displaying a certain kind of knowledge, that the principles motivating her truthfulness are appropriate. In England in the mid nineteenth century 'fear of god' establishes credibility and guarantees truth; this is what constitutes the 'condition of credibility' in this moment.

In this chapter I suggest that the scientific and public debate on memories of sexual abuse could benefit from a detailed examination of how legal systems negotiate the tensions and ambiguities surrounding children's memory of sexual abuse, including legal attempts to make children's voices heard. This means examining memory in terms of the concrete practices through which its expression is negotiated, and exploring the dynamic and shifting conditions under which credibility is assessed and established. I will illustrate this approach by exploring child witness practice in England/Wales[1] on the background of the history of sexual abuse and child witnessing. The chapter draws on interview data from a larger research project that has compared child witness practice in England/Wales and Germany against the backdrop of a genealogy of suggestibility research (Motzkau, 2006).[2] I begin by positioning the issue of child witnessing and sexual abuse in a contemporary context.

Situating the problem: child witness practice in England and Wales

As a result of an increasing awareness of child sexual abuse since the 1970s, courts across Europe and North America are now admitting children as witnesses more frequently. Yet, there has been persistent wariness about the reliability of children's memory, and their ability to give evidence in legal proceedings. Since the late 1980s legislators in England/Wales have systematically consulted psychological research on children's memory and suggestibility to inform measures that could ensure better access to justice, particularly for child victims of sexual abuse. In 1991 they began to introduce special measures that protect child witnesses by accommodating their perceived needs, while at the same time ensuring the admissibility of their evidence in court (Spencer and Flin, 1993). This laudable effort stands in stark contrast to the fact that conviction rates for cases of rape and sexual abuse in England/Wales have dropped from 32 per cent in 1977 to an all time low of 5.5 per cent in 2002 (Kelly *et al.*, 2005), and 6 per cent in 2005/2006 (Feist *et al.*, 2007). With this England/Wales (alongside Northern Ireland) continue to register the lowest conviction rates in Europe (Kelly *et al.*, 2005; Westcott, 2006). In this context it is worth asking, what exactly constitutes the concrete conditions of credibility, and how do they relate to the apparent countereffectiveness of the measures introduced to accommodate child witnesses?

While courts of law have always played a notorious (and often tragic) role in the heated international and national debates around memory and sexual abuse, the literature on these debates lags in terms of an examination of the actual minutiae of national legal practices. These details, I would suggest merit close scrutiny because legal practices shape the powerful institutional processes that make memory matter in a range of contexts with lasting consequences for the lived realities of many.

I am focusing on child witnesses in particular because discourses around childhood and child protection are key to understanding the conditions under which recollections of abuse come to matter. In a critique of developmental psychology Burman (1994, 1997) points out that the way in which children are represented as 'natural origin', or the biological starting point of human functioning, turns them into 'methodological devices' that are used to understand adult memories of the past, warranting the classification of such memories as 'normal'/'abnormal', true/false. In this sense 'children' and the concept of 'childhood' function as a powerful currency within psychological and cultural practices, as Burman (1997) puts it, because they appeal to core cultural assumptions about origin, (sexual) innocence, goodness and immanence. My analysis will focus particularly on discourses around gender, agency and protection. I will demonstrate how conflicting repertoires around protection, gender and agency contribute to the paradoxical constitution of children's credibility, creating ambiguous and ultimately silencing positions for children.

Methods perspective

This analysis is situated within a critical qualitative and discourse analytic framework. The challenge of understanding childhood memories of abuse in relation to child witness practice comprises a methodological dilemma. While taking seriously the 'material truth' claims guiding the legal discourse's (proper) concern with justice, I will also examine the efficacy of the practices 'generating' those material truths. My perspective thereby straddles between that of 'realism' and 'constructionism'. In order to face up to this methodological dilemma I pursue this analysis in an exploratory spirit, adopting a syncretic methods perspective. I deliberately combine two different discourse analytic frameworks that some consider to be incommensurable (MacMartin, 1999), because they are seen to adopt contrary theoretical and methodological stances. First, the interview data is approached by utilising analytic tools associated with discourse and conversation analysis (Wetherell and Potter, 1992; Potter and Wetherell, 1987). Second, the broader analysis of the historical and socio-political context of child witness practice draws on what Parker termed 'critical discursive research' (Parker, 1992, 2002; Burman, 1994). Here the interview material is discussed through a critical account of historical, political and cultural dynamics that shape the acute reality of child witness practice, and the conditions of credibility. By simultaneously utilising these two analytic frameworks I hope to productively suspend the issue of constructionism versus realism that has in the past led to polarised debates between representatives of these two approaches (Edwards *et al.*, 1995; Parker, 2002). This way I hope to illustrate the possibilities emerging from what Latour expresses so pointedly in his comment on the debates around constructionism and realism.

> So we do not have to choose between realism and social construction because we should try to imagine a sort of mix up between the two ill-fated positions. Rather we have to decide between two philosophies: one in which construction and reality are opposite, and another in which constructing and realising are synonymous.
> (Latour, 1997: xiv)

Inspired by Latour's suggestion, we will see that it is by adopting the latter of these two philosophies (the one that considers constructing and realising as synonymous) that we might gain a more productive understanding of the dynamics that constitute the conditions under which memories of sexual abuse can be understood: the truth about the memory of trauma is at once 'constructed' and 'realised'. On a theoretical level Latour herein echoes theorists such as Hacking (1995), who suggests, in discussing issues around sexual abuse, 'It *is* a real evil, and it was so before the concept was constructed. Neither reality nor construction should be in question' (Hacking, 1995: 68).

Focusing on the concrete instant when memory is expressed, as well as the contexts and the conditions of its expression, will alert us to the fact that constructing and realising are always in play at the same time when memory emerges. This chapter will demonstrate that realising and constructing are both constitutive dimensions of memory as it is expressed. I argue that exploring this dynamic tension in the context of child witness practice can open a new perspective for the broader debate around the matter of memory.

Memory, suggestibility and child sexual abuse

The history of research on memory and suggestibility and the history of child witnessing and sexual abuse are intricately connected. I begin my analysis by mapping the broad historical, scientific and legal conditions under which children's memories of abuse are expressed and assessed at the intersection of psychology and law.

Children have traditionally held a dubious reputation as witnesses in courts of law. One of the most notorious set of cases, routinely cited as a cautionary tale of the unreliability of child witnesses, are the Salem witch trials in the USA in the seventeenth century.[3] Ceci and Bruck (1995) suspect that these trials were partly responsible for the deeply rooted mistrust practitioners in North American and European legal systems hold towards child witnesses. This mistrust is for example reflected in the corroboration laws that applied in a number of Western countries, including the USA and England/Wales, until the mid 1980s. These laws admitted children's testimony only if it was corroborated by an adult eyewitness (Spencer and Flin, 1993; Motzkau, 2006). It was found that this criterion posed particular problems for the prosecution of sexual abuse cases because in many of these cases the child victim may have been the only witness.

The concept of child sexual abuse, perceived as a social phenomenon, has only formed within the last few hundred years and, as Haaken (1998) puts it, has since had a long history of being forgotten and remembered. Throughout the eighteenth and nineteenth centuries numerous documented cases and scientific references reflect public awareness of child sexual abuse. Yet in the early twentieth century such cases became rare and Dalgleish and Morant (2001: 8) observe that 'there is almost no published work on the consequences of CSA in the first 60 years of the twentieth century'. While isolated legislative efforts, for example in England, reflected some awareness for the issue of child sexual abuse, 'there is an absence of any real professional or public debate about the issue until the 1960s or 1970s' (Dalgleish and Morant, 2001: 8).

Child sexual abuse re-entered public awareness and discussion in the late 1960s and 1970s, when the feminist movement gained political momentum and put issues like domestic violence, rape and child sexual abuse back into the public arena (Haaken, 1998; Levett, 2003). As a result of this increased awareness of child sexual abuse the corroboration laws came under scrutiny, and during the 1980s changes to judicial systems in North America and some European countries meant that courts admitted children's testimony in cases of alleged sexual abuse much more frequently (Westcott *et al.*, 2002).

Yet the new public trust in children's memory and testimony was undermined again. During the 1980s courts in North America and parts of Europe (e.g. England and Wales, and Germany) saw a number of high profile miscarriages of justice in child abuse cases that hinged on evidence given by children. In some cases children were reporting the most bizarre scenarios of ritualistic abuse by multiple perpetrators. Yet, the accounts were later dismissed as the result of suggestive and coercive questioning techniques by (presumably) well-intentioned carers or investigators (Ceci and Bruck, 1995; Ceci and Hembroke, 1998; Bell, 1988; Lee, 1999; Bull, 1998; Steller, 2000). These cases sparked an unprecedented research interest in children's suggestibility, a topic that had so far been entirely absent from the scientific agenda. At this point in the history of child sexual abuse, the question of children's suggestibility becomes crucial for assumptions about children's ability to remember traumatic events. So from this point on children's conditions of credibility are largely constituted by the varying concepts and assumptions about suggestibility. At this point, it is worth taking a brief look at the history of suggestibility research, because it forms the backdrop against which children's credibility is now assessed.

The history of suggestibility and child sexual abuse

Around 1880 both memory and suggestibility constituted central research topics for the nascent discipline of psychology. While memory remained a central topic, the interest in suggestibility waned in the early twentieth century, and between the 1950s and the late 1970s suggestibility vanished completely from the scientific agenda (Gheorghiu, 2000; Motzkau, 2006). Suggestibility only re-emerged as a research topic in the 1980s in the context of the growing concern over children's evidence in sexual abuse cases. Yet, researchers have continually struggled to define suggestibility. A rather broad definition that is used frequently states that suggestibility is 'the degree to which children's encoding, storage, retrieval, and reporting of events can be influenced by a range of social and psychological factors' (Ceci and Bruck, 1993: 404).

Throughout the 1990s the re-emerging concern of child sexual abuse is more and more dominated by this turn to suggestibility. Rather than attending to the variable determinants of children's memories as such, a myriad of studies then turned towards an investigation of the potential malleability of children's testimony. Research in this field remained riddled with contradictory results, and while numerous studies underlined children's ability to remember and to testify reliably (Goodman and Clarke-Steward, 1991), research also demonstrated that children could be made to deliver credible reports of events that had not happened. Such research concluded that it was possible, by using suggestion, to implant false memories into children (Ceci *et al.*, 1994; Leichtman and Ceci, 1995). It is interesting to note that the equally plausible reverse case, i.e. abused children being coached (e.g. by the abuser) into reporting (or even believing) nothing had happened, hardly featured as a research focus at all until very recently (Lyon and Saywitz, 2006; Pope, 1996).

'Implanted memory research' with children fascinated the public and attracted the attention of the international media (Burman, 1997). However, this research also raised methodological as well as ethical questions and generated heated international public and academic debates. Stephen Ceci (Ceci *et al.*, 1994), who was the first to claim having experimentally implanted false memories, was criticised harshly on ethical grounds for what the critics considered a violation of children's rights. His experiments, the critics feared, could irretrievably change and thus damage participating children's memories (Herrman and Yoder, 1998; Yoder and Herrman, 1998). Other researchers in the field criticised Ceci for methodological and experimental inaccuracies, pointing to unfounded or vastly overstated results and inaccurate statistics (Goodman *et al.*, 1998; Erdmann, 2001; Ceci, 1998; Motzkau, 2005). These debates were widely covered by the media, which fuelled a simplistic understanding of suggestibility research among the general public. Ultimately this fostered an exaggerated fear of children's vulnerability to suggestion. A number of researchers pointed out that the resulting wariness about children's suggestibility also filtered into legal procedure and decision-making, reinstating a general atmosphere of disbelief in children's testimony (Greuel, 2001). This atmosphere is also thought to have discouraged children and parents from reporting abuse, and was seen to dispose jury members against child witnesses (Goodman *et al.*, 1998).

Implanted memory research and the net-effects of the debate surrounding it had wider international repercussions. In England/Wales, for example, the Judicial Studies Board decided to use a film about Ceci and Bruck's implanted memory research as part of a training course for judges (Westcott, 1998). Academics in the field criticised the use of this film, because they felt that Ceci and Bruck's work gave 'the impression that [. . .] children's accounts of abuse are often false' (Myers, 1995: 392). Given the multiple methodological and ethical problems surrounding this research, the critics feared that, rather than providing the balanced scientific advice intended by the Judicial Studies Board, this film would prejudice judges against child witnesses by offering an unfounded but 'convincing demonstration of the unreliability of children's evidence' (Plotnikoff and Woolfson, 2002: 302).

Critics worried that the use of this film reflected the generally negative attitude towards children's credibility as court witnesses and would make the prosecution of child sexual abuse even more difficult.

Let me sum up the shared history of memory, suggestibility and child sexual abuse so far. The emerging trust in children's ability to accurately remember and report events that had triggered the legal changes of the 1980s has once more been overcome by the persistent wariness over the reliability of children's testimony and their vulnerability to suggestion. However, over the decades there has been a marked shift in the criteria that define the conditions of credibility. Since the late 1990s the guiding theme has not been 'sincerity' (or fear of god for that matter), or the capacity of children's memory as such; instead children's vulnerability to suggestion is now the main issue determining the conditions of their credibility. Suggestibility, however, remains an elusive and contested phenomenon, sparking debates that illustrate the complex scientific and legal stakes involved. The scientific community itself is inadvertently drawn into heated public and legal debates, thereby potentially affecting real life court cases. As a result of such net-effects, debates about children's credibility become increasingly polarised and charged, further complicating the prosecution of child sexual abuse.

To get a more complete picture of what this 'turn to suggestibility' means for current child witness practice in England and Wales, the history of child sexual abuse also needs to be considered against the backdrop of changes in international law.

Children's rights, memory and credibility

Since 1989 international law has unequivocally established that children must be given a voice in legal proceedings concerning them. Article 12 of the UN Convention on the Rights of the Child (1989)[4] states that:

1   States Parties shall assure to the child who is capable of forming his or her own views the right to express those views freely in all matters affecting the child, the views of the child being given due weight in accordance with the age and maturity of the child.
2   For this purposes the child shall in particular be provided the opportunity to be heard in any judicial and administrative proceedings affecting the child, either directly, or through a representative or an appropriate body, in a manner consistent with the procedural rules of national law.
(General Assembly of the UN, 1989)

This article is clearly intended to improve children's access to justice by establishing that they need to be given a voice in court. However, on closer inspection we can see that this article contains a twofold conditional clause, illustrating that the ambiguity surrounding children's conditions of credibility also pervades international law. The capability of forming own views and 'age and maturity' are not 'given' by the law, but article 12 leaves it open as to how they are established locally, in context and with regard to each particular child. For this to work there have to be criteria for judging this 'maturity', and depending on country and context these criteria will be delivered by cultural and/or developmental psychological knowledge. So by introducing open concepts such as 'maturity' the law implicitly refers the question of children's voice back to the specific context and to developmental psychology. The second conditional clause is to be found in the formulation that the 'opportunity' provided to be heard will be realised according to the existing rules of the respective national law. Again article 12 leaves the provision of a voice widely open to interpretation, and rather than solving it, passes the question back to individual rules of legal procedure. Lee (2001) argues that this apparent ambivalence towards children, which seems implicitly to invalidate the very promise it is attempting to make, was an unavoidable ingredient of this law at the time of its creation. If article 12 functions, Lee argues, it functions to generate and expose, rather than to resolve, the otherwise implicit childhood ambiguity and 'then lays the responsibility for managing that ambiguity on the legislatures and policy-makers of the states that have ratified it' (Lee, 2001: 96). What Lee terms childhood ambiguity is the issue at the heart of societal and scientific issues around child sexual abuse on the one hand, and children's credibility and suggestibility on the other. Article 12 of the UN Convention on the Rights of the Child demonstrates that children's memory and credibility remain a problem situated somewhere between psychology and law, between psychological and legal truths, and thus are negotiated and produced at the intersection of psychological and legal practices. They have to be managed locally and continuously via the practices implemented to handle, negotiate and contain such ambiguity.

The ambiguous stance of international law within the history of memory, suggestibility and child sexual abuse clearly highlights the importance of exploring concrete legal practice for understanding children's conditions of credibility. We found earlier that over the past decades there has been a shift in focus from a concern about children's memory to a wariness of their suggestibility. We can now see that this shift in focus from memory to suggestibility has two central implications for legal practice.

First, with suggestibility as the primary issue, the focus shifts from potential deficits in memory encoding or storage to the instant of remembering as such, i.e. attention is directed to the expression of memory. Now the concrete conditions under which remembering is called for and occurs, and the circumstances under which memory is reported, become key to legal considerations of accuracy and credibility. Thus legal procedure now has to acknowledge that remembering is a reciprocal and contextual dynamic: remembering involves the rememberer as much as those who listen/ask, and it depends on the circumstances under which this process takes place. Inevitably this poses a dilemma for legal practice which now has to take into account its own unwitting influence on child witnesses' memory, and the way it is expressed and perceived. And legal practice has to do this in the light of contradictory and inconclusive research about suggestibility.

Second, the concept of suggestibility itself affords an intriguing shift in the attribution of the 'ownership' of memory. With suggestibility the idea is introduced that children, particularly, are not in control of their own memories, i.e. that they cannot exercise authority over the contents of their memory and thus cannot be trusted to assess the truth value of events they remember. On the one hand, assuming children are not in control of their own memories solves the dilemma of having to suspect children had deliberately given false accounts in court cases. But on the other hand, assuming children are not in control of their memories also means that the criteria for their credibility cannot be found within them. Following this rationale credibility always has to be established via external criteria. Yet, this means such judgements would have to rely on the guidance of research findings or ultimately the public's common sense. Considering the lack of clarity about the phenomenon of suggestibility and the ambiguous ways in which research itself became drawn into the net-effects of public and legal debates about sexual abuse and suggestibility research, this seems a circular solution.

So by referring the problem back to the ambiguous criteria and operations at the intersection of psychological and legal practice, the conditions of children's credibility are effectively rendered paradoxical. It is the same kind of paradoxicality we can observe in article 12 of the UN Convention on the Rights of the Child, which makes the promise of giving children a voice, while implicitly invalidating this promise through the way it is passed on as an ambiguous task for psychological and (in particular) legal practices. In the following I will examine in more detail how legal practices in England and Wales handle this promise.

Child witness practice in England/Wales: creating reliable witnesses

How and at what cost do different legal practices address the dilemma of having to give children a voice while systematically distrusting their ability to satisfy the legal 'call to truth'? How do they handle the paradox of credibility and what are the specific conditions of credibility for children's memories as they emerge in legal practice? I have examined these questions in detail in a study that compared child witness practice in England/Wales and Germany (Motzkau, 2006). In the following I will draw on two exemplary interview excerpts from this study, and explore child witness practice in England/Wales in the light of latest procedural changes. Tracing the way the expression of memory is negotiated in these excerpts, I focus in particular on colliding discourses around child protection, gender and the child's agency within the context of sexual abuse.

In 1988 England/Wales had abolished the corroboration laws that previously excluded children's evidence unless corroborated by an adult eyewitness.

In the following decade legal procedure saw further dramatic changes. The 1991 Criminal Evidence Act[5] and the Youth Justice and Criminal Evidence Act 1999 implemented a number of special measures for children and other 'vulnerable witnesses'.[6] Crucially these measures include the facility for children's evidence to be video recorded during their initial police interview. This video can be passed on to be reviewed by the prosecution, and where it comes to a trial, the video will be played in court to the jury to replace the child's 'evidence in chief' (initial witness statement in court). Other measures aim to assist children's potential courtroom appearance, and children are routinely cross-examined via live CCTV link, avoiding their courtroom appearance altogether. Overall these measures create conditions under which children are hoped to provide the most detailed and accurate information because they are less intimidated or confused. Effectively one could say that these measures act as a filter for information; they are a form of informational hygiene. The measures purify or filter information by minimising fear, or the conditions under which children might become fearful or confused, while still allowing for useful information to emerge and be communicated. At the same time the measures are designed to maintain a fair trial, by making sure the evidence can be tested, is reliable/consistent, and expressed unambiguously. This is, for example, achieved by capturing the child's statement on video at the earliest possible time, and thus separating the child from their account. The video then acts as a proxy witness for the reliable storage and stable expression of memory throughout the investigative and legal process. The aim is to provide a mechanism whereby children's voices will emerge and be heard, while their testimony is 'cleansed' of the ambiguity, unreliability and irritability characteristic of child witnesses (Motzkau, 2007). The video, as a proxy memory and proxy witness, is intended to preserve, disambiguate and amplify children's voice in order to express their memory and make it matter in court.

Childhood, gender, credibility

The following excerpt is part of an interview with a crown prosecutor, who explains how helpful she finds the video recorded evidence when assessing the credibility of a child witness, and deciding whether to prosecute or drop a case.[7]

Excerpt 1

CP1:
```
1  [. . .] I think they're go:od I think they're I think they're (2) as a way of
2  looking at the child  and seeing how the child will come across to the
3  jury ((hmhm)) I mean I had one (2) I  was really chuffed about this [. . .]
4  I had ahm a video tape that I watched for a five year old ((hmhm)) now
5  (1) that's young for here we don't normally prosecute on the evidence
6  of a five year old ((hmhm)) that's it's unusual ((hmhm)) (1) ahm and she
```

7   was an absolute   sta:r ahm it was an indecent assault [. . .] and she
8   descri:::bed it (3) perfectly (1) this and this was a child who could not
9   have made it up (1) you know her innocence shone through on the
10 video (1) absolute (1) o::h she was a doll absolute doll ahm (1) and you
11 watched it and there was n:o corroboration at all (1) nothing absolutely
12 nothing except her word and normally you'd think long and hard about
13 that with just such a small child but (2) [. . .] she was s:o good I said well
14 let's let's prosecute because I think a jury will believe every word she says
15 [. . .] and he got three years he was convicted ((hmhm)) that's a really
16 good example of I think how helpful having a video can be because it
17 helps to ass' you to you know ((hmhm)) just assess °what they are like° (2)
18 you know you get you get some that're (3) sort of look shif:t::y but then
19 it's it [. . .] must be (3) hideous so you I think you've got to take into
20 account (2) that they might look shifty and uncomfortable because they
21 are uncomfortable you know so ahm (3) but it's I think they're very good
22 they're very useful I much prefer them [. . .]

What does the prosecutor's account and the way it is presented reveal about the way the conditions of credibility are negotiated and established in this specific case, and at this moment? The prosecutor reports an unusual case she was particularly 'chuffed about' (line 3), because she considers this a particularly good example of how helpful videos are. In accordance with English/Welsh legal procedure the frame of reference outlined by the prosecutor for the assessment of credibility is the anticipated gaze of the prospective jury (how it 'will come across to the jury', lines 2–3). When tracing the prosecutor's careful elaboration of the criteria of credibility, however, her account shifts between issues of 'looking'/'seeing' on the one hand, and 'hearing' the account on the other. She shifts between reference to what the girl said ('she described it perfectly', lines 7–8) on the one hand, and '*looking* at the child' (line 2) and '*seeing* how the child will come across' (line 2) on the other hand. But what made this evidence so impressive? Why could this child 'not have made it up' (lines 8–9), and why would the jury 'believe every word she says' (line 14)?

Initially it seems it is the girl's account that convinced the prosecutor, as the girl 'described it perfectly' (line 8). But then she qualifies this by adding that 'this was a child who could not have made it up' (lines 8–9) because 'her innocence shone through on the video' (lines 9–10), which again is underscored by the prosecutor's emphatic exclamation that the girl was 'absolute (1) ohh she was a doll an absolute doll' (line 10). Highlighting the absence of corroboration, which would be a key criterion of credibility, the prosecutor emphasises repeatedly that there was '*no* corroboration *at all* (1) *nothing* (.) *absolutely nothing* except her word' (lines 11–12). Here the last phrase is crucial, because it establishes the distinction between what the girl said, that is, 'her word', and what the girl 'was', i.e. 'innocent', a 'doll'. This clearly indicates that 'her word' would not have sufficed. Yet, the evidential weakness of her word (uncorroborated evidence of a five-year-old) was of no concern because 'she *was* an absolute star' (lines 6–7). But what makes 'innocence' and 'doll-likeness' such powerful signifiers of credibility?

Notions of 'innocence' and 'doll-likeness' resonate directly with the problematic and gendered implications of the dominant discourses of developmental psychology and child protection. As Erica Burman (1997) suggests, 'Repertoires about children embody conflicting assumptions concerned with innocence, vulnerability, dependency, nostalgia for the past, hopes for the future, original sin or intimations of the unquashed, unalienated spirit here to come' (p. 294). Let me sketch out these conflicting assumptions in some more detail.

Over the past decades a number of scholars have deconstructed the traditional concept of development and exposed its powerful role within scientific, institutional and political discourses around childhood (e.g. Burman, 1994, 1997; Walkerdine, 1988, 1993; Morss, 1990, 1996). In various ways these scholars have problematised the traditional representation of development as a process of natural maturation and linear progressive change by showing that it obscures the powerful political, cultural and emotional dynamics that are implicated within this purportedly 'natural maturation' of children. Unravelling these hidden agendas, Morss (1996) outlines how the assumption of childhood as a 'natural' state of developmental origin implicitly positions children as deficient, and thus warrants their representation as partial, provisional members of society. They are not yet 'beings' but merely 'becomings', not fully present yet as Morss (1996) puts it, and thus not autonomous but dependent and in need of guidance. Burman (2003) points out that implied within these apparently unproblematic (natural) categories of dependency and need for guidance there are broader cultural-political rationales of governing and controlling children as future citizens: 'it seems there are broad cultural-political investments in maintaining children and young people as docile and dependent through educational, legal and welfare practices that portray them as deficient and therefore in need of training and/or protection' (Burman, 2003: 39). Following this critique, the dominant discourse of child protection is constructed around an imagery of children as passive, vulnerable, dependent, and thus deserving of protection. However, implicitly this concept of 'protecting the vulnerable' also provides a rationale for 'keeping' them dependent and controlling them.

Another discourse closely linked to naturalness and dependency centres on the way 'normal' childhood has been idealised as an untainted state of bliss and naïve innocence (Bradley, 1989). Crucially 'innocence' also implies a moral dimension. In the narratives of the modern Western world the child has come to be constituted as an asexual being. Stainton Rogers and Stainton Rogers (1992, 1998) have minutely traced this 'desexualisation' of childhood showing that it resulted in an atmosphere where any association of children with sexuality has become so unspeakable and unthinkable that issues like sexual abuse can only feature as the unspeakable paramount evil. They argue that it is this 'special-ness' of sex in relation to children and our imaginary identification with their innocence that causes the polarisation and panic that is so characteristic of debates around child sexual abuse. It is this 'visceral terror', as they put it, that creates the seemingly 'instinctive', but often counterproductive urge to protect children. In this context Burman (2003) points to the gendered dimension within the developmental narrative where the 'child of development' is typically the active, white, rational, autonomous little boy, while the 'state' from which development takes place is 'typically a feminised and infantilised arena' (p. 39). Hence it is young girls who most clearly represent development as a state of neediness and vulnerability. However, girls at the same time engender desirability in its most ambiguous force, appealing as much to fantasies of protection as to fantasies of seduction and possession (Stainton Rogers and Stainton Rogers, 1992). This is where discourses of childhood and gender ultimately collide around child protection. They collide because 'vulnerability' resonates with passiveness and dependency while seductiveness resonates with an ambiguous form of agency and (sexual) knowledgeability (if not 'cunning'). As we will see in the following analysis, this collision creates an additional complication around sex and gender, posing a particular problem where a girl's credibility is concerned.

The 'child' as such is usually represented as asexual, innocent and thus devoid of gender. In the context of sexual abuse, however, this conception is fractured because the different gendered positions of boys and girls in relation to the (predominantly male) abuser inevitably become relevant. Here it is the 'girl child' that is cast in a doubled position of vulnerability, both on the basis of youth and of gender. With vulnerability and the need for protection, on the one hand, and seductive desirability on the other hand, girls become the complex site of surplus moral investments and social control because they threaten the dominant conceptions of childhood innocence.[8]

So while different and similarly problematic dynamics apply to boys, it is girls in particular who must be denied any kind of knowledge and agency in relation to sexuality, in order for them to be seen as untainted by implications of active seduction or even complicity. This discursive collision creates paradoxical conditions for girls' credibility as witnesses in abuse cases, because they inevitably end up displaying forms of knowledge that collide with and threaten the dominant discourse of childhood innocence and protection. Let me return to the transcript segment to develop these points in more detail, and to see how and at what cost the conditions of credibility are established in the example reported by the prosecutor.

The video, as a proxy witness, does work in favour of the girl in this example. But rather than amplifying her voice, as was intended, the video renders the child passive. As indicated earlier, it is not her word that convinces the prosecutor, but as we can see now, it is the degree to which the video demonstrates the girl to fit the criteria of a protectable child. She is a *pretty little girl* ('a doll'), sufficiently 'little' to 'radiate' *natural innocence*, still naïve and thus untainted; she is asexual like a doll and hence not just unambiguously pretty (i.e. beautiful but not seductive) and vulnerable, but also perfectly *dependent* and *passive* (like a doll), in need of protection and with no mind of her own to fantasise or the capacity to construct or even contemplate a lie. Crucially a 'doll' does not speak, but a doll radiates these qualities. They do not have to be voiced or claimed explicitly, but they can be seen 'shining through' (line 9) on the video. These are the discursive resources mobilised within the repertoires of 'doll-likeness' and 'shining innocence'. Hence these are the discursive resources that give meaning to the prosecutor's claim that 'this was a child who could not have made it up' (lines 8–9).

These conditions of credibility operate at a cost. While they work in favour of the girl in this particular example, when considering them in the context of child witness practice in general it becomes clear that they create problematic positions for the majority of child witnesses. When unable to fit the 'doll-category', 'looking shifty' (line 18) as the prosecutor puts it, or indeed having reached an age where girls as adolescents are very often seen as 'not quite so innocent', 'too knowledgeable', or prone to deceit and promiscuity, they stand less chance of appearing credible or even getting to court. I will examine this problem in more detail in relation to the next interview excerpt.

Innocence, agency, gender: credibility colliding with protection

In the following excerpt an English high court judge replies to a challenge by the interviewer about the appropriateness of the jury system for the assessment of child abuse cases. While initially defending the jury system, he moves on to report that juries do make unexpected acquittals in cases where children have failed to complain about an ongoing abuse.

Excerpt 2

Judge:
1 [...] most of us feel that jurors come up with the right verdicts ((hmhm))
2 ahhhm and you can always find an answer well I know wha' y' know °y' ca'
3 why did they find not guilty the:re° then you always know OHHH it was
4 because you know he didn't tell the teacher or you know ((hmhm)) I
5 mean that's usually the fatal thing is when they don't tell their parents
6 the 's what juries don't understand and a little girl said it once (2) I'm
7 only a child I didn't know what I you know she was sort of four years at
8 doing it °why didn't you anyone you could tell your mother when that
9 started° *[voiced softly as if addressing a child]* (1) I was only a child I
10 didn't know what to do I was frightened he was my father (1) NOW you
11 hope juries would understand that but cases where there're acquittals
12 acquit u::sually where kids have failed to complain in circumstances
13 where you would think they would ((hmhm)) ahhhm but they not
14 because as this one said I I was only a child she was nine or ten °I think°

15 ((hmhm)) never want to do it which I didn't say like I'm saying well this 's
16 what she was saying which was very good [. . .]⁹

Just as in the previous example, this excerpt refers to a young girl, but in this case the girl is not deemed credible. Interestingly the child in this example is reported to have spoken openly and unambiguously to the court. Following the judge's account, the girl delivered a clear and plausible explanation for why she had failed to complain at the time. Notably the girl herself explicitly enlists the traditional developmental discourse; more precisely, she enlists the protection discourse and appeals to her own helplessness. She appeals to her qualities as a victim by presenting herself as being '*only* a child' (lines 6–7) hence innocent and dependent, which meant she 'didn't know what to do' (lines 9–10), was passive and helpless. She was 'frightened' (line 10), vulnerable and unable to act for herself. Given this elaborate recruitment of the 'protection discourse', why is her voice still problematic? Why will juries 'usually' (line 12) acquit in such cases, when in the previous excerpt the jury was reported to have believed 'every word' the girl said (excerpt 1, line 14)?

To untangle the conflicting discourses operant in this excerpt, we need to examine what it is that 'you hope juries would understand' (lines 10–11), as the judge puts it. Further, we need to see why it should be 'fatal' (line 5) for children not to 'complain in circumstances where you would think they would' (lines 12–13). In saying '*you* would think' the judge presents this as a generalised common sense 'we all share' about children and when they 'should' complain. But what constitutes this apparent common sense notion of such circumstances? Referring back to the work of Burman (1994, 2002, 2003) and Stainton Rogers and Stainton Rogers (1992, 1998), we can see that the girl in this example is caught at the paradoxical intersection of three colliding discourses. These are the discourses around innocence/protection, agency/credibility and gender/sexuality.

The child protection discourse, arranged around the developmental metanarrative of children as asexual, dependent and innocent victims (Stainton Rogers and Stainton Rogers, 1992), implies that children should display what could be called an immediate response to harm, and an 'instinctive' repulsion against anything of a sexual nature. Hence it 'should' come 'natural' to a child to instantly complain had something as terrible as sexual abuse happened to them. This runs counter to established findings by researchers and clinicians, who have pointed to multiple reasons why abuse is often not disclosed (Cawson *et al.*, 2000; Jones, 2000). Jury members' common sense, however, as reflected in the judge's account, clearly resonates with the implications of discourses around childhood innocence/protection. Juries struggle to 'understand' that a child would not complain, which implies that the failure to do so would be considered suspicious and can serve to undermine the child's credibility.

Further, the colliding issues of agency and credibility at work here can be illustrated in relation to the ambiguous rendering of article 12 of the UN

Convention on the Rights of the Child discussed earlier in this chapter. This article refers to those children who are 'capable of forming' their own views, and it states that due weight should be given in 'accordance with age and maturity'. Yet maturity and the capability to form one's own views are intricately linked to agency, accountability and thus responsibility. That is, displaying independency, agency and accountability is commonly taken to be an indicator of maturity. Thus, being able to display signs of maturity and agency will also contribute favourably to being perceived as a credible witness. A person who is seen to be independent, accountable and in charge of their life, someone who can present themselves as a responsible agent within their own narrative, will be considered capable of speaking the truth in a mature, accountable and responsible manner.[10] Yet, for child witnesses in abuse cases these competing demands are difficult to balance because appearing too capable of forming views ('being a little too assertive'), or appearing too independent (or indeed 'aggressive'), will render them unable to lay claim to the protection discourse.

Finally, and crucially for the girl in this second example, appearing too 'active' and 'knowledgeable' in relation to sexuality, turns her into a dubious witness. She is not passive enough and not sufficiently detached from issues of a sexual nature. In the context of the 'failure to complain' or resist, such doubts could even amalgamate into the implicit or explicit suspicion of her own complicity or guilt.[11]

The girl is not seen as credible precisely because she is speaking up in court and trying to account for her story. The paradoxical conditions of credibility operating in this practice mean that while the girl in the first example manages to strike the delicate balance of passive, yet innocent vulnerability, the girl in the second case is too passive (in the past) and at the same time not passive enough (in court), and even though the judge appreciates her explanation (line 16), this girl is not considered credible. By definition, passiveness, innocence and vulnerability cannot be voiced or 'argued', they need to 'shine through', they need to radiate, express themselves 'naturally' to be recognised by the spectator.

Since the circumstances of the girl in this second case are by no means unusual, it is clear that child witness practices resolve the paradox of credibility at the expense of making a potentially large number of child witnesses seem lacking in credibility. Ultimately the conditions of credibility that operate around the expression of children's memory in this practice are in danger of systematically rendering children speechless or in turn positioning them in such a way that their 'speaking' becomes problematic in court, as they seem to be speaking up *against* justice.

To avoid misunderstanding let me clarify my analytic position in relation to the cases described here. Both excerpts refer to very serious 'real life' cases. In the absence of any further information it is impossible to even speculate about what exactly led to the respective trial outcomes. In this analysis I did not mean to examine or compare the actual cases, nor did I mean to make

Speaking up against justice   79

claims about the appropriateness of legal procedure or decisions. My analysis focused exclusively on the way the legal professionals presented those cases, giving us an exemplary glimpse at how the conditions of credibility are expressed and negotiated in this specific context.[12]

The expression of memory: constructing and realising

I would like to take another look at the prosecutor's and the judge's account, because they both express a peculiar, if transient, paradox that is worthy of further examination. Looking at lines 19–21 in the prosecutor's account (excerpt 1), we can see that the prosecutor concludes her statement with the paradoxical plausibility that 'you've got to take into account that they might look shifty and uncomfortable because they are uncomfortable' (lines 19–21). This is paradoxical because the prosecutor has just elaborated at length that videos are helpful in assessing credibility precisely because they allow her to see that some witnesses are 'shifty' while others display the 'shining innocence' she refers to in her example of the young girl. By adding that 'shiftiness' could also be a ubiquitous sign of (justified) discomfort, rather than an indication of insincerity, she contradicts the dominant criteria of credibility she has identified as being so distinctly helpful a moment earlier. This would mean that 'just' assessing 'what they are like' (line 17) is not at all straightforward, and the video creates more ambiguity than it resolves. What I find remarkable about this paradox is not the personal self-contradiction (or her potential awareness of it). Rather, this ambiguous turn shows more generally that the paradox of credibility is not permanently resolved by the dominant discourses the prosecutor employs and that we could see underpinning this practice (see earlier analysis of the prosecutor's account). The prosecutor's account illustrates that the paradox of credibility remains at the heart of these concrete practice operations, demonstrating the constitutive volatility of this practice. This paradox, or as we can say transient openness, at the heart of this practice, communicates itself briefly via the contradictory turn the prosecutor adds, apparently casually, to conclude her account.

The judge's overall statement (see excerpt 2) expresses a transient paradox very similar to that expressed by the prosecutor. He says he feels 'that jurors come up with the right verdicts' (line 1), but then he moves to present a case example where, even though he avoids explicitly saying so, the jury 'usually' does *not* get it quite right, or indeed fails to understand something that 'you hope juries would understand' (lines 10–11). As with the video in the prosecutor's example, we can see that the jurors' 'common sense' in this case adds more ambiguity than it resolves. It is not surprising that an English judge should trust the jury system, and as in the previous example, I am not so much interested in the self-contradiction (or the judge's potential awareness of it). But at the moment of utterance the judge's statement demonstrates that the paradox of credibility is not eradicated by the dominant discourses that are implicitly guiding the 'common sense of the jury'. The paradox communicates itself through the judge's account, and while it is transient in its expression (i.e. judge and prosecutor ultimately gloss over it and it does not 'overthrow/contradict' practice as such), its persistent recurrence indicates that the concrete operations of practice, as they occur, are quite unstable and volatile. In advancing this point, my aim is not to depict individual instances of 'bad practice', 'unprofessional conduct' or legal 'malpractice'. On the contrary, my main point is to observe that these 'operative paradoxes' are constitutive elements of legal practice as such.

Understood in this way we can see that these paradoxes are not rare occurrences or special instances of personal doubt. A broader look at child witness practice reveals that it is riddled with such transient paradoxes (Motzkau, 2006). They pervade the powerful institutional structure through which the expression of memory is negotiated. They express the ambiguities that underpin the concrete operations of this practice, and they highlight that children's credibility is not as such set and defined by the dominant discourses. In this sense the paradoxes express the fact that the ambiguities surrounding children have to be negotiated and contained actively and continuously for practice to function. Such a dynamic depiction of legal practice collides with the traditional picture of legal practice as driven by static rules and a concern for an objectifiable, absolute truth. Clearly, the law must orient towards 'what really happened', and this determines its call to truth. Still, having traced the fact finding dynamic of the law and some of the concrete operations that negotiate the conditions of credibility, it becomes clear that we cannot determine what constitutes this 'absolute truth' of memory independently of its expression within those practices. The continuous process, the dynamic of the expression of memory within practice, is an inextricable part of the 'truth of memory'.

This is why in order to function, legal practice must operate dynamically. The manifestation of truth, or indeed 'fact finding', is a momentary punctuation, and thus realisation of and within the ongoing dynamics of practice, as it is performed. This finding need not imply that the law is simply 'relative' or systematically 'fabricating' its truths. Recognising the importance of the concrete 'fact-finding-process' of legal practice means to become alert to the fact that legal practices (just as other practices) need to continuously and actively reassert and establish their relation to this truth and the way it is expressed by memory. In a very real sense legal practice is in the simultaneous business of realising and constructing.

Concluding

In this chapter I have aimed to demonstrate how a detailed exploration of history, theory and practice surrounding child witnessing and sexual abuse could open up new perspectives for the debate surrounding memory and sexual abuse.

The analysis presented here does not conclusively explain the apparent ineffectiveness of the reformed child witness practices in England/Wales. However, it does suggest that we need to adopt a more detailed perspective towards the ways in which special measures operate in the context of legal proceedings. Even beyond potential issues of 'bad practice' or 'unprofessional conduct', special measures constitute a systematic structural problem within legal practice. The attempts by the legal system to create 'opportunities' for children's voices to be heard end up rendering them passive and inaudible. Thus the well-intentioned special measures systemically perpetuate the problematic implications of discourses around childhood, protection, gender and credibility. Further, we could say that these measures in effect protect the courts from the ambiguity children carry. Special measures could be considered as an attempt by the legal system to produce the kinds of child witnesses it can handle – passive victims whose 'innocence shines through' on videos, while they do not actually say anything or even speak up. In this context we could see that the child's voice is doubly precarious (i.e. endangered and dangerous), and the (justified) call for children's protection ends up undermining their credibility and eclipsing their actual right to speak. Considerations of child witnesses' credibility are pertinent for problems surrounding adult reports of childhood trauma. The dynamics surrounding child witnesses inevitably feed into the public and legal discourses through which the truth value of adult recollections of child sexual abuse is negotiated, making their stories even harder to tell. In a perfidious twist, we could speculate that the more our current legal systems are (perceived to be) struggling to deal with child witnesses/victims of sexual abuse, the larger the number of those who might only report/disclose their sexual abuse when they are adults.

In order to understand memory, we need to examine the concrete and shifting conditions of its expression. This means attending to the conditions of credibility as they are continuously constituted through the operations of, and encounters within different practices (e.g. legal, therapeutic, research). Legal practice is one of the most powerful institutional practices concerned with the expression of memory; hence examining the micro-dynamics of legal practice encounters could make a valuable contribution to wider debates around the way memory matters.

Notes

1 Northern Ireland and Scotland form independent legal jurisdictions with different legal procedures.
2 'Cross-Examining suggestibility: memory, childhood, expertise' (Motzkau, 2006). The transdisciplinary approach combined a genealogy of the history and theory of suggestibility research with the analysis of empirical data gathered in interviews with legal practitioners and psychological researchers/experts in England and Germany.
3 In 1692 in Salem (Massachusetts) 19 villagers were convicted of witchcraft and executed based on evidence given by a group of children (in spite of the children withdrawing their accusations during the trial) (Spencer and Flin, 1993).

4 Ratified by all nations (exceptions: Somalia, USA).
5 Acts of Parliament: http://www.opsi.gov.uk/acts.
6 Children are now defined as 'vulnerable witnesses'. The term 'vulnerable and intimidated witnesses' includes all witnesses under the age of 17, elderly, disabled witnesses and adult victims of sexual and physical violence (for details: articles 16.–17., Youth Justice and Criminal Evidence Act 1999).
7 The interview was conducted in 2004 for Motzkau (2006). For this chapter the excerpts were edited with omissions indicated by square brackets '[. . .]'. The overall character of the exchanges is not altered by the omissions. The transcript notations used are a simplified and modified version of the system developed by Jefferson (1984). Transcript notations: Pauses: rounded brackets indicating seconds '(1)'; speaker emphasis: '<u>underlining</u>'; acknowledgement by other speaker: '((double rounded brackets))'; silently voiced utterances: '°degree signs°'; words drawn out: 'col::ons'; loudly voiced utterances: 'CAPITALISED'.
8 This ambiguity and thus need for control is reflected, Burman (2002) argues, in repertoires about girls being dominated by a discourse of original sin, rather than innocence (e.g. debates around teenage pregnancies, prosecution of rape, issues of consent and the increasingly popular 'girls-asking for it' discourse).
9 J2: 753–83.
10 Ingrid Palmary (2005) delivers an intriguing analysis of a dynamic closely related to my example. Palmary analyses the accounts of refugee women in Johannesburg, South Africa, who have been displaced from the African Great Lakes region. She explores how the romanticised positioning of women as politically inactive, not guilty of, or accountable for conflict, positions them as pure victims of violence and persecution. However, this positioning will in return silence them in their own resistance and claims to agency. Innocence here resonates with deserving of help as well as with passivity and not having a politically credible or active voice. For a related but slightly different take on 'agency' see Reavey and Brown (2006).
11 Clare MacMartin's research (MacMartin, 2001) offers an intriguing example of a very similar dynamic at work in Canadian courts. She analysed offence descriptions in criminal trial judgements (in Canada judges will provide an elaborately reasoned, written account of the judgement). She found that in some cases descriptions of complaints provided resources that judges 'mobilized as a warrant for doubt by contrasting children's negative reception of sexual abuse with the innocuous or positive character of subsequent social contact with offenders. This argument emphasizes the agency of children in consenting to affiliate with offenders, presuming that authentic victims can and would avoid further involvement' (MacMartin, 2001: 9).
12 I would like to express my gratitude to the prosecutors and judges who agreed to be interviewed for this research, and to the Crown Prosecution Services and the Royal Courts of Justice who approved this research. Without their engagement and collaboration this research would not have been possible!

References

Bell, S. (1988) *When Salem Came to the Boro. The True Story of the Cleveland Child Abuse Crisis*. London: Pan Books.
Bradley, B. S. (1989) *Visions of Infancy: A Critical Introduction to Child Psychology*. Cambridge: Polity Press.
Bull, R. (1998) 'Obtaining information from child witnesses', in A. Memon, A. Vrij and R. Bull (eds) *Psychology and Law. Truthfulness, Accuracy and Credibility*. London: McGraw-Hill Publishing Company.
Burman, E. (1994) *Deconstructing Developmental Psychology*. London: Routledge.

Burman, E. (1997) 'Telling stories. Psychologists, children and the production of "false memories" ', *Theory and Psychology* 7(3): 291–309.

Burman, E. (2002) *Children and Sexuality: Contested Relationships Around the Control of Desire and Action*. Paper for 'Contested Childhood in a Changing Global Order', University of Michigan, USA, 3 April, 2002.

Burman, E. (2003) 'Childhood, sexual abuse and contemporary political subjects', in P. Reavey and S. Warner (eds) *New Feminist Stories of Child Sexual Abuse*. London: Routledge.

Cawson, A., Wattam, A., Brooker, K. and Kelly, L. (2000) *Child Maltreatment in the United Kingdom: A Study of the Prevalence of Child Abuse and Neglect*. London: NSPCC.

Ceci, S. J. (1998) 'On the ethics of memory implantation research', *Applied Cognitive Psychology* 12: 230–40.

Ceci, S. J. and Bruck, M. (1993) 'The suggestibility of child witnesses: a historical review and synthesis', *Psychological Bulletin* 113: 403–39.

Ceci, S. J. and Bruck, M. (1995) *Jeopardy in the Courtroom*. Washington DC: American Psychological Association.

Ceci, S. J. and Hembroke, H. (1998) *Expert Witnesses in Child Abuse Cases*. Washington DC: American Psychological Association.

Ceci, S. J., Huffmann, M. L. C., Smith, E. and Loftus, E. F. (1994) 'Repeatedly thinking about a non-event: source misattributions among preschoolers', *Consciousness and Cognition* 3: 388–407.

Dalgleish, T. and Morant, N. (2001) 'Socio-historical perspective', in G. M. Davies and T. Dalgleish (eds) *Recovered Memories. Seeking the Middle Ground*. West Sussex: Wiley & Sons.

Edwards, D., Ashmore, M. and Potter, J. (1995) 'Death and furniture: the rhetoric, politics and theology of bottom line arguments against relativism', *History of the Human Sciences* 8: 25–49.

Erdmann, K. (2001) Induktion von Pseudoerinnerungen von Kindern. Dissertation. FU-Berlin.

Feist, A., Ashe, J., Lawrence, J., McPhee, D. and Wilson, R. (2007) 'Investigating and detecting recorded offences of rape', *Home Office Online Report 18/07*.

General Assembly of the United Nations (1989) *UN Convention on the Rights of the Child*. www.un.org.

Gheorghiu, V. A. (2000) 'Suggestion und Suggestibilität: Stiefkinder der Psychologie' ['Suggestion and suggestibility: stepchildren of psychology']. Presentation for the XV International Conference for Hypnosis, Munich 2000. Unpublished manuscript.

Goodman, G. S. and Clarke-Steward, A. (1991) 'Suggestibility in children's testimony: implications for child sexual abuse investigations', in D. L. Doris (ed.) *The Suggestibility of Children's Recollections*. Washington DC: American Psychological Association.

Goodman, G., Quas, J. A. and Redlich, A. D. (1998) 'The ethics of conducting "false memory" research with children: a reply to Herrman and Yoder', *Applied Cognitive Psychology* 12: 207–17.

Greuel, L. (2001) *Wirklichkeit – Erinnerung – Aussage*. Weinheim: Psychologie Verlags Union.

Haaken, J. (1998) *Pillar of Salt. Gender, Memory and the Perils of Looking Back*. London: Rutgers University Press.

Hacking, I. (1995) *Rewriting the Soul. Multiple Personalities and the Sciences of Memory*. New Jersey: Princeton University Press.

Herrman, D. and Yoder, C. (1998) 'The potential effects of the implanted memory paradigm on child subjects', *Applied Cognitive Psychology* 12: 198–206.

Jefferson, G. (1984) 'Transcript notation', in J. M. Atkinson and J. Heritage (eds) *Structures of Social Action: Studies in Conversation Analysis*. Cambridge: Cambridge University Press.

Jones, D. P. H. (2000) 'Editorial. Disclosure of child sexual abuse', *Child Abuse and Neglect* 24: 269–71.

Kelly, L., Lovett, J. and Regan, L. (2005) 'A gap or a chasm? Attrition in reported rape cases', *Home Office Research Study 293*. London: Home Office Research, Development and Statistics Directorate.

Latour, B. (1997) 'Foreword. Stenger's Shibboleth', in I. Stengers (ed.) *Power and Invention. Situating Science*. Minneapolis: University of Minnesota Press.

Lee, N. (1999) 'Distributions of childhood's ambiguity in adult institutions', *Childhood. A Global Journal of Child Research* 6(4): 455–74.

Lee, N. M. (2001) *Childhood and Society. Growing up in an Age of Uncertainty*. Buckingham: Open University Press.

Leichtman, M. D. and Ceci, S. J. (1995) 'The effects of stereotypes and suggestions on preschoolers' reports', *Developmental Psychology* 31: 568–78.

Levett, A. (2003) 'Problems of cultural imperialism in the study of child sexual abuse', in P. Reavey and S. Warner (eds) *New Feminist Stories of Child Sexual Abuse*. London: Routledge, pp. 52–76.

Lyon, T. D. and Saywitz, K. J. (2006) 'From post-mortem to preventive medicine: next steps for research on child witnesses', *Journal of Social Issues* 62(4): 833–61.

MacMartin, C. (1999) 'Disclosure as discourse. Theorizing children's reports of sexual abuse', *Theory and Psychology* 9(4): 503–32.

MacMartin, C. (2001) '(Un)reasonable doubt? The invocation of children's consent in sexual abuse trial judgements', *Discourse and Society* 13(1): 9–40.

Morss, J. R. (1990) *The Biologising of Childhood: Developmental Psychology and the Darwinian Myth*. London: Laurence Erlbaum Associates.

Morss, J. R. (1996) *Growing Critical. Alternatives to Developmental Psychology*. London: Routledge.

Motzkau, J. F. (2005) 'Cross-examining suggestibility: memory, childhood, expertise. Children's testimony between psychological research and juridical practice', in A. Czerederecka, T. Jaskiewicz-Obydzinska, R. Roesch and J. Wojcikiewicz (eds) *Forensic Psychology and Law: Facing the Challenges of a Changing World*. Krakow: Institute of Forensic Research Publishers.

Motzkau, J. F. (2006) *Cross-examining suggestibility: memory, childhood, expertise*. Loughborough University, unpublished doctoral thesis.

Motzkau, J. F. (2007, January) 'Matters of suggestibility, memory and time: child witnesses in court and what really happened. *Forum Qualitative Sozialforschung/ Forum: Qualitative Social Research* [On-line Journal], 8(1), Art. 14. Available at: http://www.qualitative-research.net/fqs-texte/1-07/07-1-14-e.htm (accessed: 24.2.2007).

Myers, J. (1995) 'New era of skepticism regarding children's credibility', *Psychology, Public Policy and Law* 1: 387–98.

Palmary, I. (2005) 'Family resistances: women, war and the family in the African Great Lakes', *Annual Review of Critical Psychology. Feminisms and Activisms* 4: 54–66.

Parker, I. (1992) *Discourse Dynamics: Critical Analysis for Social and Individual Psychology*. London: Routledge.

Parker, I. (2002) *Critical Discursive Psychology*. New York: Palgrave.

Plotnikoff, J. and Woolfson, R. (2002) 'What do judges know about young witnesses?', in H. L. Westcott, D. M. Davies and R. H. C. Bull (eds) *Children's Testimony. Handbook of Psychological Research and Forensic Practice*. New York: Wiley & Sons.

Pope, K. S. (1996) 'Memory, abuse and science. Questioning claims about the false memory epidemic', *American Psychologist* 51(9): 957–74.

Potter, J. and Wetherell, M. (1987) *Discourse and Social Psychology: Beyond Attitudes and Behaviour*. London: Sage.

Reavey, P. and Brown, S. D. (2006) 'Transforming agency and action in the past, into present time: adult memories and child sexual abuse', *Theory and Psychology* 16(2): 179–202.

Spencer, J. R. and Flin, R. (1993) *The Evidence of Children. The Law and The Psychology*. London: Blackstone Press.

Stainton Rogers, R. and Stainton Rogers, W. (1992) *Stories of Childhood: Shifting Agendas of Child Concern*. Hemel Hempstead: Harvester Wheatsheaf.

Stainton Rogers, R. and Stainton Rogers, W. (1998) 'Word children', in K. Lesnik-Oberstein (ed.) *Children in Culture*. London: Macmillan.

Steller, M. (2000) 'Forensische Aussagepsychologie als angewandte Entwicklungs- und Kognitionspsychologie', *Praxis der Rechtspsychologie (Sonderheft 1)* 9–28.

Walkerdine, V. (1987) 'No laughing matter: girl's comics and the preparation for adolescent sexuality', in J. M. Broughton (ed.) *Critical Theories of Developmental Psychology*. New York: Plenum Press.

Walkerdine, V. (1988) *The Mastery of Reason. Cognitive Development and the Production of Rationality*. London: Routledge.

Walkerdine, V. (1993) 'Beyond developmentalism', *Theory and Psychology* 3(4): 451–69.

Westcott, H. L. (1998) 'Jeopardy in the courtroom', *British Journal of Psychology* 89: 525–7.

Westcott, H. L. (2006) 'Child witness testimony: what do we know and where do we go?', *Child and Family Law Quarterly* 18(2): 175–90.

Westcott, H. L., Davies, G. M. and Bull, R. H. C. (2002) *Children's Testimony. Handbook of Psychological Research and Forensic Practice*. New York: Wiley & Sons.

Wetherell, M. and Potter, J. (1992) *Mapping the Language of Racism: Discourse and the Legitimation of Exploitation*. Chichester: Columbia University Press.

Yoder, C. and Herrman, D. (1998) 'Revisiting the ethics of implanted memory research with children', *Applied Cognitive Psychology* 12: 245–9.

5 Transformations of public and private knowledge
Audience reception, feminism and the experience of childhood sexual abuse[1]

Jenny Kitzinger

This chapter examines an extraordinary cultural transformation in public and private knowledge: the '(re)discovery' of child sexual abuse in the late twentieth century.[2] It draws on interviews and focus group discussions conducted during the 1980s and 1990s to explore how dramatic changes in mass media coverage influenced public and personal perceptions of this issue. Focusing on the experiences of women and girls in the UK, my research highlights the media's role in helping to shape the way we understand and frame sexual abuse. Media coverage made a crucial contribution to a spiral of recognition. It encouraged the formation and expression of private identities around previously fragmented and silenced experience. It helped sexual abuse, particularly incest, to enter public discourse. This research throws into question any simple and inevitable division between those with 'recovered memories' and those who 'always knew' by exploring the complex processes through which individuals come to recognise, name and articulate experience in the light of a changing cultural context. Media coverage of sexual violence continues into the twenty-first century. However, the lessons from this research – conducted through a time of radical transition – highlight the way in which cultural resources are mobilised in constructing memory/experience and narratives about the self.

Media discovery of child sexual abuse

Child sexual abuse, particularly incest, became a high profile issue in many different countries during the 1980s and 1990s. In the UK and US the foundations for this change were laid by feminist initiatives addressing physical and sexual abuse of adult women. Workers in battered women's refuges established during the 1970s began to find women seeking help because of sexual abuse of their children. Similarly, some of those ringing Rape Crisis lines were calling, not because they had been attacked recently, but because of abuse during childhood, often by men that they knew. The issue was also exposed in consciousness raising groups and through testimonies from individual survivors (Armstrong, 1994). During the late 1970s and early 1980s, childhood sexual abuse was addressed in a series of key feminist texts: theory, testimony, fiction and autobiography. These included: *Kiss Daddy Goodnight* (Armstrong, 1978), *The Best Kept Secret* (Rush, 1980), *Incest: Fact and Myth* (Nelson, 1982), *Father-Daughter Rape* (Ward, 1984) and *I Know Why the Caged Bird Sings* (Angelou, published in the US in 1969, but not in the UK until 1984).

It was not until 1986, however, that the UK mass media began to pay attention to the issue (a similar discovery having occurred in the US a little earlier). Prior to this media attention to child sexual abuse was characterised by flurries of coverage around abductions and rapes by strangers. Incest was barely mentioned. Sexual abuse was known by a roll call of murdered children and profiles of particular individuals (most notoriously, in the UK, Ian Brady and Myra Hindley). The start of broader public recognition, particularly of abuse by family and friends, was signalled in 1986 with Esther Rantzen's programme, *Childwatch*, which launched the children's helpline, Childline. This was accompanied by a remarkable expansion in attention from the rest of the UK media. Analysis of *The Times* newspaper, for example, shows that coverage of sexual abuse increased by 300 per cent between 1985 and 1987 and attention shifted toward sexual abuse within the family (Kitzinger, 1996). Such abuse also became an issue for documentary programmes, featuring in flagship series such as *Brass Tacks* (BBC2, 7 July 1987); *Everyman* (BBC1, 8 May 1988); *Antenna* (BBC2, 10 May 1989) and *Horizon* (BBC2, 19 June 1989). It also became a topic for discussion programmes and chat shows (e.g. *Oprah*) and was the focus of several TV films (e.g. *Something about Amelia*, BBC2, 6 March 1989). By the early 1990s child sexual abuse began to appear in regular police, hospital and legal drama such as *The Bill* (ITV, 29 January 1993), *Casualty* (BBC1, 6 February 1993) and *LA Law* (Channel 4, 16 March 1994). It also featured in soap opera story lines, most extensively the 'Beth Jordache' story on *Brookside*, which ran from March 1993 (see Henderson, 1996).

These examples of recent history of media coverage provide a crude but striking index of a revolution in the public profile of sexual abuse. This was not a smooth and unproblematic transition. Although media coverage acknowledged widespread abuse, much of it evaded the full implications of assaults within the family and still treated each incident of such abuse as an isolated aberration (Kitzinger and Skidmore, 1995). In addition, peak news coverage focused on contested allegations, including the Cleveland and Orkney scandals and, more recently, the phenomenon of so-called 'false memory syndrome' (see Nava, 1988; Campbell, 1997; Kitzinger, 1998, 2000). In any case journalists' attention was seldom informed by feminist analysis. Indeed, media coverage has been extensively criticised for everything from promoting stereotypes of abusers and disempowering children (Kitzinger, 1988, 1999) to exploiting an incest entertainment 'industry' in which sexual abuse is used to titillate and fascinate (Armstrong, 1994).

However, these critiques are not the focus of this chapter. Here attention is drawn, instead, to the overall growth in coverage and the way in which this marked a decisive swing from cultural vacuum to, at times obsessive, media attention. This chapter demonstrates how this shift in media recognition impacted on public consciousness and how it influenced, and was used by, those with personal experiences of abuse. I argue that the sheer fact of media acknowledgement challenged abusers' monopoly over definitions of reality and undermined some of their power to silence victims. It created the potential for redefinition of women's experiences into the public domain.

The research: recording personal accounts during the 1980s and 1990s

The material that informs this chapter was collected as part of two separate research projects, one conducted in the 1980s, the other in the 1990s. I started work around child sexual abuse as a feminist activist, coming from a background in social anthropology with little knowledge of media studies. In the early 1980s I became involved in a collective setting up a helpline and then a refuge for teenage girls seeking to escape sexual abuse at home. The young women who contacted us needed accommodation and support; they also expressed a desire to learn about other survivors' experiences. This was the original impetus behind my first research project. It involved tape-recorded interviews with 40 sexual abuse survivors and mothers of sexually abused children. The interviews explored their experiences of dealing with sexual abuse and the process of survival. The youngest interviewee was 16 years old, the oldest was 59. These interviews were conducted over a time period which proved to be one of decisive social change: 1984 to 1989 (with most interviews being conducted between 1985 and 1987). Although media representation was not the focus of this research, it emerged as a crucial issue for my research participants.

The second research project which informs this chapter was conducted in the mid 1990s. By this point I had developed an interest in media studies and joined the Glasgow University Media Research Group. After conducting a series of projects about audience reception of health issues (such as AIDS), I obtained an ESRC grant to study the production, content and reception of media coverage about child sexual abuse. The audience reception part of this study involved 49 focus group discussions with 275 participants, aged between 14 and 79. These research participants included both men and women, and those with and without personal experience of sexual abuse.

This chapter draws primarily on my first piece of research. However, it also uses some data from the more recent focus groups. The time span covered by the two projects (1984 to 1995), combined with the wide age range of the research participants (14 to 79), yields data spanning a broad historical period. Many of the abuse survivors I spoke to had been children between the 1940s and 1970s while others, interviewed for the second project, grew up during the 1980s and early 1990s. Most of those interviewed in the first project were abused during a time when the subject was completely taboo. Some were interviewed while that taboo still prevailed. Others, interviewed *after* 1986, had lived through a dramatic transition in public discussion of sexual abuse. By the time I conducted the second project the context had changed. Some younger participants who spoke to me during the mid 1990s had grown up surrounded by a plethora of media representation of sexual abuse. Teenage focus group participants interviewed in 1995, for example, had been abused during the late 1980s or early 1990s (after the launch of Childline and during the media furore about the Orkney scandal – a famous case of contested allegations – see Kitzinger, 2004). Re-reading both sets of transcripts I was struck by the strong sense of history that emerges. The transcripts highlight how dramatic changes in media recognition during the course of the two projects transformed public knowledge. They also demonstrate how the media is implicated in 'private' knowledge: making sense of intimate experiences of violence within domestic space, providing a framework for personal interaction and reference points for building a sense of identity.

From cultural vacuum to media mediation: survivors' accounts of the media's role

Prior to 1986 incestuously abused children and adult survivors had to process their experiences in an almost total cultural vacuum. Some grew up thinking that abuse was perfectly normal. 'He told me it was something that all daddies do with their little girls.' Others believed that no one else had ever 'participated' in anything so unnatural and disgusting. (Although some had sisters or brothers who were also victimised, it was never discussed between them at the time.) Even as adults, survivors often had no words to define what was happening to them, other, perhaps, than the explanations offered by abusers. As one woman explained: 'I had absolutely no words for it, all the words I had were the ones *he* gave me'.

In interviews conducted during the early 1980s women struggle to articulate the literally unspeakable. They often consciously experienced the interview itself as an arena for discourse construction, a process of 'putting together the pieces of the jigsaw'. During the course of talking to me they tried to unpick ideas imposed on them by their abusers ('you are my little princess', 'this isn't happening', 'you want this', 'you deserve this'). They also often made observations about the interview process such as 'I'd never seen it that way until just now' or 'I've never said this before but . . .'.

I always offered to send women copies of their own transcripts. I adopted this practice in response to feminist theory about ethical research processes (Kelly, 1988). This practice also helped generate new data. Several responded to reading their own transcripts with remarks such as: 'This is the first time I've seen anything like this in black and white'. I read one young woman's transcript to her over the phone because it was not safe to post anything to her home. Even though it recorded her own words she commented that it was the first time she had even heard such a story. She found it very shocking and it made her look at her experiences differently

Obviously, there are structural aspects to child sexual abuse that make articulating issues around the experience difficult. Abuse may always generate a sense of isolation, dislocation and confusion. Complex feelings can be generated by abusers' manipulation of reality and their insistence on secrecy. Issues will also arise because of the early (even pre-verbal) age at which children might be abused and their efforts to accommodate to repeated victimisation (see Summit, 1983; Kitzinger, 1990a). Many survivors today will recognise feelings described by those talking in the 1980s. However, the contemporary scene in the UK (as in the US) means that there are now far more cultural resources for confronting abuse and women who spoke to me during the late 1980s were starkly aware of this change.

As children, teenagers and adults, prior to 1986, survivors recollected struggling to make sense of what had been done to them within the conventional categories available to them at that time. Many had, for many years, been confused or unsure about how to understand or define what had happened to them. They made comments such as: 'I just had these funny ideas floating around in my head – I had no way of making sense of them'. One interviewee described her confusion and distress about her stepfather's 'fondling' and contrasted this with her sense of clarity when he finally forced her to have sexual intercourse. Then, and only then, could she identify his acts as assault. She recalled this generating a sense of 'relief'.

> Afterwards I thought, 'Jesus, I've been raped, I've been raped'. Like all the stuff before was just other things. I'd never seen it as rape because whenever you're told about it in newspapers or school it's always that, it's never anything else. So I thought: 'I've actually been raped this time. He's actually raped me now'. It felt quite real. *It felt real because I could call it something* [my emphasis]. It really happened. (Liza)[3]

Another young woman, however, was unable to name her experiences as rape in spite of her father penetrating her. This was because she felt that she had displayed insufficient resistance and she saw rape in stereotyped terms as an encounter in a dark alleyway with 'a man with a knife'. In fact she argued that she could *never* be raped by anyone because, even if she were attacked by a stranger with a knife: 'I would just lie down and take it, to get it over with'.[4] Her 'consent' to sex under these circumstances would thus, in her view, mean that she had not been raped.

The absence of media discussion of the range and subtlety, as well as the power dynamics, of incestuous assault made it hard for children to resist pressure to dismiss what had happened to them as consensual. Some women felt they had never been able to identify what was happening. The lack of cultural tools to understand what was occurring and the inability to 'call it something' was also highlighted by mothers of abused children. Deficiencies in everyday language prior to 1986 were vividly illustrated by one mother who recalled searching through the dictionary for information about 'incest'. It was the only place she could think to turn to for information. The dictionary definition simply talked about marriage between blood relations and was of no help. Another interviewee, who I shall call Kathy, described how ill equipped she felt to confront the possibility of sexual abuse until she actually walked in on her husband with her daughter.

> [I felt] totally as though I was just in a nightmare and when daylight came I would wake up and it hadn't happened. And daylight came, and it didn't go away. [. . .] [Finding my husband in there] confirmed what I knew, although I didn't know I knew it. (Kathy)

Throughout her account Kathy stressed the absence of cultural reference points and having to respond by 'instinct', 'like an animal', without any guidance:

> It felt just as though it were a primitive kind of instinct. I had to protect her. It was just like an animal, you know, the young have been threatened and you just have to close round them and just protect them. And that is what I did, in any way I knew how. But I had absolutely no model whatever, *that was the horrible part of it*. [my emphasis] [. . .] I just didn't know anything about sexual abuse. I remember thinking: 'if only I had read something about it'. But I had never read anything about it. [. . .] only awful stories in the paper [about abduction], but no useful articles in women's magazines that said 'I did so and so'. These things just weren't around then. (Kathy)

Only two of my research participants described media coverage prior to 1986 as a positive resource. In both cases this was not because the media represented abuse, but rather the opposite. One young woman said she would watch TV sitcoms and use them to make up stories about her own family life in order to disguise the abuse and neglect she suffered. Another explained that media representations of happy families helped her to realise that her experience was not normal.

> Because if you've been brought up with it [abuse] all your life then you can't even think about a different situation . . . So you don't actually have a vision of how life could be different, to motivate you to get something different. All I've got is [. . .] the situations I see on television or when I go round to a friend's house and see the family altogether. [. . .] Their dads don't go in and say goodnight the way my dad did. Their dads just go in and say: 'Goodnight, sleep well' and go back to their beds again. That never happened in my family. (Samantha)

From 1986 onwards, however, the rapid rise in media coverage helped to increase general public awareness and inform parents, as well as becoming a resource for children and adults recognising their own abuse. This was clearly acknowledged in the focus groups I conducted during the mid 1990s. Research participants made comments such as: 'Nobody knew about such things when I was young, now it's even on children's programmes like *Grange Hill*' (Group 35) and 'I recall my parents saying: "Now don't talk to strangers" [. . .], that was about the end of it. But now everyone's looking round every corner [. . .] the whole culture's changing or it's changed' (Group 37). People often reported that this coverage altered their own views on the subject:

> We never talked about it in my day. I've no doubt it went on, but it just wasn't discussed. It's right to be out in the open now. I realise now it's going on. (Group 58)

> Ten years ago I found it hard to believe that fathers abused their daughters. But now I realise it's often just like that. I know that largely because of the telly, it comes back to the media. (Group 5)

This recognition of a cultural transformation was even more acute among those with direct experience of abuse and often had profound personal ramifications. Abuse survivors who had grown up without their experiences recognised by the dominant culture began to find words and images for what had happened to them. Many adults began literally to 're-collect' and 're-member' abusive childhoods. Some of my interviewees described how they had begun to re-assess what had happened to them – finally realising that it was wrong or 'not normal' or that they did not deserve it. Others found that media coverage forced them to confront memories that they had been trying to ignore. It was media coverage, rather than comments from friends or family, which was most often identified as a trigger for confronting childhood abuse.[5] Amy, for example, described how she first sought help in the second half of the 1980s because: 'It were too much, it were all coming on the telly and it were starting to really get to me'. Others described a slow process of making sense of what had happened in the context of increased publicity:

> It started being talked about a bit more in the media and then I heard a radio programme, that made me start thinking about it . . . Whenever he abused me he never said a word I always found this silence around it a very loud thing. It's all been so silent. (Joanne)

Recognition on TV and radio, in newspapers, magazines and films became a vital part of women's process of naming and making sense of their memories. Women referred to the importance of representation in every form: from the 'agony' column in magazines to TV news reports, from soap opera to current affairs discussions. The interviewees did not usually distinguish between genres or formats for these purposes (hence this chapter does not discuss such distinctions). As Joanne explained:

> [What ever it is] it legitimises your experiences, it is saying 'yes, it does happen' and you know that other people are reading it and are accepting it. Whether it's fact or fiction, whether it is research or autobiography or whatever, it's adding to this. I know when I read Sarah Nelson [a journalist who also published a book on sexual abuse in 1982] it was wonderful seeing all the basic feelings that I had there. [. . .] [And] it moves people forward all the time, and it isn't just odd people saying things [. . .] it is actually down on paper. [. . .] it's not just me having a fantasy in my head about this, many people believe this. (Joanne)

As well as legitimating the reality of incest ('it's not just me having a fantasy'), media reporting about sexual abuse also, in very practical ways, helped people both to tell, and to ask, about such experiences. One young woman, for example, saved up two early articles about incest from women's magazines and used these to tell her mother what was happening.

> I was hysterical. I'd been smoking a lot of dope and I was feeling really, really low . . . I ran into the house screaming 'Mum, come and help me, I need to talk to you' and she came out and said 'Oh, what?' And she pushed me into the caravan and she couldn't understand what I was saying and I shoved these two articles from women's magazines under her nose. (Melissa)

Another woman explicitly relied on a particular programme to help her to find out whether her daughter was being abused.

> I didn't know how to approach it. But I remembered Esther Rantzen's programme which suggested asking: 'Has anyone ever touched you or made you feel uncomfortable?' So I asked her, and she said: 'Yes, today a boy threw a ball and it hit my head' [. . .] I said: 'Yes, that was today, what about anyone else?' And she said: 'Yes, dad' and started screaming. She wept and wept, I'd never heard a child cry like that. (Shiobhan)[6]

The media coverage could trigger discussions of their abuse memories with other family members: a sister, brother, cousin or aunt. Sometimes they would then discover that this relative had also been victimised by the same perpetrator (e.g. the grandfather). For many interviewees there was also a quite complex interplay between media representation, public discussion and a re-definition and revelation of experience. One woman, for example, was in her early twenties when she attended a feminist film and post-viewing discussion about pornography held in her local arts cinema. This film, *Not a Love*

Story, included footage of explicit and violent pornography. She was familiar with such images because her abuser had forced her to look at porn magazines as a child. The film and surrounding discussion made her re-evaluate what he had done to her. It also provided a context for talking about it in public for the first time.

> Everyone in the audience was really shocked [by the porn] and I was thinking: 'God, I have seen all this before'. What got me in a state of shock wasn't that it was new, but that I had seen it all before and nobody else seemed to have. For the first time it made me think what a real bastard he is. It really brought it home to me what he had done. [. . .] After about three-quarters of an hour of them all talking about how upsetting it was, I told them that I had seen all that when I was eight. (Liza)

Examples of engaging and using the media were even more prevalent in the focus groups I conducted in the mid 1990s.[7] Films, television programmes, newspaper reports and magazine articles had become an important resource in identifying, exploring and comparing experience. One group of young survivors for example, emphasised the value to them of the in-depth portrayal of incest survivor, Beth Jordache, in the soap opera, *Brookside*:

> You can watch it and say – I had those feelings like Beth, that happened to me. [. . .] We've got some kind of communication with the telly and can talk to each other about the way Beth is. (Group 48, f3)

Another member of this group commented on how a TV film, *Liar, Liar*, had improved relations with her mother:

> My mum watched it with me. In the film the mother doesn't believe – my ma watched it and saw what pressure the girl went through and it made her see how *I* could feel. (Group 48, f2)

A third girl, whose mother was less understanding, had videotaped and repeatedly watched an audience discussion programme (*Kilroy*) because it showed supportive family reactions:

> It was on about two years ago – families talking about how they'd reacted. I've got that on video and I kept re-watching it, wishing my mum had so much sympathy. (Group 48, f1)

Far from feeling that their experiences were invisible, some survivors in the 1990s felt that their experiences had become public property. One, for example, described becoming upset while watching the film *Liar, Liar* with her little sister: 'My wee sister says: "What are you greeting [crying] for? It's only a film". But then she said: "Oh, that was *you*" ' (Group 48, f3). Another member of this group agreed, adding: 'You don't know if they are watching it, or putting *you* in the film and watching you' (Group 48, f1).

Indeed, media representations (even positive ones) could cause considerable discomfort and distress, especially when a viewer was taken off-guard: 'When it comes on the telly, and I'm not expecting it, I go dead cold inside and it brings back memories' (Group 48, f1). In this context of media construction of the problem, women also became vulnerable to stereotypical, gratuitous or destructive representations. The character of Beth Jordache in *Brookside* was not only important as a cultural resource for talking about feelings (see above), but offered an unusual and important model of survival (at least before this character was killed off and written out of the series). One research participant summarised the sentiments of many other survivors:

> Victims on TV, they're like a big shadow, all blacked out. That makes me feel terrible, they're hiding away. [. . .] I thought: 'I'm going to grow up and I'm going to be scared of everything'. But Beth [in *Brookside*], she's so strong, she's got a grip of everything. Before that, everything I saw seemed to say that if you were abused you'd be strange, different, keep yourself in a wee corner. Watching Beth has really helped me. (Group 48, f3)

This young woman was not alone in her feelings. When news leaked that the character of Beth Jordache was to be written out of *Brookside* through a fatal heart condition, incest survivors' groups demonstrated outside the TV studios to try to save this valuable representation of survival.

The media, identity, and social change

The interviews and focus group discussions with survivors of childhood sexual abuse demonstrate the crucial significance of the media. Because this data spans a decade during which there were highly significant changes in media coverage, the research also highlights the role the media played in shaping the memories and accounts of survivors over time. Prior to 1986 survivors could glean little useful information from a media (and broader culture) that failed to acknowledge their experiences. In the second half of the 1980s, however, sexual abuse, particularly within the family, gained a dramatic public profile. Media coverage helped many survivors to identify their own abuse and to speak out about what had happened to them. It led many parents to recognise the possibility that their children might be victims and provided a context for asking about abusive experiences. Media attention, whether through television, films or newspapers, in the form of documentary or fiction narratives, had profound implications for what people could imagine, what they could say, and what they felt they had the right to resist. It influenced how survivors constructed their identities and envisaged possibilities for the future. The media discovery of sexual abuse fundamentally transformed private and public discourse about this issue: opening it up for both personal reflection and community discussion.

The media have a key role in popularising new discursive repertoires and shaping personal identity (Grodin and Lindloff, 1996). The interaction between individual experience and culturally available narrative can generate further social change – mobilising professional and expert knowledges and policies, which, in their turn, impact on the objects of that knowledge. As Hacking notes: 'You might think that the experiences speak for themselves, at least for the victims. Yes – and yet events, no matter how painful or terrifying, have been experienced or recalled *as child abuse* only after consciousness-raising. That requires inventing new descriptions, providing new ways to see old acts – and a great deal of social agitation' (Hacking, 1995: 55). Once a new idea takes root it can, in turn, transform the 'object of knowledge'. As Hacking puts it: 'There is a feedback effect. Classification of people and their actions affects the people and their actions, which in turn affects our knowledge about them and classification of them [. . .] The people who are the objects of our concept of child abuse become different' (Hacking, 1998: 55, 62). Hacking's argument resonates with perspectives which have emerged from the radical survivor movement. Alcoff and Gray, for example, argue that in order to theorise personal experience it is important to realise that 'subjectivity will be constituted by our discourses' and vital to be 'aware of the danger that even in our own confessionals within autonomous spaces we can construct ourselves as reified victims or as responsible for our own victimization' (Alcoff and Gray, 1993: 284). There is, they argue, no such thing as 'pretheoretical' experience. Recognising this does not mean one has to be a complete relativist about how we experience reality. Instead it is important to recognise that:

> [T]here are multiple (not infinite) ways to experience sexual violence: as deserved or not deserved, as humiliating to the victim or as humiliating to the perpetrator, or as an inevitable feature of women's lot or as a socially sanctioned but eradicable evil. And this more adequately reflects the experience most of us have had of 'coming to' our anger and even our hurt only after we have adopted the political and theoretical position that we did not deserve such treatment or bring it on ourselves.
> (Alcoff and Gray, 1993: 284; see also Worrell, 2003)

Press and TV reports can be part of this process. My interviews show how media representations can help to reconfigure memories and transform the ways in which experiences are interpreted ('I know now that I never deserved it'; 'It really brought it home to me what he had done'). The media, for better or for worse, are implicated in the very way in which we think about ourselves and relate to one another.

Recognising the media's role in this process of transformation does not mean that the media achieved this in isolation from social movements. Nor can the media be credited with initiating the 'discovery'. The groundwork for change lay in earlier activities by feminists and survivors. However, the transformations witnessed since the 1980s could not have happened without mass media involvement and some campaigning journalists who made crucial contributions. The media's role in defining the public domain is such that, had newspaper, radio, magazine and television reporting continued to ignore incest, obstacles to public recognition of the problem would have been far more daunting. Alternative press and other grassroots avenues for bringing sexual abuse into public discourse were limited. The isolation, stigma and taboo around abuse were such that it was a difficult subject to raise, even though the fact that many survivors *did* speak out publicly was crucial to media coverage. The mass media's discovery of sexual violence against children facilitated, and may have been a prerequisite for, its transition from shameful, individual secret to public, social issue. Mass media attention ricocheted through the general population and became a catalyst for change at an intimate, private, as well as public, level.

However, media recognition of sexual abuse is, of course, not a cause for uncritical celebration. It can be a double-edged sword in that silence and invisibility are not the only ways in which power can operate. Power also operates through representation and 'the gaze' (Foucault, 1990; Haaken, 1999; Bell, 1993). The media selectively publicises *certain kinds* of stories and in *certain kinds* of ways. As society has increasingly recognised incest, the incest survivor has increasingly been 'subject to discourse', scrutiny and control (over and above that imposed by the abuser). Survivors are now targeted as mental health clients and offered terminology ranging from discovering their 'inner-child' to 'multiple personality disorder' in ways which may constrain and discipline as much as they enable and liberate (Hacking, 1995; Haaken, 1998). Indeed, we now see a new identity of victimhood being peddled by the media. The complexity of the early feminist analysis of how women's narratives are shaped has been obscured (Alcoff and Gray, 1993; Armstrong, 1994; Scott, 1998: 1.6). Instead the media (along with some self-help and therapy texts) have psycho-pathologised survivors (Brown and Burman, 1997). Sexual abuse has become increasingly enmeshed in expert vocabularies (Kelly, 1996) and the path to survivorhood is mapped through self-help and therapy guidelines in ways which neutralise feminist analysis (Kitzinger, 1992). Sometimes sexual abuse is adopted as a 'master narrative' to explain a host of less readily articulated female ills, promoting simplistic redemption narratives (Lamb, 1999; Haaken, 1999; Reavey and Warner, 2003).

Many of these problematic developments are discussed in subsequent chapters in this volume. Here, however, I conclude by reflecting on the implications of my research on child sexual abuse and the media for future directions in feminism and media studies.

Conclusions: future directions for feminist media studies

We now have an established, if still contested, canon of feminist media research which highlights the operations of gendered power relations in media consumption. Studies have examined how women's use of the media reflects or challenges traditional female roles of wife and mother. Feminist writers have reclaimed pleasure, fantasy and feminine genres of popular culture as serious objects of study. They have documented, and demanded recognition of, women's cultural competencies. (See, for example, Ang, 1985; Brunsdon, 1981; Gray, 1987; Hobson, 1980, 1982; Modleski, 1984; Radway, 1984; Seiter *et al.*, 1989; Winship, 1987). These areas of enquiry have been very significant in the development of media and cultural studies. However, gaps remain in the field of feminist critical enquiry, particularly in relation to how the media influences public and private understandings of key social problems. Media scholars have focused less, for example, on how women's activism has impacted on popular culture or how media representations of 'women's issues' have been received (exceptions include Skidmore, 1998; van Zoonen, 1994; Schlesinger *et al.*, 1992). Indeed, there is often a clear division, and sometimes mutual antagonism, between feminist work (focused on women's activity as audiences) and research into the production and formation of popular culture. I think this division should be challenged.

We urgently need more feminist work on media production, representation and influence. Such work is important *politically* because media advocacy has historically formed a vital strand of feminist activism and is likely to continue to do so. After all, a great deal of feminist activism has been concerned with ensuring that 'private' issues are placed on the public agenda. Media advocacy has been an essential part of campaigns to change laws around provocation when women kill violent partners (Hester *et al.*, 1996). It has also formed a fundamental strategy for activists fighting for public recognition of, and policies against, everything from mass rape in war to the international traffic in women as well as being extensively used to promote women's health issues (e.g. around childbirth or breast cancer) (Gallagher, 2001; Byerly and Ross, 2006). At the same time the media are, of course, also targeted by 'the opposition' such as those wishing to discredit equal rights legislation or to challenge feminist analyses of sexual violence (Kitzinger, 1998).

The study of how feminist activism and media advocacy impact on public understandings of a social issue also holds important implications for media *theory*. We are in a promising historical period in being able to review and reflect on momentous social changes initiated by the Women's Liberation Movement. Studying such changes can generate insight for media studies precisely because they explore boundaries between private and public, personal and political boundaries disrupted by feminist interventions around the family, relationships, the body, sexuality and domestic violence.

Research into how 'public knowledge' is constructed is a crucial part of feminist studies, and indeed, of media studies in general. It is equally important that 'public knowledge projects' (Corner, 1991) enlist the insights of feminists. Feminist scholars have criticised the traditional 'public knowledge project' on several counts: accusing it of focusing on 'male' over 'female' news and displaying a concern with ostensibly gender-neutral issues such as citizenship while neglecting the problematic relation of non-white, non-male (and, one might add, non-adult) citizens to the public sphere (van Zoonen, 1994 cited in Gray, 1999). Feminist critics, along with others from a critical cultural studies perspective, have suggested that some media studies academics unreflectively replicate a cultural hierarchy of 'hard' fact over 'soft' fiction, highbrow over lowbrow, and masculine over feminine (Gray, 1999). These critics have pointed to the importance of popular culture to political communication and understanding (van Zoonen, 2000). They have also questioned traditional male concepts of what constitutes 'the political' and argued against a focus on what people 'know' without looking at the constitution of imagination or feeling.

My research supports arguments for recognising the significance of fictional accounts as well as factual ones, 'soft' news as well as 'hard' news. The role of soap opera in representing child sexual abuse, for example, was vital (see also Henderson, 1996). Other research projects, such as those examining media coverage of breast cancer or human cloning, reveal similar findings about the importance of soft or fictional genres ranging from radio plays to science fiction films (see Henderson and Kitzinger, 1999; Haran *et al.*, 2007). Research which explores audience responses shows how people respond to media reporting of a scientific discovery, illness, social problem or political dispute. Further, these related studies suggest that empathy, personal interest, and identification come into play and intersect with the ways that people interact around media representations. Feminist insights in relation to the 'public knowledge project' have a vital contribution to make in expanding definitions of key public issues, developing multi-layered enquiries, and investigating the intersections between the public and private, the individual and collective.

Feminist media studies can also make a crucial contribution to contemporary debates about media influence and effects. One way in which we can do this is by giving due attention to the interplay between cultural resources and self-narration. For example, a crude 'hypodermic effects model' (the term developed by the Frankfurt School in the 1930s) suggests that media messages flow directly into the hearts and minds of the public. Such a model could suggest that the 'epidemic' of adult survivors recalling sexual violence during recent years is simply due to the media injecting people with wrong-headed ideas and false memories. Indeed, it is precisely this sort of model which appears in literature from the false memory societies based in the UK and US. Examples of adults recalling childhood abuse after viewing a television programme are seen as incontrovertible evidence of misleading cultural saturation and distortion. Most media scholars now view the 'hypodermic' model as discredited; media influence is far more nuanced and contextual than the hypodermic model implies (Eldridge *et al.*, 1997: 126–32).

Any attempt to 'explain away' memories as merely a product of media brainwashing therefore needs to be considered in a wider social and historical context. This is not to deny the potential role of the media; it is, however, to consider the context in which claims, and counter-claims, are produced. Dismissive explanations have accompanied each new wave of exposure of sexual violence. Even before the discovery of 'false memory syndrome', various experts were noting that the Women's Liberation Movement was leading to an increase in what they called 'pseudo' or 'subjective rape' and women artificially reinterpreting past events. Such dismissal oversimplifies complex relations between cultural representation and the ways in which experiences are labelled, identified, recalled and reinterpreted, as well as how they may be suppressed, obscured and silenced.[8] My research suggests that we can track media effects, without falling into a simple hypodermic needle model. It is possible to see the media as helping to 'put together pieces of the jigsaw puzzle', to 'make sense' of abuse or 'grasp it', without assuming that the media falsely convinces people that they have been abused when they have not in actual fact.

Further, feminist media scholars can ensure that the breadth of women's perspectives are taken seriously and that our experiences are used to interrogate existing theory. This means respecting women's active engagement with the media without denying questions of power or the possibility of media influence. Some media scholars assert that concern about media misrepresentation or under-representation is based on dubious or non-existent evidence and is theoretically naive (Gauntlett, 1995; Cumberbatch, 1998). Audiences are cast as cultural dupes incapable of inventive identifications and re-readings. Those wishing to take a progressive stance often argue that instead of seeing audiences (especially women and children) as victims of the text we should identify the ways in which oppressed peoples appropriate images from the media in order to reflect on their lives. Such work highlights the complexity of audience/text relations. However, the extent to which audiences are free to make creative use of mainstream media may also be exaggerated. In addition, research which demonstrates audience 'power' and 'creativity' is often conducted with particular types of cultural groups and with 'fans' (those who have constructed passionate and intricate ways of engaging with a media product). It is important to recognise audience activity; however, such recognition need not negate critical perspectives on the power of commercial culture, including the media.

Survivors of abuse emphasise the need for positive and realistic media representations (a point also repeatedly asserted by women who have experienced physical domestic abuse; see Schlesinger *et al.*, 1992). Their accounts demonstrate the value of such representation and how *lack* of representation undermines victims' sense of reality and, in effect, colludes with abusers. My early interviews highlighted how media resources were vital for abused children – and how, prior to the media's 'discovery' of the problem in the 1980s, abused children could only use the media as a way of learning about 'normal'/ 'happy' families and disguising their own abuse. In this context it is important to fully acknowledge the conditions which facilitate or inhibit audience creativity, appropriation or resistance. Sexually abused children have no homeland, no common language, no sense of belonging from which to forge alternative 'readings' or appropriations of media images. Dilemmas arise, then, in transferring theories about the media's role in relation to national, class, gender or ethnic identity onto the identity of abuse survivor. One question that has to be asked is how audience responses depend on communities of interpretation. Although most people are brought up in families or communities that include *identifiable* members of their own national, class, gender or ethnic identity, this is not true about the experience of sexual abuse. By contrast most survivors grew up with their childhood experiences being ignored, invisible and isolated.

In conclusion, this chapter has offered one detailed case study of the shifting ways in which survivors were able to engage with the media coverage of sexual violence through a period of social transformation. The media's role in helping to frame experience and memory is just one illustrative case showing how feminist analyses can have far-reaching implications for both media studies theory and the debate about memory, identity and sexual violence.

Notes

1 This chapter is based on an article which first appeared as: Kitzinger, J. (2001) 'Transformations of public and private knowledge: audience reception, feminism and the experience of childhood sexual abuse' in *Feminist Media Studies* 1(1): 91–104.
2 As Linda Gordon points out, child abuse has been perpetually repressed and re-discovered in modern history (Gordon, 1988).
3 All names are pseudonyms. Names indicate that the quotes come from interviews conducted for the first project, Group ID numbers indicate that quotes come from the focus groups conducted for the second project.
4 There are complex issues here about survival strategies that go beyond media representation and might feature in the accounts of children being abused today. I am not implying that such dynamics are *entirely* dependent on media stereotypes about sexual violence.
5 There were other factors which acted as a trigger (such as the death of the abuser, or becoming a mother herself). For discussion see Kitzinger (1990b).
6 By the late 1980s, post-Cleveland, parents not only had information about how to approach the subject, they also knew about the highly publicised dangers of social services involvement. As Shiobhan went on to explain, she delayed seeking help because of this: 'I was so scared, the first thing I asked the social workers when I *did* see them was, "Are you going to take my children off me?" You hear it on the telly, they just grab the children off you and I thought I'd be seen as incompetent. But it didn't turn out that way.'
7 Certain types of coverage also inhibited children from seeking help. For example, one young woman who participated in my research had been just 11 years old during the high-profile Orkney crisis (a scandal around contested allegations – see Kitzinger, 2004). She explained why she had been reluctant to confide in anyone for so long: 'I used to think I'd get sent away if I told. [Journalists] make social workers out to be big and bad [. . .]. They sort of put a barrier up.' (Group 48)

8 Some self-help books equally over-simplify the process of 'discovery'. There is also an issue about the way in which identity becomes a commodity to be policed or 'sold' to consumers via an entertainment and therapeutic industry.

References

Alcoff, L. and Gray, L. (1993) 'Survivor discourse: transgression or recuperation?', *Signs: Journal of Women in Culture and Society* 18(2): 260–90.

Ang, I. (1985) *Watching 'Dallas': Soap Opera and the Melodramatic Imagination*. London: Methuen.

Angelou, M. (1984) *I Know Why the Caged Bird Sings*. London: Virago Books.

Armstrong, L. (1978) *Kiss Daddy Goodnight*. New York: Profile Books.

Armstrong, L. (1994) *Rocking the Cradle of Sexual Politics: What Happened When Women Said Incest*. Reading, MA: Addison-Wesley.

Bell, V. (1993) *Interrogating Incest: Feminism, Foucault and the Law*. London: Routledge.

Brown, L. and Burman, E. (1997) 'Feminist response to the "false memory" debate', *Feminism and Psychology* 7(1): 7–21.

Brunsdon, C. (1981) 'Crossroads: notes on soap opera', *Screen* 22(4): 32–7.

Byerly, C. and Ross, K. (2006) *Women and Media: A Critical Introduction*. London: Blackwell.

Campbell, B. (1997) *Unofficial Secrets: The Cleveland Case*. London: Virago.

Corner, J. (1991) 'Meaning, genre and context: the problematics of "public" knowledge in the new audience studies', in M. Gurevitch and J. Curran (eds) *Mass Media and Society*. London: Edward Arnold.

Cumberbatch, G. (1998) 'Effects: media effects: the continuing controversy', in A. Briggs and P. Cobley (eds) *The Media: An Introduction*. Longman: Pearson.

Eldridge, J., Kitzinger, J. and Williams, K. (1997) *The Mass Media and Power in Modern Britain*. Oxford: Oxford University Press.

Foucault, M. (1990) *The History of Sexuality*. Harmondsworth: Penguin.

Gallagher, M. (2001) 'The push and pull of feminist action and research in feminist media studies', *Feminist Media Studies* 1(1): 11–15.

Gauntlett, W. (1995) *Moving Experiences: Understanding Television's Influences and Effects*, Academia Research Monograph, 13. London: John Libbey.

Gray, A. (1987) 'Behind closed doors: video recorders in the home', in H. Baehr and G. Dyer (eds) *Boxed In: Women and Television*. London: Pandora.

Gray, A. (1999) 'Audience reception research in retrospect: the trouble with audiences', in P. Alasuutari (ed.) *Rethinking the Media Audience: The New Agenda*. London: Sage, pp. 22–37.

Gordon, L (1988) *Heroes of Their Own Lives: The Politics and History of Family Violence*. New York: Viking.

Grodin, D. and Lindloff, T. R. (eds) (1999) *Constructing the Self in a Mediated World*. London: Sage.

Haaken, J. (1998) *Pillar of Salt: Gender, Memory and the Perils of Looking Back*. London: Free Association Press.

Haaken, J. (1999) 'Heretical texts: the courage to heal and the incest survivor movement', in S. Lamb (ed.) *New Versions of Victims: Feminists Struggle with the Concept*. New York: New York University Press, pp. 13–41.

Hacking, I. (1995) *Rewriting the Soul: Multiple Personality and the Sciences of Memory*. Princeton: Princeton University Press.

Hacking, I. (1998) 'The sociology of knowledge about child abuse', *Nous* 22: 53–63.

Haran, J., Kitzinger, J., McNeil, M. and O'Riordan, K. (2007) *Human Cloning in the Media: From Science Fiction to Science Practice*. London: Routledge.

Henderson, L. (1996) *The Issue of Child Sexual Abuse in TV Fiction: Audience Reception of Channel 4's 'Brookside'*. London: Channel 4.

Henderson, L. and Kitzinger, J. (1999) 'The human drama of genetics: "hard" and "soft" media representations of inherited breast cancer', *Sociology of Health and Illness* 21(5): 560–78.

Hester, M., Kelly, L. and Radford, G. (1996) *Women, Violence and Male Power: Feminist Activism, Research and Practice*. Buckingham: Open University Press.

Hobson, D. (1980) 'Housewives and the mass media', in S. Hall., D. Hobson, A. Lowe and P. Willis (eds) *Culture, Media, Language: Working Papers in Cultural Studies 1972–79*. London: Routledge.

Hobson, D. (1982) *Crossroads: The Drama of a Soap Opera*. London: Methuen.

Kelly, L. (1988) *Surviving Sexual Violence*. Cambridge: Polity.

Kelly, L. (1996) 'Weasel words: paedophiles and the cycle of abuse', *Trouble and Strife* 33: 44–9.

Kitzinger, J. (1988) 'Defending innocence: ideologies of childhood', *Feminist Review* 28: 77–87.

Kitzinger, J. (1990a) 'Who are you kidding? Children, power and the struggle against sexual abuse', in A. James and A. Prout (eds) *Constructing and Reconstructing Childhood*. London: Falmer Press, pp. 157–83.

Kitzinger, J. (1990b) 'Recalling the pain: incest survivors' experiences of obstetrics and gynaecology', *Nursing Times* 86: 38–40.

Kitzinger, J. (1992) 'Sexual violence and compulsory heterosexuality', *Feminism and Psychology* 2: 399–418.

Kitzinger, J. (1996) 'Media representations of sexual abuse risks', *Child Abuse Review* 5: 319–33.

Kitzinger, J. (1998) 'The gender-politics of news production: silenced voices and false memories', in C. Carter, C. G. Branston and S. Allan (eds) *News, Gender and Power*. London: Routledge.

Kitzinger, J. (1999) 'The ultimate neighbour from hell? Stranger danger and the media representation of "paedophilia"', in B. Franklin (ed.) *Social Policy, the Media and Misrepresentation*. London: Routledge.

Kitzinger, J. (2000) 'Media templates: patterns of association and the (re)construction of meaning over time', *Media, Culture and Society* 22: 64–84.

Kitzinger, J. (2004) *Framing Abuse. Media Influence and Public Understandings of Sexual Violence Against Children*. London: Pluto Press.

Kitzinger, J. and Skidmore, P. (1995) 'Playing safe: media coverage of the prevention of child sexual abuse', *Child Abuse Review* 4: 47–56.

Lamb, S. (ed.) (1999) *New Versions of Victims: Feminists Struggle with the Concept*. New York: New York University Press.

Modleski, T. (1984) *Loving With a Vengeance – Mass-produced Fantasies for Women*. London: Methuen.

Nava, M. (1988) 'Cleveland and the press', *Feminist Review* 28: 103–21.

Nelson, S. (1982) *Incest: Fact and Myth*. Stramullion: Edinburgh.

Radway, J. (1984) *Reading the Romance: Feminism and the Representation of Women in Popular Culture*. Chapel Hill: University of North Carolina Press.

Reavey, P. and Warner, S. (2003) *New Feminist Stories of Child Sexual Abuse: Sexual Scripts and Dangerous Dialogues*. London: Routledge.

Rush, F. (1980) *The Best Kept Secret: Sexual Abuse of Children*. New York: McGraw-Hill.

Schlesinger, P., Dobash, R. E., Dobash, R. P. and Weaver, C. K. (1992) *Women Viewing Violence*. London: BFI.

Scott, S. (1998) 'Here be dragons: researching the unbelievable, hearing the unthinkable. A feminist sociologist in uncharted territory', *Sociological Research Online* 3, 3. Available at: http://www.socresonline.org.uk/socresonline/3/3/1.html (accessed: 6/26/2001).

Seiter, E., Borchers, H., Kreutzner, G. and Warth, E. M. (1989) *Remote Control: Television, Audiences and Cultural Power*. London/New York: Routledge.

Skidmore, P. (1998) 'Gender and the agenda: news reporting of child sexual abuse', in C. Carter (ed.) *News, Gender and Power*. London: Routledge.

Summit, R. (1983) 'The child sexual abuse accommodation syndrome', *Child Abuse and Neglect* 7(2): 177–93.

Van Zoonen, L. (1994) *Feminist Media Studies*. London: Sage.

Van Zoonen, L. (2000) 'Popular culture as political communication: an introduction', *Javnost – The Public* 7(2): 5–18.

Ward, E. (1984) *Father-Daughter Rape*. London: Women's Press.

Winship, J. (1987) *Inside Women's Magazines*. London: Pandora.

Worrell, M (2003) 'Working at being survivors: identity, gender and participation in self-help groups', in P. Reavey and S. Warner (eds) *New Feminist Stories of Child Sexual Abuse: Sexual Scripts and Dangerous Dialogues*. London: Routledge.

6 'Alternative memories' and the construction of a sexual abuse narrative

Jo Woodiwiss

A central belief within the sexual abuse recovery literature is that childhood sexual abuse (CSA) is a devastating experience that inevitably has devastating long-term effects, allowing for the idea that 'knowledge' or 'memories' can be recovered from the minds and bodies of victims. For many women who enter adulthood with no memory of CSA, coming to 'know' they were abused relies on a redefinition of memory to include not only 'recall memory' but also 'alternative memories' such as imagistic memory, body memory, feeling memory and acting-out memory (Fredrickson, 1992; Herman, 1992; Whitfield, 1995). These memories, often shown as lists of symptoms, can take the form of dreams and flashbacks, physical or bodily experiences, feelings such as sadness or anxiety and other events or difficulties experienced in adulthood. They are often said to be held by an inner child, or children, who may be stuck at the time of the abuse and influence the thoughts, feelings and behaviours of adult victims. Alternative memories occupy a central position in the sexual abuse recovery literature but there are many other interpretations for such symptoms. It is only because they are defined as such within this literature that these 'symptoms' can be identified as 'memories' of sexual abuse.

This chapter, drawing on an Economic and Social Research Council (ESRC) funded research project, explores the role of alternative memories for women coming to 'know' they were sexually abused in childhood, and the narratives or life stories they come to tell. For many of the women in this study alternative memories are the only evidence they have for a history of CSA and I look at these memories, often thought to be held by an inner child, as a source of knowledge on which women base their narratives and sense of self. I explore how and why some women may be content with a simple correlation of symptoms with perceived abuse, whilst others may embark on a quest for further knowledge, some sharing their life with one or more inner children, and yet others come to reject memories they once believed to be true. I locate these stories within the context of an increasingly pervasive therapeutic culture in which ideas around healing, recovery, the inner child, and recovered memories permeate many aspects of our everyday lives.

Introduction

The recovered memory wars of the 1990s were set against the background of a therapeutic culture (Furedi, 2004) in which the reflexive self is seen as an ongoing project (Giddens, 1991), and we are 'educated in a therapeutic discourse of the emotions' (Rose, 1989: 257). Within this culture we are encouraged to engage with therapeutic and self-help literature and to reconstruct ourselves as damaged and in need of healing (Furedi, 2004; Woodiwiss, 2005, 2007). It is against this background that women, and it is primarily women, engage with a particular aspect of the body of knowledge surrounding CSA, recovery and healing that constitutes the 'harm story' (O'Dell, 2003) and its therapeutic corollary, the 'healing discourse' (Davies, 1995). These revised stories of abuse are constructed within an increasingly psychologised language that is closer to the language of mental health and illness than it is to the language of women's political activism (Armstrong, 1994; Reavey, 2003). Much of the recovered memory wars focuses on the perceived role of therapists and constructs those whose stories are at the centre of these debates as passive 'victims' of either CSA (e.g. Bass and Davis, 1988; Blume, 1990; Courtois, 1992; Fredrickson, 1992; Herman, 1992; Olio, 1989; Whitfield, 1995) or misguided or malicious therapists (e.g. de Rivera, 1998a, 1998b; Ofshe and Watters, 1995; Pendergrast, 1997, 1999; Yapko, 1994a, 1994b). However, as Rose points out, we can use therapeutic discourses to 'turn our own "cases" into stories, and become the authors of our own plot' (Rose, 1989: 257). However, more complex and nuanced readings, in which we do not have to choose between true and false and in which the tellers of these stories may themselves have taken an active part in the construction or telling of their own stories, are also possible (e.g. Haaken, 1998a, 1998b; Hacking, 1991, 1995; O'Dell, 2003; Reavey, 2003; Showalter, 1997; Spence, 1998; Woodiwiss, 2005, 2006). In the following pages I explore how sixteen women negotiated their own path through the CSA recovery literature and engaged with concepts such as recovered memories, alternative memories and false memories.

A central argument at stake in the recovered memory wars focuses on the perceived truth or falsity of previously unknown or inaccessible memories of CSA. Participants in this argument often wrongly assumed that the memories under debate are always 'recall memories' whereby the individual is remembering or falsely remembering past experiences of sexual abuse in childhood. However, as I demonstrate in this chapter, for some of those who come to construct their life story or narrative based on 'recovered memories' of CSA, it is not 'recall memories' that they recover, but rather 'alternative memories' (a range of perceived 'symptoms' reinterpreted as memories which it is believed are stored in, and can be recovered from, the minds and bodies of victims). The concept of 'alternative' or 'recovered' memories is not based simply on the wrongfulness of CSA but rather on the belief that CSA is a devastating experience that inevitably has deep and long-term effects on victims, combined with a failure to recognise a range of external factors which may well be the cause of many women's unhappiness or dissatisfaction, whether or not they are victims of CSA. Further, traumatic memories, such as those relating to CSA, are thought to be not encoded and stored in the same way as non-traumatic memories. These 'alternative memories' can take the form of imagistic memory, body memory, feeling memory and acting-out memory (Fredrickson, 1992; Herman, 1992; Whitfield, 1995). They are often shown as lists of symptoms and can take the form of dreams and flashbacks, physical or bodily experiences such as pain and nausea, feelings such as sadness, depression, anxiety or fear and other (common) events or difficulties experienced in the lives of adult women (Bass and Davis, 1988; Blume, 1990; Fredrickson, 1992; Herman, 1992).

Within much of the CSA recovery literature recovered memories of trauma are also viewed as unmediated (and therefore 'true') versions of past external events (Bass and Davis, 1988; Blume, 1990; Courtois, 1992; Fredrickson, 1992; Herman, 1992; Olio, 1989; Whitfield, 1995), and as such should not be challenged or subjected to (re)interpretation. This is often linked to feminist struggles to have women's stories of rape and abuse heard, making it particularly difficult for feminists participating in the 'recovered memory' debate to question such memories (Haaken, 2003; Showalter, 1997). The surfacing of these memories is thought to be spontaneous and inevitable and therefore neither the individual who remembers nor, if she has one, her therapist, is thought to be responsible for the emergence or construction of such memories. However, this fails to acknowledge the active role played by those who come to tell their own stories of CSA in the process of making sense of, and attempting to improve their lives, which for some might involve making a break with a (familial) past (Haaken, 1999).

The CSA recovery literature addresses those with continuous knowledge of past sexual abuse as well as those who hold no memories but believe they may have been victims of CSA. 'Symptoms' or 'alternative memories' can, some argue, provide more solid knowledge and enable victims to 'validate concretely what they know intuitively' (Dinsmore, 1991: 65). For those whose mind 'chooses to forget', it is claimed, the 'body remembers' and these memories 'are stored in our bodies', so it is 'possible to physically re-experience the terror of the abuse' (Bass and Davis, 1988: 74–5). Victims are told, 'everyone has a child within her' (Hall and Lloyd, 1989) and that 'within all of us there is an inner voice telling us how we feel' (Bass and Davis, 1988: 117). Victims may experience this voice in a variety of ways, such as through dreams, headaches, exhaustion or obsessive cleaning, but as Bass and Davis suggest, 'the important thing is not what you experience, but that you recognise it as a message' (Bass and Davis, 1988: 117). As Cameron argues, for those with no conscious knowledge it may be that their unconscious:

> had for years been speaking to them in a variety of languages – bodily

symptoms, emotions, sexual problems, compulsive self-abuse, and strange dreams and fantasies.

(Cameron, 2000: 158)

Validation of this knowledge is said to take the form of 'sense memories, childhood coping skills, childhood and adult behaviour patterns and acquired survival skills' (Dinsmore, 1991: 64). As this implies, within much of the CSA recovery literature based on recovered memories, knowledge of abuse is believed to be a continuous presence in the minds and bodies of victims, and either held by an inner child or stored in a damaged, childlike part of the adult victim. The expression of this knowledge is not thought to be a conscious act but rather a spontaneous and inevitable display of the effects of past trauma. These 'implicit memories of trauma have a life of their own' (Hovdestad and Kristiansen, 1996: 43) and neither therapist nor victim is thought to be responsible for their emergence. As Cameron claims, in such memories, 'reality had broken through' (Cameron, 2000: 178). According to Dinsmore, flashbacks, a term she uses to include bodily sensations and feelings as well as visual images, 'occur because the survivor is ready to deal with the memories of her abuse' (Dinsmore, 1991: 66). The accuracy of these memories and the view of the inner child as an 'objective observer' or recorder of events is reinforced by the idea that for her 'time was frozen' or 'stopped at the moment of trauma' (Dinsmore, 1991: 59). By contacting her inner child the survivor gains access to knowledge which she either 'sees' or 'experiences', and so startle reactions, flashbacks and sleep disorders, such as nightmares occur, replicating the experience as if it were happening at that moment (Dinsmore, 1991: 59). The victim is said to 're-experience the original abuse' (Bass and Davis, 1988: 73), which is seen 'through the child's eyes' (Cameron, 2000: 195). In placing such emphasis on knowledge held by an inner child, this literature can also be seen to encourage those who, although they might have identified 'symptoms' in their adult lives, are not certain of past abuse, to contact an inner child or even inner children in their search for 'proof'. Representing recovered memories as straightforward or literal accounts of past trauma also fails to recognise the motivational aspect of searching for memories or to acknowledge the variety of ways we can understand or interpret representations of the past (Haaken, 1999), whatever form they might take in the present.

Remembering or recovering memory is thought by some to play a central role in a victim's journey to healing (Olio, 1989; Herman, 1992). However, for others the recovery of memories is not so important, as long as the victim recognises, and deals with, the affects of having been sexually abused (Bass and Davis, 1988; Dinsmore, 1991). Memory, counsels Dinsmore, is 'not needed for survivors to begin the acknowledgement process' (Dinsmore, 1991: 56), or even the healing process as 'one does not need memory to heal from abuse' (Dinsmore, 1991: 65). Whereas some believe memories are crucial, others acknowledge that: 'Instances of regaining such memories are rare' (Dinsmore, 1991: 64) and 'Many women don't have memories, and some never get memories. This doesn't mean they weren't abused' (Bass and Davis, 1988: 81). What is important is that the 'survivor' recognises the existence of hidden or alternative memories, either held by her damaged inner child or stored in her damaged psychology, and the unhealthy influence they exert on her adult life. Some of the CSA recovery literature therefore contains advice on how to recognise or identify symptoms in the lives of adult women, but this is often based on a simple correlation between 'symptoms' and perceived past abuse which fails to recognise other possible causes of unhappiness or dissatisfaction in women's lives (Haaken, 1999; Showalter, 1997; Tavris, 1992). Some of the literature also includes encouragement or suggestions on how to make contact with an inner child (or children) in order to gain access to (additional) knowledge or memories, which fails to recognise the rich, textured nature of 'memory' (Haaken, 1999), our interpretations of which are as much about making sense of the present as they are about uncovering the past.

The research

This chapter draws on data from an Economic and Social Research Council funded research project looking at women's engagement with sexual abuse narratives. The research sought to look at how and why women engaged with CSA, recovery and therapeutic discourses, and why they entered therapy or read self-help manuals aimed at victims of CSA, often with no knowledge of having been sexually abused. It is informed by my own position as a feminist and a poststructuralist sociologist. There is now a large body of literature aimed at adults who have come to believe they are (based on continuous or recovered memories) victims of CSA. This research explored women's engagement with such literature. I use data from written accounts or interviews conducted with women who had, by their own definition, 'continuous', 'recovered' or 'false' memories of CSA and analyse literature that the majority of the participants in this study engaged with. I contacted women through an article in a national newsletter produced by a survivor's organisation named Cisters, through the British False Memory Society (bfms) newsletter, and through a letter sent to female members of the bfms.

The research was based primarily on eleven in-depth, semi-structured interviews, and five written accounts which followed a similar structure, in which women were asked about their lives and what led them to engage with the sexual abuse recovery literature, their experiences of therapy/counselling, and their experiences of self-help literature. A total of sixteen women took part in the research, eleven of whom replied to the article in Cisters and five to material they received from the bfms. Of the sixteen, five had continuous memories, six had recovered memories and five believed they had recovered false memories of sexual abuse in childhood. Ten of the eleven participants who 'recovered' memories recovered only 'alternative memories'. Three of the five participants who identified as being victims of false memory syndrome (FMS) did not reject entirely the idea that they were victims of CSA, but only that their fathers were the perpetrators of that abuse.

Much has been written about victims of CSA and the stories they come to tell, but very often the voices of those women whose lives are at the centre of these stories are absent within a debate that seeks to establish the 'truth' or falsity of their stories. This chapter attempts to give voice to these women whilst recognising that they are constrained by the stories that can be told. I do not attempt to establish whether the participants' 'memories' are 'true' in the sense that they relate to 'real' experiences of CSA but begin with the understanding that their 'memories' and their narratives are true to them. I recognise the agency of those who shared their narratives with me but also acknowledge that there is more than one 'truth' that can be spoken. The participants were, like all of us, constrained by the stories that can be told (Bauman, 2001; Gergen, 1994; Plummer, 1995, 2001) and therefore the narratives they have constructed are not the only possible narratives. I treat their stories as accounts that are informed by discourses and currently circulating narrative frameworks that have been constructed by the women themselves in an attempt to make sense of and give meaning to their lives. In doing so I recognise that there is not one single 'truth' out there that makes sense of women's lives but many truths that make sense of different aspects of women's lives, in different circumstances, and at different times. Instead of looking to see how our past histories are entwined with our present needs and desires I show how our present needs and desires, themselves constructed in discourses, can inform our understanding of our pasts. This line of inquiry does not evade the question of 'truth' but rather allows us to move beyond it to explore how and why some women may come to construct a narrative which relies on a correlation of 'symptoms' with perceived past abuse (see also Woodiwiss, 2005). This approach also enables us to look at why some women may ultimately reject as false, memories they once believed in. For more detailed discussion of the research methods see Woodiwiss (2005).

Adult behaviour patterns: symptoms as 'alternative memories'

We live in a world of storytelling where culturally available stories are enlisted to make sense of our lives and who we are. We do not simply slot ourselves into ready-made narratives but are constrained by the stories that can be told (Bauman, 2001; Gergen, 1994; Plummer, 1995, 2001; Woodiwiss, 2005). In Western societies during the late twentieth and early twenty-first centuries the genre of storytelling that has taken centre stage in the media and popular culture derives from a therapeutic culture (Furedi, 2004) in which we are encouraged to look inward for the cause of and solution to our unhappiness or dissatisfaction. Examples of this therapeutic ethos (Furedi, 2004) are not only found in the consulting rooms of counsellors and the pages of self-help and self-improvement literature but can be seen to permeate all aspects of our everyday lives. Whether through reading self-help manuals and psychology textbooks, magazines and newspapers, or through listening to the radio and watching films and television, we are introduced to 'alternative memories' of CSA in the form of potential symptoms on a daily basis. These symptoms might take the form of, for example, 'adult behaviour patterns', 'acquired survival skills', or 'compulsive self-abuse', or they might take the form of 'dreams' or 'flashbacks', many of which need interpreting, or they might take a more bodily or physical form, which may also require interpretation. Like other forms of 'alternative memories', these 'symptoms' can be seen as evidence of a damaged psychology or an inner child exerting an unhealthy influence on the adult woman.

When women read much of the CSA recovery literature and are presented with lists of possible symptoms, the ideas are not entirely new to them. From the novels of Margaret Atwood to episodes of *The Bill*, docudramas of women living with multiple personalities, or films about adult women wreaking havoc on their own lives and the lives of those around them, we are introduced to the idea that traumatic experiences can be stored as 'alternative memories' in the minds and bodies of, often unsuspecting, victims. *The Courage to Heal* (Bass and Davis, 1988) is one of the most popular self-help books aimed at adult victims of CSA and in this text Bass and Davis list over 70 symptoms, many of which take the form of 'adult behaviour patterns', 'acquired survival skills' or 'compulsive self-abuse'. They are grouped by Bass and Davis under a number of themes or headings such as self-esteem and personal power; feelings; your body; intimacy; sexuality; children and parenting; and families of origin.

The checklists of 'symptoms' include:

- Do you have a full range of feelings in your body? Or do you sometimes go numb?
- Are you aware of the messages your body gives you (hunger, fear, tiredness, pain)? Do you respond to them?
- Do you feel powerless like a victim?
- Do you have a hard time nurturing and taking care of yourself?
- Are you able to enjoy feeling good?
- Do you feel unable to protect yourself in dangerous situations?
- Have you ever experienced repeated victimization (rape, assault, battery) as an adult?
- Do you have trouble feeling motivated?
- Can you accomplish things you set out to achieve?
- Do you feel you have to be perfect?
- Are you comfortable with anger? Sadness? Happiness? Calm?
- Do you have a hard time loving and accepting your body? Do you feel at home in it?
- Do you often feel taken advantage of?
- Do you find your relationships just don't work out?

- Can you say no?
- Do you often have sex because you want to, or only because your partner wants it?
- Do you find it hard to set clear boundaries with children? To balance their needs with your own?
- Have you had trouble protecting the children in your care?
- Are you overprotective?
- Are you satisfied with your family relationships? Or are they strained and difficult?
- Do you feel crazy, invalidated, or depressed whenever you see your family?
- Have you ever been rejected by your family?

(Bass and Davis, 1988: 35–9)

Women find these symptoms listed elsewhere in the CSA recovery literature, which not only reinforces the messages but also underscores their authority. Parks, for example, suggests that adult victims of CSA are 'guilt ridden, self-sabotaging, sexually dysfunctioning on-going victims' (Parks, 1990: 13). Herman believes the adult victim of CSA to be at 'great risk of repeated victimization' who 'finds it difficult to form conscious and accurate assessments of danger' (Herman, 1992: 111) and Bass and Davis suggest that 'Survivors were programmed to self destruct' (Bass and Davis, 1988: 179). Dinsmore includes in her list of possible symptoms chronic depression, drug and alcohol abuse, anxiety, suicide attempts and a history of revictimisation (Dinsmore, 1991: 114) and Blume includes depression, phobias, low self-esteem, fear of the dark, wearing baggy clothes, and a pattern of ambivalent or intensely conflictive relationships (Blume, 1990).

The central premise of these checklists, which are 'general enough to include everybody' (Tavris, 1992: 323), and can apply to most women at some time in their lives (Tavris, 1992; Haaken, 1999; Showalter, 1997), is that the cause of the symptoms is likely to be located within the psychology of the reader, who is encouraged to dismiss external factors and look to themselves for explanations. However, what these symptom lists also do is to suggest to the reader what is appropriate and what is inappropriate in terms of thoughts, feelings and behaviours, both in adulthood and in childhood. Much of this literature 'gives a clear story of what a good/normal woman should be' (Warner, 1996: 47), and constructs the victim of sexual abuse as both long suffering (Lamb, 1999) and 'other' (O'Dell, 2003; Haaken, 1998b; Reavey, 2003). It is therefore not only women who are unhappy or disaffected with their lives who could be seen to carry evidence of past trauma but so too can those who deviate from prescribed norms.

For the majority of the women who participated in this study their life stories were based on 'alternative memories' which, for the most part, involved such a redefinition of memory to include perceived symptoms of CSA. Identifying some of these symptoms was for many their first introduction to the idea that they had been sexually abused in childhood. As one woman stated after reading a self-help manual:

> When I read I still didn't have any memories then, but I went yes. I mean if that's what happened that would explain it so much. That would really completely make sense but I still didn't have any memories then. (Beccy)

All sixteen of the women in this study were able to identify 'symptoms' in their adult lives which could be seen or interpreted as evidence of sexual abuse, including general unhappiness or dissatisfaction with their lives, problematic relationships with sex and being overweight. For a number of the women in this study it was a desire to address such 'problems' that first led them to engage with therapeutic discourses, not necessarily in the first instance those aimed at adult victims of CSA. For many, the identification of such 'symptoms' or 'alternative memories' was their first and often most significant 'memory' of CSA. This was enough for some women to 'know' they were victims of sexual abuse in childhood but others needed more concrete knowledge to be certain. For many of those who participated in this study, the process of developing and telling their stories was more dynamic than simply identifying symptoms, even when this included an element of 'knowledge' or 'memories' bursting through.

The understandings of CSA, memories and knowledge promoted within much of the CSA recovery literature offered women a way to gain the more concrete knowledge they needed to be certain they had been sexually abused in childhood, together with an explanation for why they previously lacked such knowledge. It could be stored as 'alternative memories' in the minds and bodies of victims, held by an inner child who split at the time of the abuse, or stored in the unconscious mind of the adult victim. This knowledge might surface spontaneously in the form of alternative memories bursting through, or contact with that part of their 'inner child' thought to hold the alternative memory could be actively sought. Those who participated in this study did not feel constrained to remain loyal to particular texts or explanations, but were able to draw on a range of ideas at different times. Those who developed a relationship with an 'inner child' did not necessarily rely on a static relationship with 'her' but were able to develop different or evolving relationships with their inner child (or children), as their own needs and understandings changed. Through their inner child they could try and access different or additional knowledge but an inner child could also perform different functions and/or serve different purposes. Through her inner child Fiona was able to engage in activities she perceived as inappropriate or childlike, whereas for Anne her inner children often acted as friends or companions.

Fiona and Anne were among those who relied on an inner child or children to access otherwise unknown knowledge. Whilst there were times when they actively sought out their inner child or children, there were also times when both felt overwhelmed by knowledge held by an inner child 'breaking through':

> It was as if I wasn't able to keep the lid on it anymore and the memories just popped out, just came out. But I didn't at first understand. I thought it was because I was depressed and having horrible thoughts. It was because I was depressed that these thoughts were ... I wasn't able to control them anymore and out they came. (Fiona)

It was, they felt, their inner child who was in control:

> We'd get more upset and you know, she [the therapist] would follow my upset. (Anne)

Whereas for Beccy accessing knowledge was often harder work and at times she had to actively seek out her inner child:

> Try and connect with myself as a child because, to help me get the memories back. (Beccy)

Elsewhere in her account Beccy refers to a different form of knowledge coming to the surface, over which she felt she had no control:

> I get emotional flashbacks, I'm not reacting to what's happening. (Beccy)

Knowledge that surfaced in the form of emotions and feelings was important to a number of women and could, they believed, provide them with a direct connection to their abuse:

> I don't know what age I began to be abused at but that seems to be the age that now if I get really upset, that seems to be the age that emotions regress back to. And where I can't talk about what's going on, I'm not able to verbally express or tell anyone or ask for help and I feel really upset because I can't do that at that age. All I can do is express how I feel and you know, in emotions, in crying or shouting or rage, whatever physical way I can I'm expressing these strong feelings. I'm too young to be able to talk about them and that wee person wants listening to. (Fiona)

At times Anne, who believed that knowledge of her abuse was held by hundreds of inner children, also gained access to this knowledge by putting herself in a trance, because she said:

> that's what you have to do to let the little ones talk. (Anne)

This knowledge might not provide detailed information but, as it was seen as the inner child re-experiencing the sexual abuse, many women felt it provided enough information for them to 'know' they had been abused. As the source was understood to be their child self, or inner child, this knowledge was seen as an accurate reflection of feelings and emotions relating to sexual abuse. It was a form of knowledge, the women believed, that did not lie. Angela, for example, who had employed a number of techniques to access information held by her inner child, felt that connecting with her child's emotions was the more powerful:

> It's much more intense than just writing to your inner child if you like, because it's feeling what she's feeling. (Angela)

A similar intensity can be seen in the words of Jenny and Fiona:

> What we are doing is feeling the pain that we couldn't feel as a child. (Jenny)

> The past was a daily reality to me, I was living in the past I couldn't escape it, it was with me all the time. Memories erm, . . . feelings, the past was haunting me I wasn't able to get on with my present. (Fiona)

At times Fiona felt her inner child took over her life. It was her inner child who held the knowledge of abuse and who chose when to bring it to the attention of the adult Fiona who did not see herself as responsible for the surfacing of her memories or the content of her sexual abuse narrative. The memories were there, believed the adult Fiona, before she was aware of them:

> They were just squished down, now they're out in the open and here's a chance to sort them out. (Fiona)

She did not choose to look for buried knowledge of abuse but seized on an opportunity presented to her, by implication, by someone other than her adult self who had access to this knowledge. In attributing her memories to an inner child Fiona, like many of the participants, was able to distance herself from the process by which they surfaced.

Although Anne also relied on her inner children to 'know' she was abused. As she said,

> We knew something had happened. The children knew something had happened but not quite why or how it happened. (Anne)

The aim for the majority of women in this study was to uncover knowledge of CSA but for Anne making contact with her inner children was more important than uncovering knowledge. Within her understanding the very existence of these 'alters' was evidence that she was sexually abused as a child.

Anne's inner children all had their own memories and often the memory and the inner child surfaced together, in what Anne described as a traumatic experience:

> After a time your mind gets so used to the horrors that, I mean you are shattered ... because there's another child each time that surfaces and each memory is different. I suppose it's different each time. (Anne)

Often the children surface when Anne was not awake:

> The children come with the dreams into the memories. (Anne)

Although many of the women understood their emotions and feelings as an inner child reliving the abuse, they did not require an inner child to access this knowledge. This knowledge could also be understood to come from their unconscious or from a damaged part of their adult selves. Even those who did recognise their inner child as an important source of information did not rely solely on that part of herself for knowledge. Fiona, for example, identified strongly with the idea of a child self, both in terms of needing to heal and of holding memories. However, she was also able to access other memories which she did not have to attribute to a child self:

> Not visual memories, more memories of touch and smell and sound because this happened at night. Either it was dark or I was closing my eyes but I don't remember really seeing a lot of things going on. (Fiona)

She was able to do this because, informed by the CSA recovery literature, she said:

> I remember my other senses have got memories. (Fiona)

Of those who recovered memories of CSA only Sarah did not rely on identifying perceived symptoms or 'alternative memories' as she had also recovered 'recall memories' which had been validated by others. She talked of how her memories 'came through', which implied a level of spontaneity, and believed that additional memories would surface if they needed to. She had also been able to use different concepts to explain, and access, hidden knowledge which she believed lay waiting to be uncovered. Whilst she believed this knowledge might be brought to the surface by her unconscious, and therefore not under the control of her adult self, she had also considered taking a more proactive approach:

> Yes because if my conscious or whatever needs to bring it out, it will bring it out. I don't know if I go to hypnosis it might bring it up then. (Sarah)

Like others, Sarah believed she could actively seek out knowledge of her abuse, but saw this process as one of finding existing knowledge. She might have played an active role in bringing this knowledge to the surface but she did not see herself as responsible for it.

Beccy also believed that a childlike part of herself held knowledge of her abuse but, unlike Anne, she had not seen this as a separate personality. This inner child she believed:

> has the memories that me as a child who was abused . . . Yeh. Obviously it's myself telling myself but it's that part of my mind that's been shut out. I think I don't want to listen to it. I want to, consciously I want to but obviously subconsciously I don't otherwise I would know. (Beccy)

Beccy was very clear that her child self was not a separate personality:

> Yes I see it as part of my mind rather than something separate. (Beccy)

Although she did not see this inner childlike self as a separate personality, Beccy did credit this 'inner self' with a degree of control over her adult self and over the process of healing and recovery. Beccy had considered a variety of techniques, such as hypnotherapy and regression therapy, to help her recover knowledge, and she attributed failure to fully engage with these techniques to her inner childlike self. In doing so, she not only distanced the adult Beccy from responsibility but also reinforced the idea of an inner child(like) self carrying the knowledge and effects of CSA into adulthood. Although Beccy attributed knowledge or memories to her childlike self, her sexual abuse narrative was at the same time based on a particular understanding of CSA and its consequences. Whether she was sexually abused or not, without this understanding, Beccy would not have been able to uncover, or recognise, memories of sexual abuse, or interpret her failure to access some memories as further evidence of CSA:

> I haven't done much of it because I'm quite resistant to it. I want to but my mind's resistant to it so it's not quite worked so far. (Beccy)

Not all of those who participated in this study recognised or developed a relationship with an inner child. For those who entered adulthood with no memories and did not recognise an inner child in possession of knowledge, the idea that memories were stored in their unconscious minds and/or bodies was something that made sense to them and again provided an explanation for how they could recover memories that they appeared to have forgotten. Even where women did believe their inner child held memories, they did not rule out the possibility that other memories were stored in their unconscious minds and bodies. They could therefore work with techniques for contacting their inner child as well as ways of interpreting these other memories. What these women shared was the belief that past knowledge was waiting to be uncovered, but, like Beccy, their interpretations of this knowledge relied on a particular understanding of CSA and its consequences. The knowledge or memories they recovered (whether 'true' or not) cannot be seen as straightforward or literal accounts of past trauma. To see them as such not only fails to recognise a variety of possible meanings and interpretations which are themselves constrained by the narrative frameworks within which they are positioned but also fails to recognise our reasons for looking to the past and searching for memories which are intricately linked with making sense of, and improving, the present.

Interpreting spontaneous knowledge

Whether or not the memory came to them from an inner child, this newfound knowledge was not always readily understood by the participants in this study. Often it came in the form of dreams and, whilst they might be sure it related to sexual abuse, the participants did not always know what the dreams were telling them. Fiona was certain that the knowledge she uncovered related to a history of CSA but she also felt she needed the help of others to understand:

> When I realised what it was about, what the memories were about then I sought out a counselling service specifically ... they could help me understand what I was feeling and what was happening and what was the best way forward. (Fiona)

Whilst Fiona believed it was her inner child who was responsible for bringing memories to the surface, like many of the women in the study, she identified an active role played by her adult self in making sense of this knowledge. The memories may have come unbidden but, as alternative memories, they required someone to interpret or make sense of them. Anne was also certain that in her dreams her alters were telling her about the abuse but that this information often needed additional work, either because it was not in a form that was easily understood but more often because it was incomplete:

> It was extraordinary at the beginning. We maybe have been having dreams I would go ... I mean the pattern now, the best pattern is that I go with my dreams and often it's just a fragment when I wake up. It's just a sentence and the whole thing comes out of that. In the therapy session we just work on the fragment. (Anne)

Not all of the women put in the additional work on their memories as did Anne, who was unique in the amount of time and energy she invested in contacting her inner children and recreating or uncovering what she believed to be hidden knowledge of past abuse.

Written communication, often in the form of letters written between the inner child and the adult self, is one of the techniques suggested in the literature. Although not many of the participants made use of this technique, the idea of communicating with a child self did reinforce to them the view of an inner child who held knowledge that they could gain access to.

Actively seeking knowledge

The majority of participants with no memories relied on 'hidden knowledge' which they believed surfaced spontaneously and inevitably. However, many also reported that there were times when they actively sought out additional knowledge, or supporting evidence. The literature suggested a number of techniques for accessing knowledge and although most were centred on making contact with an inner child, such as letting or enabling the child to write letters and draw pictures, much of the CSA recovery literature also suggested other techniques such as guided flashbacks which could be used even by those who did not recognise a child within.

Anne, for example, employed a range of techniques to make contact with her inner children. Ultimately, however, she found the technique of using guided flashbacks too traumatic:

> Early on, I read that thing here and I did a sort of guided flashback if you like, sort of jiggling about in a chair and things, as if I was being raped and then it was clear that I was being raped by different people if you see what I mean . . . So the memories – some came in that guided flashback. (Anne)

The driving force for Anne was making contact with her inner children, and therefore she did not have the same incentive as others to persevere when those techniques proved difficult. The technique had served its purpose for Anne if it enabled an inner child to surface. Other participants were more concerned with accessing knowledge, which itself might relate to the degree of certainty they had both in the narrative they had constructed and their identity as victim/survivor. For some the search for additional knowledge might also have been related to the extent to which they felt their lives had improved since they recovered memories of CSA.

At one point Fiona claims that:

> There's enough in my memory that I know what happened, I know who did it. (Fiona)

But there were other times when this was not the case. At those times she had considered returning, to:

> get in touch with my wee self at two-and-a-half/three. (Fiona)

Fiona hoped that contacting her 'wee self' would increase the information she had, which she felt to be only partial and limited. The paucity of her knowledge, she believed, indicated a greater depth to her trauma and therefore also to some of her memories. She contemplated other forms of therapy as a way to address the limitations of her knowledge:

> Then I thought perhaps some of these feelings I have are so deeply hidden that consciously I'm not going to be able to get at them and maybe if I went to see a psychotherapist or psychodynamic counsellor who was skilled in uncovering deep feelings with, I don't know, tricks of the trade that I thought they might have. They might know ways of getting at things, you know, subconscious things that consciously I wasn't really getting access to. (Fiona)

Although Fiona was thinking about accessing knowledge she did not yet hold, her understanding of the effects of CSA allowed her to identify the existence of such hidden knowledge by the feelings she had in the present. At the same time her investment in recovered memories and healing could also be seen to encourage her to look deeper for such knowledge as long as she was still unhappy with her life.

For others, contact with an inner child was seen as being more spontaneous and less under the control of their adult selves. Beccy believed the information provided by her inner child was an accurate reflection of past events and therefore not open to interpretation. She also believed there was a relationship between the proximity of knowledge and what she referred to as the 'main problem' and the difficulty this knowledge had in getting to the surface:

> And then sometimes I do get memories coming back and sometimes I don't. But sometimes I just get feelings I don't get any images. I mean mostly I never get nothing, when it's a bigger thing that's touching on the main sexual problem erm, I err ... I get feelings but I don't get any memories. So all the feelings come but I can't remember anything ... I think it's just a question of time just getting at it bit by bit and doing the less kind of sensitive beliefs first to sort of get to it bit by bit. (Beccy)

This is not the only way Beccy believed she could discover the knowledge held by her child self. Using photographs of her self as a child, particularly those where she looked very unhappy, she would:

> look at them before I go to bed at night and to try to communicate. Sort of ask that little girl that I was what happened, just to help remind me, you know ask her. (Beccy)

Beccy believed she had to work with her child self to recover memories but there were also times when she believed patience might be more useful than recovered memory work.

Not the first author

Not all of those who recovered memories of CSA were the first authors of their stories. Of those who did recover memories of CSA, five were first introduced to the idea that they had a history of CSA by a therapist and did not gain access to 'alternative memories' without assistance. Ultimately all five came to reject as false the memories they recovered during therapy and identified themselves as victims of false memory syndrome (FMS) but their explanations for this rejection varied as they negotiated their own paths through the literature on recovered and false memories. However, three of these five, although they maintained an identity as a victim of FMS, did not reject entirely the belief that they had been sexually abused in childhood, only that the abuse was perpetrated by their fathers.

It was during a hypnosis session in the cases of Hazel and Rae, and a scientology session in the case of Pat, that their memories surfaced. Hazel and Rae both wanted to lose weight and Pat wanted to address her ME type symptoms. The idea that their concerns, whether related to weight or ill health, resulted from being unhappy made sense to these three women. Therefore when a therapist suggested that they needed to discover the cause of their unhappiness he tapped into ideas that resonated to some extent with the women's own belief systems. As Rae commented:

> I've always been like that and I used to wonder what I was pushing to the back. (Rae)

For some, their first knowledge of abuse came in the form of dreams, although they had not necessarily interpreted these dreams as evidence of abuse. Hazel did not recognise an inner child but relied instead on regression and the interpretation of dreams by her hypnotist as a way of accessing knowledge of past abuse. She would either take her dreams to be interpreted by the hypnotist or, whilst hypnotised, regress to recover other 'memories' which also needed interpretation, again by her hypnotist. Of her dreams she says:

> he would analyse them. It could be like I said about a house and a red box and I would be the house and dad would be the red box and it had been squashed . . . Things like that. (Hazel)

At the time Hazel believed the interpretation she was offered but later, when she came to question her CSA narrative, she recognised that there was a range of interpretations of dreams and that it was possible to read them in different ways:

> I mean sometimes a dream makes sense. Yeh sometimes they do don't they, they do make sense sometimes. But those dreams I don't know he just made things out of them. (Hazel)

Although Hazel came to question the interpretation of her dreams, like Pat and Rae, she did not reject the idea that hypnosis could uncover hidden knowledge of traumatic events. It was this belief in knowledge stored in the unconscious which all three brought with them to therapy and which perhaps made it difficult to reject entirely the idea that they had been sexually abused as children.

> See I've always believed that anything that comes out in hypnosis is the truth. (Rae)

A belief in knowledge stored in the unconscious had contributed to their acceptance that they were victims of child sexual abuse. When they came to doubt these memories it was this same belief that enabled them to construct an alternative explanation, in which they could reject the specifics of their memories but not the underlying theme. For Pat and Rae it was a belief in past lives that not only enabled them to maintain their belief in hypnosis or the unconscious and the retrieval of buried memories but also provided a way of removing their fathers from the story of sexual abuse:

> I had to say well look if I haven't been abused in this life I must have been abused in a previous life. That has to be the answer. Whether or not it is I'll never know but I had to believe that that was the answer because I had to cling on to something. (Rae)

All three struggled with the question of how they could have memories of abuse and although Pat also saw past lives as a credible and acceptable explanation she was also aware of alternative explanations:

> this could have been in a past life or it could have been something I'd seen on television or something initially. (Pat)

Although Hazel did not share this belief in past lives, she too was able to accept an explanation which did not challenge her view that she had been abused, but only challenged the role her father was said to have played in that abuse. As she suggested:

> I just think it's real, that I really do think it's real. I've said to K . . . I'm sure something happened but not with my dad. Absolutely positive something happened. (Hazel)

All three acknowledged that their own wishes and motivations played a role in the explanations they eventually put forward. In ruling out any possible role her father may have played in sexually abusing her, Rae acknowledged that her reasoning was based to some extent on the outcome she wanted. This might have included feelings about her father together with a desire to maintain a belief in hypnosis which she had returned to since rejecting her memories:

> But I couldn't rule out the possibility that I'd been abused, I could only rule out dad's part of it. But whether I have ruled that out in my head because I loved him so much and protected his image I don't know, I honestly don't know and I'll never know will I. Well it's just one of those things you've got to live with isn't it. (Rae)

Like Rae, Hazel also recognised a motivational aspect to the construction of her own narrative. Not only did her abuse story enable her to avoid a sexual relationship with her partner but, in rejecting only that aspect of her narrative that implicated her father, she was also able to maintain a positive image of her father. Both women were also able to maintain a belief in hypnosis, which was important to them and may have provided additional impetus for the construction of their narratives. Such a motivational element was clearest in those participants who had come to reject some, but not all, aspects of their abuse narrative as they recognised the driving force behind the particular narratives they constructed was not simply a desire to uncover the 'truth'. They wanted an interpretation that made sense of their adult lives but which also fitted with their own needs.

Hazel, Rae and Pat's understandings of how knowledge could be stored in the unconscious mind had enabled them to explain hidden knowledge of sexual abuse, and later to explain how they had come to uncover 'false' memories of abuse. However, their explanations for recovering false memories did not challenge the idea that this knowledge could have been buried and therefore, although they were able to construct new narratives based on, and located within the narrative frameworks of, both recovered memories of CSA and false memory syndrome (FMS), they could not do so with certainty. Whilst some were able to construct a narrative or life story with confidence, others were condemned to a state of autobiographical limbo (Tietjens-Meyers, 1997). As Hazel said:

> When I think about my dad and I look at his photo in the dining room, yeh I always wonder; did you or didn't you? (Hazel)

Whether they continued to believe they were victims of CSA or rejected at least some aspects of their sexual abuse narratives, the participants were all constrained as well as helped by the narrative frameworks currently available to them. Those who came to identify themselves as victims of false memories were constrained by a narrative framework based on false memory syndrome (FMS) in much the same way as those who identified themselves as victims of CSA were constrained by a narrative framework based on the harm story and the healing discourse.

Conclusion

As O'Dell and Reavey have argued, drawing on a psychologised language to demonstrate the harmfulness of CSA, not only to the child but also the adult, can lead to the positioning of victims in problematic ways (O'Dell and Reavey, 2001). However, this positioning is also implicated in the construction of sexual abuse narratives based on 'alternative memories' by those who have no knowledge or recall memories of having been sexually abused in childhood. As this chapter shows, although the recovered memory wars focus on the 'truth' versus 'falsity' of recovered memories, some women do not in fact recover what we might call recall memories. Instead, they recover, or identify, 'alternative memories' – or perceived symptoms of CSA. We should recognise that in constructing their narratives, reinterpreting their lives, or uncovering 'hidden' knowledge of the past, women do so from the vantage point of the present. 'Alternative memories' say less about memory, even traumatic memory, than they say about the world in which we now live. They say more about the pervasiveness of therapeutic culture, the harm story and the healing discourse; limitations in currently circulating stories and narrative frameworks available to unhappy or dissatisfied women, and contemporary understandings of CSA in which the wrongfulness of CSA is recognised only when equated with inevitable and devastating psychological damage. It is this that enables the identification of perceived symptoms and their redefinition as 'alternative memories' of CSA.

Whilst I cannot speak for all those whose narratives are based on recovering alternative memories this chapter does illustrate that for some (the majority who participated in this study) their narratives relied on a redefinition of memory in which perceived symptoms – which in different contexts might attract a political, economic or social interpretation – are identified as 'alternative memories' or evidence of CSA. The women in this study did not adopt off-the-peg stories or slot themselves into readymade narratives but they did draw on those narrative frameworks currently available to them. In doing so they identified 'alternative memories' in their own lives in the process of making sense of those lives, who they were and the circumstances they found themselves in, and with the promise of a better, happier life to come. Sexual abuse narratives may appear to be empowering (Showalter, 1997) but they do not equip women to deal with the variety of social, economic and political factors that might delimit the possibilities of all women, whether or not they were sexually abused. Perhaps more importantly they do not even recognise these factors, but instead separate 'abused' from 'non-abused' women and thereby personalise any problems that survivors (Reavey, 2003), or indeed any other women, may have.

The participants did not draw on currently circulating narrative frameworks uncritically and indeed many recognised that a sexual abuse narrative based on 'alternative memories' was not the only way they could make sense of their lives. Rather than focusing on the question of truth or falsity I have tried to move beyond this debate – not least because, when sexual abuse narratives are based on 'alternative memories', we cannot say whether the tellers of these stories were abused or not. What we can say is that their stories are not the only stories that can be told, given the available evidence. If we dispensed with the harm story and the healing discourse, recognised the wrongfulness of CSA without having to equate it with inevitable and devastating psychological damage, and recognised the contexts of women's lives, we would free a significant number of women (the majority in this study) to draw on narrative frameworks that did not encourage them to identify 'symptoms' in their lives and reconstruct themselves as psychologically damaged. Instead they could construct narratives which, in acknowledging the material, social, economic and political conditions of their lives, would be better able to make sense of and improve those lives. We should after all remember that we can be constrained as well as liberated by our stories (Tavris, 1992).

Acknowledgements

I thank the women who gave so generously of their time and energy and shared their stories, their thoughts and feelings with me, and the ESRC who funded the project (R42200034452) out of which this chapter partly arose. I would also like to thank Paula Reavey and Janice Haaken for their helpful comments on an earlier draft of this chapter.

References

Armstrong, L. (1994) *Rocking the Cradle of Sexual Politics: What Happened When Women Said Incest*. London: The Women's Press.
Bass, E. and Davis, L. (1988) *The Courage to Heal: A Guide for Women Survivors of Child Sexual Abuse*. London: Cedar.
Bauman, Z. (2001) *The Individualized Society*. Cambridge: Polity.
Blume, E. (1990) *Secret Survivors: Uncovering Incest and its Effects in Women*. New York: Ballantine Books.
Cameron, C. (2000) *Resolving Childhood Trauma: A Long-term Study of Abuse Survivors*. London: Sage.
Courtois, C. (1992) 'The memory retrieval process in incest survivor therapy', *Journal of Child Sexual Abuse* 1: 15–31.
Davies, M. (1995) *Childhood Sexual Abuse and the Construction of Identity: Healing Sylvia*. London: Taylor and Francis.
de Rivera, J. (1998a) 'Evaluating believed-in imaginings', in J. de Rivera and T. R. Sarbin (eds) *Believed-in Imaginings: The Narrative Construction of Reality*. Washington DC: American Psychological Association.
de Rivera, J. (1998b) 'Relinquishing believed-in imaginings: narratives of people who

have repudiated false accusations', in J. de Rivera and T. R. Sarbin (eds) *Believed-in Imaginings: The Narrative Construction of Reality*. Washington DC: American Psychological Association.

Dinsmore, C. (1991) *From Surviving to Thriving: Incest, Feminism and Recovery*. New York: State University of New York Press.

Fredrickson, R. (1992) *Repressed Memories*. New York: Fireside/Parkside.

Furedi, F. (2004) *Therapy Culture*. London: Routledge.

Gergen, M. (1994) 'The social construction of personal histories: gendered lives in popular autobiographies', in T. R. Sarbin and K. Kitsuse (eds) *Constructing the Social*. London: Sage.

Giddens, A. (1991) *Modernity and Self-identity: Self and Society in the Late Modern Age*. Cambridge: Polity.

Haaken, J. (1998a) 'Women's stories of hidden selves and secret knowledge: a psychoanalytic feminist analysis', in J. de Rivera and T. R. Sarbin (eds) *Believed-in Imaginings: The Narrative Construction of Reality*. Washington DC: American Psychological Association.

Haaken, J. (1998b) *Pillar of Salt: Gender, Memory and the Perils of Looking Back*. London: Free Association Books.

Haaken, J. (1999) 'Heretical texts: the courage to heal and the incest survivor movement', in S. Lamb (ed.) *New Versions of Victims: Feminists Struggle with the Concept*. New York: New York University Press.

Haaken, J. (2003) 'Traumatic revisions: remembering abuse and the politics of forgiveness', in P. Reavey and S. Warner (eds) *New Feminist Stories of Child Sexual Abuse: Sexual Scripts and Dangerous Dialogues*. London: Routledge.

Hacking, I. (1991) 'The making and moulding of child abuse', *Critical Enquiry* 17: 253–88.

Hacking, I. (1995) *Rewriting the Soul: Multiple Personality and the Science of Memory*. Princeton: Princeton University Press.

Hall, L. and Lloyd, S. (1989) *Surviving Child Sexual Abuse: A Handbook for Helping Women Challenge Their Past*. London: Falmer.

Herman, J. (1992) *Trauma and Recovery: From Domestic Abuse to Political Terror*. New York: Basic Books.

Hovdestad, W. and Kristiansen, C. (1996) 'Mind meets body: on the nature of recovered memories of trauma', in S. Contratto and M. J. Gutreund (eds) *A Feminist Clinician's Guide to the Memory Debate*. London: Harrington Park Press.

Lamb, S. (1999) 'Constructing the victim: popular images and lasting labels', in S. Lamb (ed.) *New Versions of Victims: Feminists Struggle with the Concept*. New York: New York University Press.

O'Dell, L. (2003) 'The "harm" story in childhood sexual abuse: contested understandings, disputed knowledges', in P. Reavey and S. Warner (eds) *New Feminist Stories of Child Sexual Abuse: Sexual Scripts and Dangerous Dialogues*. London: Routledge.

O'Dell, L. and Reavey, P. (2001) 'Listening and speaking: the lost and found voices of women survivors of sexual violence', *Psychology of Women Section Review* 3: 4–14.

Ofshe, R. and Watters, E. (1995) *Making Monsters: False Memories, Psychotherapy, and Sexual Hysteria*. London: Andre Deutsch.

Olio, K. (1989) 'Memory retrieval in the treatment of adult survivors of sexual abuse', *Transactional Analysis Journal* 19: 93–100.

Parks, P. (1990) *Rescuing the 'Inner Child': Therapy for Adults Sexually Abused as Children*. London: Souvenir Press.

Pendergrast, M. (1997) *Victims of Memory: Incest Accusations and Shattered Lives*. London: Harper Collins.

Pendergrast, M. (1999) 'From mesmer to memories: a historical, scientific look at the recovered memories controversy', in S. Taub (ed.) *Recovered Memories of Child Sexual Abuse*. Springfield, IL: Charles C. Thomas.

Plummer, K. (1995) *Telling Sexual Stories*. London: Routledge.

Plummer, K. (2001) *Documents of Life 2: An Invitation to a Critical Humanism*. London: Sage.

Reavey, P. (2003) 'When past meets present to produce a sexual "other": examining professional and everyday narratives of child sexual abuse and sexuality', in P. Reavey and S. Warner (eds) *New Feminist Stories of Child Sexual Abuse: Sexual Scripts and Dangerous Dialogues*. London: Routledge.

Rose, N. (1989) *Governing the Soul*, 2nd edn. London: Free Association Books.

Showalter, E. (1997) *Hystories: Hysterical Epidemics and Modern Media*. New York: Columbia University Press.

Spence, D. (1998) 'The mythic properties of popular explanations', in J. de Rivera and T. R. Sarbin (eds) *Believed-in Imaginings: The Narrative Construction of Reality*. Washington DC: American Psychological Association.

Tavris, C. (1992) *Mismeasure of Woman: Why Women Are Not the Better Sex, the Inferior Sex, or the Opposite Sex*. New York: Touchstone Books.

Tietjens-Meyers, D. (1997) 'The family romance: a *fin-de-siecle* tragedy', in H. L. Nelson (ed.) *Feminism and Families*. London: Routledge.

Warner, S. (1996) 'Constructing femininity: models of child sexual abuse and the production of "woman" ', in E. Burman, P. Alldred, C. Bewley and B. Goldberg (eds) *Challenging Women: Psychology's Exclusions, Feminist Possibilities*. Buckingham: Open University Press.

Whitfield, C. L. (1995) *Memory and Abuse: Remembering and Healing the Effects of Trauma*. Deerfield Beech, FL: Health Communications Inc.

Woodiwiss, J. (2005) *Stories to live by, selves to live with: constructing the self through narratives of childhood sexual abuse*. Unpublished PhD thesis, University of York.

Woodiwiss, J. (2006) 'Alternative memories: searching for knowledge, telling a story', in K. Milnes, C. Horrocks, N. Kelly, B. Roberts and D. Robinson (eds) *Narrative, Memory and Knowledge*. Huddersfield: Huddersfield University Press.

Woodiwiss, J. (2007) 'Politics, responsibility and childhood sexual abuse', *Sociological Research Online*. Online. Available at: http://www.socresonline.org.uk/12/2/woodiwiss.html (accessed 3 June 2007).

Yapko, M. (1994a) 'Suggestibility and repressed memories of abuse: a survey of psychotherapists' beliefs', *American Journal of Clinical Hypnosis* 36(3): 163–71.

Yapko, M. (1994b) *Suggestions of Abuse: True and False Memories of Childhood Sexual Traumas*. New York: Simon and Schuster.

Section 2
Widening the lens
Cultural contexts for remembering child sexual abuse

7 The spaces of memory
Rethinking agency through materiality

Paula Reavey

> Whatever the reason may be, I find that scene making is my natural way of marking the past. Always a scene has arranged itself: representative, enduring.
> (Virginia Woolf, 1976: 142)

In this chapter I explore two major themes in relation to memory and child sexual abuse, often overlooked in debates over how to assess recollections of abuse and their impact on adult life. The chapter discusses (1) how survivors develop a construct of their own sense of agency in the past and (2) the material contexts that shape such recollections. Drawing on interviews carried out with survivors, I show how agency in memory and material contexts are interconnected and thoroughly interdependent. Material contexts, I argue, contain symbolic, imagined and actual references to relationships that surround the individual (Reavey and Brown, in press).

In discussing examples from interviews with women survivors of child sexual abuse, my aim is to provide a set of ideas that facilitate a reading that is attentive to the spatial and material aspects of memory and agency in relation to child sexual abuse. A physically grounded analysis, in other words. Further, I suggest how attending to domestic objects and spaces invoked in recollections of abuse speaks to a larger set of cultural practices that transcend the episode(s) of abuse itself. In attending to the material contexts of abuse, such as bedrooms, bathrooms and kitchens, and other spaces associated with the home, we may be better able to attend to the symbolic loadings of memories of abuse. The home often serves as the very stage on which the drama of child sexual abuse and agency is played out. The examples presented here are drawn from interviews with twelve British women survivors of childhood sexual abuse. The interviews explored (a) how women understand the relationship between their history of abuse and their current sexual relationships and sense of agency and (b) their experiences of agency as they compare the relationship between the past and the present.

Agency and memory

Agency is an important aspect of memory practices, as it enables the individual to locate themselves, as a subject in a wider political landscape. This includes how people identify themselves as active participants in their own stories. Yet, agency is a complex and multi-layered process, and does not always allow for a straightforward reading of choice and positive action. For example, our experiences of agency (when we feel we are participants) can also contain reference to dilemma and ambiguity. Recollections of abuse can be replete with such dilemmas, especially where survivors are unable to clearly define the boundaries of their own participation in the abuse (e.g. they did not object, or they had positive feelings about the person abusing them). However, attending to dilemmas and ambiguities in memories of sexual abuse has been intensely controversial in practice. Many feminists argue that any questions raised about women's 'participation' in the abuse can inevitably (and erroneously) lead to the questioning of the survivor's responsibility. A wariness about research on the ambiguities and dilemmas that might surround recollections of childhood sexual abuse is understandable given the power inequities that exist between adults and children. Yet such a denial of the complexities of agency has often led to the adoption of a literalist approach to memory, resulting in the promotion of romanticised and stereotypical portraits of female victims (Haaken, 1999), or victims who do not appear to exercise agency in any shape or form. Overall, there appear to be very few available discourses in which to situate women's agency, especially when memories of abuse form part of the picture (Haaken, 1998).

The omission of agency as a theme in recollections of childhood sexual abuse also shapes understandings of adult female sexuality, which is often portrayed as passive, weakened and victim-like (Levett, 1995; Reavey, 1998, 2003). There are many problematic consequences of the dominant victim discourse – the view that abuse produces inevitable damage, rendering 'untreated' children future victims or potential abusers (Warner, 1996; Haaken, 1998, 1999, 2003; Lamb, 1999; O'Dell, 2003). One problematic consequence involves the idea that women are passive registers of past events. One reason for this passive conception of the female victim involves storytelling conventions, and dilemmas women face as storytellers in patriarchal societies. In describing trauma therapy narratives of the 1990s, for example, Janice Haaken (2003: 80) argues that 'therapeutic attentiveness and empathy centre exclusively on the "good" victim (and that) the less culturally supported aspects of the female self may be smuggled into the clinical narrative through a perpetrator story'. Narratives of agency are less likely to be incorporated into accounts of abuse because of their association with guilt and because they disrupt the conventional cultural drama, based on the innocent and virtuous female victim and the guilty and malevolent male villain. Women's agency is not only stripped of complexity, it is 'cleaned' up by the central plot of the drama making the links between past and present more streamlined and culturally readable. This laundering of memory is further perpetuated by a lack of attention to the social and cultural identities of survivors, which preserves the idea that the central focus should remain on the individual actors of the abuse (Wilson, 1993; Levett, 2003).

Agentic stories, therefore, do not necessarily serve to relieve the burden of trauma, but call into question the survivor's moral position and status as a legitimate victim and 'good' citizen. This is due to the emphasis in discourses that prioritise the individual narrative, without sufficient attention to the material surroundings contributing to the shape of the memory. This stripping away of the world reiterates the primacy of the individual as the sole locus of psychological interest; as if the memory could have happened anywhere and at any time. Whether a memory is formed on a battlefield, a private home or in the full view of others is systematically ignored, as if the setting held no significance or individual/social relevance. Here, I argue that in reality those settings hold a very particular relevance in the shaping of agency and memory.

Space, agency and memory

The home, as captured in much of the geography literature, for instance, is situated in the category of the 'private' – a space largely divorced from the public gaze and one where individuals live out a set of practices that constitute them as active subjects (Duncan, 1996b). However, feminist geographers, in particular, have emphasised the gendered nature of such a space, wherein agency can be more limited or restricted for women. In Anglo-American societies, many children are reported to be sexually abused at home, either by a family member or someone invited into the family home (Baker, 2002). Secrecy is maintained and guarded by the abuse taking place in the private setting of the home, where doors are closed and locked to keep the public world at bay. Children abused at home by family members are then subject to an already existing physical landscape that in turn territorialises their memory in particular ways. For example, survivor testimonies can contain references to their homes being representative of the moral order, where the father's space is protected by other family members, signifying deference to his needs (see Hall, 1996). The father's authority to invade the spaces of his female partner and of his children, therefore, speaks to a set of unwritten values that family members must accept. However, the way in which this process is realised may vary and will impact on the experience, and the memory of it.

Edward Casey (1987), in a phenomenological study of autobiographical memory, proposes that 'personal memories' are indeed firmly embedded within the material spaces that we inhabit with other people, such as family homes, schools and hospitals. In short, the material setting itself can serve to mark out the ethics and organisation of the familial group (Wigley, 1992). Put this way, we can see that the home is a concrete example of how memories are shaped by the spatial 'affordance' (Latour, 2005) – whether we have physical boundaries from other family members, or whether secrets are held in particular rooms etc. Furthermore, the performance of rituals and forms of commemoration in families, involving repetitive and stylised behaviours, are largely prescribed by the organisation of space in particular ways (e.g. formal eating in a designated space) (Massey, 1995).

The material setting then holds the meaning of the group, its values and sets of power relations. Thus, abusive experiences may happen in the home and be powerfully recollected in all their specificity. However, as Haaken suggests (1999), memories may also be imbued with a larger set of sexual prohibitions, secrets and gendered relations that go beyond discrete past encounters. The home is symbolic of those larger issues, containing examples of agency, as well as oppressive practices – of play and movement, as well as pain and constriction (Massey, 1995). This is precisely the reason why an analysis of material settings in which memories emerge can provide insight into the variety of positions that can be afforded as well as limited by family spaces and experiences of child sexual abuse. The question remains as to how memories of child sexual abuse are embedded in material contexts, and in turn how these contexts afford a particular reading of agency in the past and present.

The four examples below are taken from twelve semi-structured interviews with women who experienced sexual abuse as children. Seven of the women were white, two black, one South Asian and two mixed race. Seven were university educated. Two were self-defined as bisexual, two as lesbian and eight as heterosexual. Although these various identifications are all worthy of exploration, and indeed I have explored them elsewhere (Reavey and Warner, 2003; Reavey *et al.*, 2006), the analytical aim of this chapter is to develop a more narrow focus on the role of the spatial context of the memories in making sense of agency in the past and present.

Rather than present an inductively derived set of analytical observations from the participants' life narrative (for this, see Reavey, 1998; Reavey and Warner, 2001; Reavey and Gough, 2000; Reavey, 2003; Reavey *et al.*, 2006), I introduce four examples to illustrate the ways in which spaces (material contexts) participate in the management of agency in memory. In presenting these examples, I am interested in both private and public spaces as they register dilemmas of agency. The women in these examples situate their memories in houses, bedroom and park spaces, as they describe their experiences of asserting agency or having their agency severely limited.

Analysing the limits and affordances of space: spatialising agency in memory

In the examples presented here, there are a number of references to ambivalence and dilemma in describing their sense of agency in the remembered events. In all four cases discussed, participants appear to be aware of their status as a child and how this status compromised their ability to have avoided the abuse. However, the examples also include references to their sense of childhood agency – to their desires and needs – which I argue are articulated through the spatial composition of the memory.

The reported memories contain rich details about the place where the individual was abused, even though this was not included as an explicit question in the interview. Thus the material context of the memory emerged without prompting or intervention from the interviewer. Consider the following example from an interview with a white 34-year-old woman, who I have named Sara. Here she describes in detail a scene in which a number of significant features relating to her agency and the agency of others are directly connected to the wider space of the houses, the road, and the park nearby.

> I used to go and stay with my grandma, for most weekends, because my mother was having a hard time with my two brothers, and she used to cross me over the road, for me to go to and visit these people who lived across the road, and it gave my grandmother a break in the afternoon. Er, and it was at this home where it happened, there was this man there, I can remember, having been crossed over the road by my grandma, standing at the gates of this house, and thinking, I don't want to go here, because I knew what was going to happen, but, and I also knew that there was a playground, a bit further down, and there were swings and things, which was also very exciting, and I, I can remember wondering whether I could actually go the swings instead of going and seeing this man, and em, and em, I think that I've always felt . . . why didn't I make the choice?

In the first part of the extract, it is clear that Sara lays particular stress on her childhood agency, by referring to the choice she could have made to go to the park. She clearly remembers the swings as a site of pleasure, a site which situated her sense of choice, desire and well-being. It is perhaps limiting, then, to characterise Sara as someone without access to those kinds of memories – as just a victim. Something more complex is in operation. The presentation of agency does not fit neatly into a binary framework, wherein someone has or does not have agency. For example, it is clear that what is at stake in the extracts above is the preservation of a memory *about* an active motive, as well as someone who has reluctantly followed the orders of her elders.

The next part of the extract brings into the story relational dilemmas and sources of ambivalence, which is again situated in the material context of the road and gate of the house.

> . . . part of me knows that if I'd gone to the swings my grandma would have found out, one, she would have been extremely angry, and she would have told my mum, and my mum would have been extremely angry, em, two, my grandma would have been terrified, if I wasn't where I'd ought to have been. [P yeah] so I can remember thinking all of those things, you

> know, but at six years old, it, do you think all those things, I don't know, I mean I think children are quite responsible, aren't they, in many ways, they feel they're responsible for choices, and things, they do ask questions, but you know, I didn't want to be a naughty girl really I wanted to do the right thing which was what my grandma has told me to do, was to go across the road and be a good girl and visit Mr such and such . . . my therapist used to say there wasn't an option, because er, I didn't have an option because I was a child . . . but I can't can't deal with that.

The 'road' in particular becomes a stable feature of this narrative in that it dramatises the inevitability of the choice: Sara has to cross the road because her grandma has escorted her there. To avoid being 'naughty' and disrupting familial harmony, she must cross that road and fulfil the needs of her elders. But in that crossing it is as if the 'choice' to be abused has been made, as it is also necessary to return again via this road, and if expectations have not been met (i.e. the child stays in the man's house) severe consequences would have to be faced. However, such a coherent presentation of agency, underscored in her commentary on children being responsible and capable of choices, is thoroughly embedded in the will of others – her grandma's, and her mother's needs and the unmanageable needs of her brothers. As Haaken notes, women and children are often called upon to engage in the 'emotion management' of others, which has particular resonance in the context of domestic spaces, where women feel more compelled to restore balance.

The spatialisation of events through the focus on objects makes visible a complex moral agentic order. The child may be seen to be acting responsibly towards others. She crosses the road, and in so doing avoids upsetting people who matter. However, the introduction of the swings as her 'object' of pleasure, that she could have chosen to indulge in, reiterates her emphasis on the reality of the child's agency. She refuses to take the line (as her therapist encourages her to do) that children are not capable of choice and represents the reality of children's agentic capabilities and pleasures in the objects themselves. The working through of dilemmas concerning choice, then, through the spatial distribution of the objects in the memory, is a significant feature of how narrative coherence is established retrospectively.

Some women described to me how their memories of particular spaces and objects speak to a sense of agency they have experienced that takes them out of feeling completely victimised (although this experience always looms large). Whether in parks or in their possessions or the spaces they inhabit with their friends, these pleasurable spaces also end up being the settings where they also experience and re-experience abuse. Consider the following example taken from an interview with a 37-year-old woman, who I have called Bella:

> I couldn't forfeit the important relationships in my life, just to stop this abuse happening, so it carried on for about a year . . . I mean I can

remember one time we were sitting on top of this wall, and he came out, and he lifted his daughter down, sort of like you do with a child . . . and he lifted me down, and he looked over his shoulder and he put his hand between my legs . . . he didn't have to lift me down like that. It was that that made me realise the lengths he would go to, I don't know why I put up with it and that's when it stopped.

In this example, Bella describes how the spaces she occupied with her best friend were the happiest and most important of her life (even though she continued to be abused by her best friend's father when she visited her friend). This was due to her impoverished home life and her experience of parental neglect. Once again, such a pleasurable space is intimately tied to the failings of her home life, where she experienced isolation and felt confined to her bedroom.

In the example presented, Bella remembers that she persisted with visits to her friend, despite the continuation of the abuse, as the space she shared with her friend was pleasurable and intimate. However, her decision to stop the abuse came when she recalls a specific memory of the father's intrusion into the very space (a certain wall) that was special to her and her friend. To her, this spatial violation signifies the end of agency in this situation and forces her to confront the idea that the private space of her and her friend could no longer be preserved and owned by them: 'It is then I realised that there was nowhere else to go, even though this [her friendship] was the most important relationship in my life'.

When we attend to the spaces of agency, it becomes clear that there is far more complexity as well as ambivalence. The ambivalence in the above memory centres on the expression of agency in the context of abuse, as it defies conventional narratives of memories of child sexual abuse. Stories that are ambivalent or contain agency or involve women's destructive capabilities are less well received by popular culture, as they are seen to compromise the status of the memory and the woman recalling it.

While Sara's and Bella's memories refer to the public space of the road, the wall and the park, the following example is based on memories of the private space of the home and the bedroom. The bedroom of a child (if the child has one) can signify the privatisation of sexuality, although the absence or removal of a lock on that child's door can also speak to the usurping of that private space by family members. If a child has a room of her own, the abuse can often take place within the boundaries of what she would see as 'her' space, rendering the space a privatised but 'owned' setting for inappropriate and abusive sexual activity. As the following example taken from an interview with a 29-year-old white woman, who I have named Martha, demonstrates:

It was my place [her bedroom], my zone of comfort. Even though he had reign over it when he did what he did to me, it was over before you knew it and what I was left with was my fucking room, with my stuff in it and

I protected it with my life, no one was allowed to enter, because without any of that, I had no sense of who I was, where he finished and I began.

In this passage, Martha refers to her bedroom as a space that is her own, and despite the horror of the abuse, a comfort zone containing her treasured possessions. Of interest here is how Martha constructs her sense of agency. Her agency appears to be tied to her sense of privatised space (her bedroom), ensuring that her father's reign is temporal, rather than constant. Her respite comes from her ability to reassert her agency in the private zone of the bedroom, which she protects and where she also prohibits entry. Her agency is clearly compromised by the intrusion of the abuser into her private zone but she discusses the regaining of boundaries and her sense of 'who she is' when he exits, resulting in the reclaiming of her territory. Agency is thus boundaried by the space itself and Martha's (partial) ability to defend it. Whilst this certainly has a physical demarcation (the bedroom and the outside), agency is a thoroughly relational effect (bound up in her relationships with others in the home) of Martha's way of inhabiting her bedroom. The defence of the private speaks to the success of Martha's abilities to maintain her sense of self and agency, which is dependent upon her separation from the abuser, outside the times when the abuse is taking place. Without such an ability to defend and prevent others from entering her protected private world, her ability to sense 'who she is' is impaired and the line separating her and her abuser blurred and inchoate.

This sense of gaining control over the private world of her bedroom is common in survivor testimonials. Children may also leave the privacy of their own rooms to visit their abusers, so that once they return to their room again, they can better retain a sense of boundaries and safety (Bass and Davis, 1988). These bounded places can operate as potential sites of agency, registering areas where women hold some form of control over the boundaries between self and other, and some investment in their own pleasures and activities. Agency then, to an extent, can appear to be organised around the boundaries of private spaces (Duncan, 1996a).

Privacy boundaries are certainly not available to all children, especially those who remember less defined domestic households or for those who do not have access to an exclusive privacy, such as a bedroom. Children who have stepped into the shoes of an absent mother, expected to fulfil traditional female duties, such as washing and ironing and providing for younger siblings, are particularly at risk of having no definable private territory (Baker, 2002). The 'parentification' process involves the child occupying adult roles, but with contradictory and unstable consequences. Even when the role of the adult mother is performed, the tasks can feel demeaning and denigrating, not only because the task is associated with gendered inequalities in the production of domestic labour, but also because the child feels decidedly 'out of place' in the domestic sphere (Hall, 1998). The spaces associated with childhood pleasures are, therefore, neglected, disrupted or severely compromised.

One survivor, Sukie, a 24-year-old South Asian woman, describes how her abuse by a family friend at the age of nine was facilitated by the lack of privacy she encountered at home, wherein she was required to carry out all sorts of domestic duties, as a result of her mother's absence. In order to gain space and a sense of individuality, she would regularly visit a relative's house, where the abuse subsequently took place.

> When I told my mum about the abuse, she didn't believe me and said that I must have done something to provoke it. I don't think she wanted to see me as a child though I was responsible for pretty much everything ... I was all and sundry's babysitter, it was more forced than it was anything, so I used to go and visit my aunty everyday and I loved it there, I really loved it, I think I actually preferred her over my mum because there were no demands on me there. At home I wasn't actually allowed to lock the door, so I used to just lie in bed pretending to be asleep.

Sukie's account signals a wider set of issues that go beyond her mother's rejection of her account of sexual abuse, including conflicts between mother and daughter. Sukie's lack of agency is represented through the confines of the domestic space, and the complex set of familial relations that occupy that space. She has no room to call her own, and as a result, pretends to be asleep, because of the lack of a bounded space (e.g. a private locked room). Conversely, Sukie asserts agency by spending a significant proportion of her time with her auntie, who fills the emotional void created through parental neglect and provides her with a childlike space, with no adult demands to be met.

The lack of a boundaried world (boundaries between privacy, home and the more public setting of her auntie's, where visitors were constantly passing through) and the merging of adult and child roles, in part facilitated the abuse, as adult responsibility for Sukie is unclear. As she notes, it is also unclear whether she is considered to be a child at all.

Conclusion

The link between past and present in memories of child sexual abuse often centres on a drama structured according to a plot involving the powerless female victim and powerful male villain. Memories of past abuse inform current versions of agency and selfhood, where the identity of the survivor is secured through the simplifying of agency – in the past, the female victim lacked agency and her present agency is compromised by those experiences in the past.

In the therapeutic and self-help literature women's current difficulties are presented as having a common origin in sexually abusive childhood experiences. Readers of that literature are often invited to view instances of abuse as key sites to understand the causes of present difficulties or 'vulnerabilities'.

However, recent feminist scholarship has called into question perspectives that deny the more ambivalent and agentic features of memories of child sexual abuse, arguing that women's memories should not be reduced to straightforward tales of powerlessness (Haaken, 1998, 1999; Reavey and Brown, 2006, 2007). In the research I have conducted with survivors, women's memories are laced with a multiplicity of subject positions grounded in specific material locations that produce positions of agency as well as experiences of powerlessness. The actual locations of memories can also provide instances where a whole set of subject positions are played out. Women are often encouraged to conflate passivity and acts of sexual abuse but this reading cannot possibly speak to the entirety of their experiences of their lives, where acts of agency are performed and experienced positively. This position does not negate the potency of the past or deny the devastating impact that abuse can have, though it can provide a more complex reading of the range of subject positions afforded by the private and public locating of memory. It can also make visible the complexity entailed in women's experiences of agency in the past, rendering these experiences readable, articulated and narratable. In this way, women may more easily confront conflicted feelings that challenge their status as a legitimate victim or 'real' survivor.

References

Baker, C. (2002) *Female Survivors of Child Sexual Abuse*. London: Routledge.
Bass, E. and Davis, L. (1988) *The Courage To Heal. Women's Guide to Survival*. Bolton: Cedar Press.
Casey, E. (1987) *Remembering: A Phenomenological Study*. Bloomington and Indianapolis: Indiana University Press.
Duncan, N. (ed.) (1996a) *Body Space: Destabilizing Geographies of Gender and Sexuality*. London: Routledge.
Duncan, N. (1996b) 'Renegotiating gender and sexuality in public and private spaces', in N. Duncan (ed.) *Body Space: Destabilizing Geographies of Gender and Sexuality*. London: Routledge.
Haaken, J. (1998) *Pillars of Salt: Gender, Memory and the Perils of Looking Back*. London: Free Association Press.
Haaken, J. (1999) 'Heretical texts: *The Courage to Heal* and the Incest Survivor Movement', in S. Lamb (ed.) *New Versions of Victims: Feminists Struggle with the Concept*. New York: New York University Press.
Haaken, J. (2003) 'Traumatic revisions: remembering abuse and the politics of forgiveness', in P. Reavey and S. Warner (eds) *New Feminist Stories of Child Sexual Abuse: Sexual Scripts and Dangerous Dialogues*. London: Routledge.
Hall, J. (1998) 'Geography of child sexual abuse: women's narratives of their childhood environments', *Advances in Nursing Science* 3: 980–110.
Lamb, S. (1999) 'Constructing the victim: popular images and lasting labels', in S. Lamb (ed.) *New Versions of Victims: Feminists Struggle with the Concept*. New York: New York University Press.
Latour, B. (2005) *Reassembling the Social: An Introduction to Actor-Network Theory*. Oxford: Oxford University Press.

Levett, A. (1995) 'Stigmatic factors in sexual abuse and the violence of representation', *Psychology in Society* 20: 4–12.

Levett, A. (2003) 'Problems of cultural imperialism in the study of child sexual abuse', in P. Reavey and S. Warner (eds) *New Feminist Stories of Child Sexual Abuse: Sexual Scripts and Dangerous Dialogues*. London: Routledge.

Massey, D. (1995) *Space, Place and Gender*. Cambridge: Polity Press.

O'Dell, L. (2003) 'The "harm" story in childhood sexual abuse: contested understandings, disputed knowledges', in P. Reavey and S. Warner (eds) *New Feminist Stories of Child Sexual Abuse: Sexual Scripts and Dangerous Dialogues*. London: Routledge.

Reavey, P. (1998) *Child sexual abuse: professional and everyday constructions of women and sexuality*. Unpublished PhD thesis: Sheffield Hallam University.

Reavey, P. (2003) 'When past meets present to produce a sexual "other": examining professional and everyday narratives of child sexual abuse', in P. Reavey and S. Warner (eds) *New Feminist Stories of Child Sexual Abuse: Sexual Scripts and Dangerous Dialogues*. London: Routledge.

Reavey, P. and Brown, S. D. (2006) 'Transforming agency and action in the past, into the present time: adult memories and child sexual abuse', *Theory and Psychology* 16(2): 179–202.

Reavey, P. and Brown, S. D. (2007) 'The embodiment and spaces of memory: child sexual abuse and the construction of agency', *Journal of Social Work Practice* 21(4): 5–21.

Reavey, P. and Brown, S. D. (in press) 'The mediating role of objects in recollections of adult women survivors of child sexual abuse', *Culture and Psychology*

Reavey, P. and Gough, B. (2000) 'Dis/locating blame: survivors' constructions of self and sexual abuse', *Sexualities* 3(3): 325–46.

Reavey, P. and Warner, S. (2001) 'Giving up the cure: child sexual abuse and the construction of femininity', *International Journal of Critical Psychology* 3: 59–74.

Reavey, P. and Warner, S. (eds) (2003) *New Feminist Stories of Child Sexual Abuse: Sexual Scripts and Dangerous Dialogues*. London: Routledge.

Reavey, P., Ahmed, B. and Majumdar, A. (2006) ' "How can we help her when she won't tell us what's wrong?" Professionals working with South Asian women who have experienced sexual abuse', *Journal of Community and Applied Social Psychology* 16: 171–88.

Warner, S. (1996) 'Constructing femininity: models of child sexual abuse and the production of "woman" ', in E. Burman, P. Alldred, C. Bewley, B. Goldberg, C. Heenan, D. Marks, J. Marshall, K. Taylor, R. Ullah and S. Warner *Challenging Women: Psychology's Exclusions, Feminist Possibilities*. Buckingham: Open University Press.

Wigley, M. (1992) 'Untitled: the house of gender', in B. Columina (ed.) *Sexuality and Space*. Princeton: Princeton University Press.

Wilson, M. (1993) *Crossing the Boundary: Black Women Survive Incest*. London: Virago.

Woolf, V. (1976) *Moments of Being*. Hertfordshire: Panther.

8 'Truth', memory and narrative in memoirs of child sexual abuse

Kathryn Robson

In the late twentieth century, first-person accounts of child sexual abuse generated intense controversy, exemplified in the idiom of 'memory wars', pivoting around the question of whether or not individuals' (recovered) memories of childhood abuse can be taken to be reliable.[1] Advocates of recovered memory and supporters of 'false memory syndrome' have both seen memory as intrinsically faulty (albeit in very different ways), yet simultaneously tend to imply that the 'truth' about the past can ultimately be known and verified. While debates raged over the reliability of memory, traumatic memory and childhood memory in particular, much of what was at stake went beyond the accuracy of memory to include the limits and possibilities of narrative itself. The literary critic Leigh Gilmore observes that ' "False memory" presents less a conflict about memory than one about power and narrative, specifically, *which* and *whose* story will prevail, even as the crisis of who is to control the family narrative is played out as a conflict in the realm of memory' (2001: 29).

Accounts of child sexual abuse are typically judged not according to their content, but according to the perceived authority and credibility of the narrator. Thus until quite recently, when children's claims of sexual abuse were contradicted by their parents' version of events, the child's testimony was all too frequently dismissed in favour of the authorized parental narrative. Although children's testimonies are no longer so summarily disregarded, the perceived credibility of the person giving testimony remains politically charged, particularly in the case of recovered memories.[2] Unsurprisingly, stories recounting individuals' recovered memories of childhood sexual abuse almost inevitably counter sanctioned family histories, so that two opposing narratives compete for acceptance as the 'true' version of the past. In this contested context, the political imperative to believe victims whose stories are frequently silenced acquires a decisive urgency. In defending silenced victims, many feminists have warned against adopting an over-simplified dichotomy between 'truth', on the one hand, and fabrication or fantasy, on the other, that fails to take into account the unreliability of both memory and narrative.

In the face of psychological trauma, memory is commonly accepted to be fallible. But so, too, is language. Trauma theory has repeatedly emphasized the difficulty of articulating traumatic experience in terms that can convey its impact.[3] Yet in the case of recovered memories of child sexual abuse, it is precisely through the production and interpretation of different narrative versions of the past – often in the context of a therapeutic session – that hitherto inaccessible or unassimilated memories can be revealed or recovered. These narratives are constructed and shaped by an ethical imperative to know 'what really happened', 'to tell the truth', to rework family histories which have concealed and protected instances of sexual abuse.

The need to have a more authentic version of events accepted as 'true' effectively confronts the limits in the narrative models available for discovering and giving voice to that truth. In telling their stories, survivors inevitably draw on the most familiar (and thus plausible) templates possible in a quest to be believed. Credibility in terms of (recovered memories of) child sexual abuse is culturally determined; the criteria by which these narratives are produced and judged are bound to specific notions of 'truth' and means of establishing the integrity of a recollection.

In this chapter, I analyse Sylvia Fraser's celebrated memoir, *My Father's House: A Memoir of Incest and of Healing* (1987), in order to explore how memoirs of sexual abuse produce and evaluate 'truth' in terms of integrity and coherence and how this definition of truth shapes critical responses to them. I go on to show that memoirs of sexual abuse can also experiment with different models of 'truth' and testimony by focusing on a much less well-known memoir, Janice Williamson's *Crybaby!* (1998). Williamson is a literary critic who wrote about Canadian memoirs of sexual abuse – including commentary on *My Father's House* – before publishing *Crybaby!* Both her memoir and her critical writing are experimental, blurring the boundaries between autobiography and literary criticism; both seek alternative modes of recounting sexual abuse. Williamson has insisted that 'More work needs to be done in exploring how we can admit variations on stories, half-memories and imagined reveries into our understanding of child sexual abuse', adding that this work need not be in the service of undermining children's testimony, 'but so we can more fully comprehend the effects of the abuse and the way desire is implicated in the painful drama' (Williamson, 1994: 222). Williamson is calling for alternative narrative templates that open up space for different stories about sexual abuse, without calling into question the integrity of the witness and without disregarding the importance of attempting to establish the 'truth' about the past. This project requires us to respond differently to testimonies of sexual abuse, not only by moving beyond the over-simplified binary of 'truth' versus 'fiction' or 'fantasy', but also by making room for 'variations', 'half-memories' and imagination in narratives of sexual abuse.

Memoirs of child sexual abuse: narrative recovery

In psychotherapy, part of the healing process for a survivor of trauma involves taking charge of one's own life story and putting it into words: 'the survivor [. . .] must be the author and arbiter of her own recovery' (Herman, 1994: 133). In a context in which first-person narratives of trauma have proliferated across television talk-shows, websites, magazine articles and autobiographies,[4] writing a memoir offers one way of literally authoring one's own story. Gilmore claims that 'memoir has become *the* genre' of the end of the twentieth and the beginning of the twenty-first century (2001: 1), 'energized in no small part by a surge in the publication of personal accounts of trauma' (2001: 16) covering a range of traumatic subjects, including chronic illness, loss, catastrophes, accidents, violence and torture. Within the rapidly expanding market of traumatic memoirs, the memoirs of sexual abuse survivors, particularly those authored by women, have become particularly prominent. These belong to what Christine Clegg calls a 'significant genre of women's writing [. . .] at the frontiers of speech and literature, memory and consciousness, autobiography and fiction' (1999: 70). Whilst these memoirs may be cast as straightforward narrative testimonies to sexual abuse, traumatic experiences must, as Cathy Caruth points out, be articulated 'in a language that is always somehow literary: a language that defies, even as it claims, our understanding' (1996: 5). Clegg writes that 'While incest survivor narratives represent claims to truth, as well as testimony to the trauma of remembering, they also reproduce and elaborate literary forms' (1999: 70); more than this, I would suggest, they necessarily draw on, expose and develop literary structures and strategies precisely in order to make their 'claims to truth'.

A key text in the *genre* of memoirs of recovered memories of sexual abuse is Sylvia Fraser's *My Father's House: A Memoir of Incest and of Healing*, which recounts the author's childhood, her recovery of memories of abuse as an adult, and subsequent healing. This memoir is cited in psychotherapeutic and self-help literatures on sexual abuse as 'a landmark text for those (including survivors) who [. . .] fought for the recognition of child sexual abuse as an important and neglected reality' (King, 2000: 62). The trajectory from 'incest' to 'healing' traced in Fraser's memoir reflects dominant psychotherapeutic models of trauma and recovery.

My Father's House also describes a process of dissociation and rupture followed by reconnection and recovery that finds resonances in contemporary psychotherapeutic narratives. In Judith Herman's *Trauma and Recovery*, for instance, Herman suggests that as a child experiences sexual abuse, 'the abuse is either walled off from conscious awareness and memory' or 'minimized, rationalized and excused'; the child 'tries to keep the abuse a secret from herself' and, if the process is taken to an extreme, begins 'to form separated personality fragments' that carry their own separate memories (1994: 102) in what is usually called 'dissociation'. This dissociation, figured as a fracture or splitting of the self, is clearly illustrated in *My Father's House*. Fraser asserts that as a young child and being abused by her father, 'I acquired another self, with memories and experiences separate from mine, whose existence was unknown to me' (1987: 15). She describes this process of dissociation in bodily terms as decapitation, the head (and mind) severed from the body where the abuse is lived and the mind subsequently unable to register the abuse as it occurs. In her words:

> I unscrew my head from my body as if it were the lid of a pickle jar. From then on I would have two selves – the child who knows, with guilty body possessed by daddy, and the child who dares not know any longer, with innocent head attuned to mommy.
>
> (1987: 221)

Fraser's account of dissociation encapsulates the double rupture within the self and between the child and each of her parents, showing how child sexual abuse damages the relation between self and other through an enforced framework of secrecy, shame and lies, with which the child ends up colluding (Herman, 1994: 107). Fraser makes an implicit distinction between bodily memory (the memory of sexual abuse that remains locked within the body and excluded from her conscious mind) and conscious or rational memory (that is unable to access the experience of abuse). These may correspond roughly to Herman's categories, drawn from the nineteenth century psychotherapist Pierre Janet, which distinguish between 'traumatic memory' ('wordless and static') and 'narrative memory', which is a more flexible form of story-telling that adapts and modifies the memories being recounted over time to fit a coherent life story (Herman, 1994: 175).

Until the therapy and self-analysis that unlocks the bodily memories of abuse, Fraser's sexual relationship with her father remains outside her consciousness, outside her narrative memory and her life story. The rupture in her memory is hardly visible to herself or others; her life story (like her constructed self) has adapted and shaped itself to accommodate the missing fragments of memory. As Laurence J. Kirmayer writes, 'Dissociation is a rupture in narrative, but it is also maintained by narrative because the shape of narrative around the dissociation protects (reveals and conceals) the gap' (Kirmayer, 1996: 181). The death of Fraser's father disrupts her sense of self, causing her to question her life choices and to register dissatisfaction with her life story as she currently tells it. Even before she claims to begin recovering memories, she guesses that she may have been sexually abused. She asks herself, 'Did I truly wish to open the Pandora's box under my father's bed? How would I feel to discover that the prize [. . .] was knowledge that my father had sexually abused me?' (p.211). Already, before she embarks on therapy, hypnotherapy and Freudian and Jungian self-analysis, Fraser seems to suggest that sexual abuse might offer a key to understanding her life and a means of giving meaning to her life story. She enters into therapy and seeks to recover dissociated memories at least partly in order to reconstruct her autobiography in a way that can explain her present life in relation to her past.

For Judith Herman, recovering the dissociated memories and converting them into narrative form serves a dual purpose: firstly, it exposes the silenced horror to which the child has been subjected, releasing the damaging secret between child and abusive adult. Secondly, recovery of dissociated memory heals the fractures in the self (Herman, 1994: 181). In *Shattered Subjects*, the literary critic Suzette Henke describes this as 'narrative recovery', defined as 'both the recovery of past experience through narrative articulation and the psychological reintegration of a traumatically shattered subject' (Henke, 1998: xxii). For Henke, as for Herman, narrating a past hitherto inaccessible to conscious awareness implies (re)creating a cohesive self in narrative.

My Father's House (to which Henke devotes a chapter of *Shattered Subjects*) exemplifies this model of narrative recovery. Through piecing together her memories as an adult, Fraser claims, she reconnects mind and body and her two fragmented selves to discover that 'she was I and I was she' (p.228). In *My Father's House*, as Henke argues, 'by telling her unspeakable story' – by telling the 'truth' about her past – Fraser 'worked towards a personal catharsis' (Henke, 1998: 144). This echoes Herman's emphasis on 'the restorative power of truth-telling' (Herman, 1994: 181); Fraser repeatedly stresses her compulsion to uncover and to recount the hidden secrets of her childhood in terms of a commitment to telling the 'truth'. In the prefatory author's note to her memoir, she writes:

> The story I have told in this book is autobiographical. As a result of amnesia, much of it was unknown to me until three years ago. For clarity, I have used italics to indicate thoughts, feelings and experiences pieced together from recently recovered memories, and to indicate dreams. It is important to keep this device in mind when reading this book.
>
> To provide focus and structure, I have used many of the techniques of the novelist. I have also adopted fictional names and otherwise disguised persons who appear in the narrative. No attempt has been made to create full or balanced characterizations, only to portray such persons and myself as our lives relate to this difficult story. However, to my knowledge, I have not exaggerated or distorted or misrepresented the truth as I now understand it.

Fraser's commitment to telling 'the truth' is coupled with her strategic deployment of literary techniques to recount her story, notably, the use of italics to illustrate recovered memories or dreams, the structure of 'a detective novel' (Margaret Atwood, blurb on book cover) and the characterization. Clegg describes *My Father's House* as 'an exemplary text, both in relation to the formation and circulation of a genre, and for the ways in which it is so clearly caught between the acts of witnessing and creative writing' (Clegg, 1999: 70). But Fraser's prefatory note displaces this opposition between witnessing and creative writing by suggesting that it is precisely through these creative strategies that she can bear witness to her recovered memories and strive to tell 'the truth'. As a written testimony, this text seeks to convince the reader both of the sincerity of Fraser's pledge to tell the 'truth' and of the veracity of the childhood memories that she 'recovers'. Yet clearly the preface also implicitly raises the question of how Fraser can be so sure of memories that were by her own admission unknown to her until shortly before she began to write the memoir, that is, how she can 'truthfully' represent a past that she was previously barred from accessing, and thus how the reader can assess the 'truth' of her account.

As a self-consciously literary testimony, *My Father's House* tells a double story: it narrates Fraser's memories and recounts the process through which she recovered them. She admits that it was partly through writing her first novel, *Pandora*, ostensibly a work of fiction about a Canadian childhood in the 1950s uncannily similar to her own, that she began to remember and that her 'other self', the self created and shattered by her father's abuse, began to 'speak': '*My other self has learned to type. She presses my keys, throwing up masses of defiant memories*' (p.149). These memories generated through the fictional work offer her clues to her childhood, enabling her to 'open the Pandora's box' (p.211) of memories that have hitherto been inaccessible to her conscious mind. Thus the fictional writing shapes her memory recovery, providing a preliminary narrative framework for the story that she produces out of her memories and that unsurprisingly reads like a novel. The family history that Fraser produces is coherent because every effect has a clear cause; she can make sense of her adult choices and problems (a failed marriage; an affair with her old friend's married father) by attributing them to her father's sexual abuse. Within her own memoir, Fraser constructs herself and her father as cohesive characters whose every decision can be readily explained (even her father's abuse, deemed the result of his difficult childhood). She can thus forgive both herself and her father: 'Fraser's split female subject is reconciled finally in a version of the "happy ending", an epiphanic scene of forgiveness where the child imagines the father as victim also' (Williamson, 1994: 229). Fraser ends her story by asserting: 'My father is dead. The king is dead. The princess is dead. "Hi ho, the wicked witch is dead"' (p.242), self-consciously drawing on a fairy tale intertext of kings, princesses and wicked witches, within which the parameters of good and evil are clearly defined and happy endings are requisite.[5] Narrative recovery, in *My Father's House*, has a fairytale dimension and ending. It magically empowers Fraser to become 'author and arbiter of her own recovery'.

As my reading of *My Father's House* shows, the notion of 'narrative recovery' is intrinsically tied to a model of a cohesive self with a coherent life story shattered by trauma and reconstructed. This cohesive, meaningful self as constructed through narrative is also implicitly shown to be bound up in cultural notions of 'truth' and integrity according to which 'truth' is somehow connected to coherence. Fraser judges her recovered memories to be 'true' because they make sense and cohere to her pre-constructed narrative models. Her main witnesses – her mother and her sister Helen – follow suit. When Helen hears Fraser's story, she immediately believes it, claiming that 'I always felt something strange was going on' and adding that her father's sexual preference for her sister explains 'why I got fat' (p.222). Helen accepts the story of abuse because it offers an explanation and justification for her current situation, imputing her weight gain to her father's neglect of her and privileged relationship with her sister. When Fraser's mother hears her story, she 'pick[s] up the pieces of her life as if it were another plate to be mended' (p.237), so that her daughter's testimony, far from shattering her life, offers her the wherewithal to put it back together. For Fraser's family, the story of abuse provides an alternative, more cohesive, shared family history. If Fraser's mother and sister are witnesses to her story, they do not themselves remember the events that she recounts; they believe her mainly because her story reshapes their shared family history in a credible way that makes their own past and current lives feel more coherent.

This is echoed in critical responses to *My Father's House*, which also evaluate the veracity of Fraser's memoir in terms of its narrative plausibility. Henke asserts that Fraser's story 'proves so vivid and convincing that we, as readers, do indeed believe her' (1998: 122), whilst Elaine Showalter insists that 'Fraser's narrative raises questions about its authenticity as a reconstruction' (Showalter, 1997: 166) because 'the abuse memory "returns" at a moment when Fraser is desperately trying to retain her self-image and self-esteem' (p.166), that is, it seems somewhat too convenient in allowing Fraser to excuse herself by casting herself as victim of her childhood trauma. What is striking in these contrasting reactions to *My Father's House* is that they are both based on how the memoir is written, rather than on its content; the 'truth' behind her memories is implicitly assessed in relation to its narrative structure. Nicola King observes that *My Father's House* 'is so highly and tightly constructed, and the recovery and representation of memory so apparently complete, that doubts arise about the truth status of the events she reconstructs' (King, 2000: 62). It seems that to be plausible as 'truth', a narrative must be consistent enough to convince, but not so cohesive as to appear contrived.

Rather than debate the 'truth' of Fraser's story, I would suggest that we need to reconsider both how we assess 'truth' in relation to expected models of narrative cohesion and how our notions of truth in terms of coherence limit the narratives told about sexual abuse. As Gilmore observes, 'autobiography draws its authority less from its resemblance to real life than from its proximity to discourses of truth and identity, less from reference or mimesis than from the cultural power of truth telling' (2001: 3); implicit here is the connection between 'truth and identity' on the one hand and 'the cultural power of truth telling' on the other. As readers of Fraser's memoir, we are cast into the position of witnesses urged to corroborate her story mainly because it makes sense.

Janice Williamson claims that memoirs of sexual abuse implicitly invoke the reader as 'witness', as 'one who will not misread' (1992: 226), which might suggest that the reader is ethically compelled to be sympathetic to the narrator's story and to believe. This may also, however, be interpreted differently if taken as an injunction to think beyond prevalent cultural discourses on 'truth' as coherence. *My Father's House* leaves little space for reading differently; few gaps or contradictions appear in Fraser's tightly constructed narrative. To explore further how we might renegotiate models of truth, identity and coherence in the context of narrative recovery of child sexual abuse, I turn to Janice Williamson's own memoir, *Crybaby!*

Relocating 'truth' and testimony

In 'Writing aversion', Williamson notes 'the proliferation of child sexual abuse in contemporary writing' in Canada (1994: 199), citing Elly Danica's *Don't: A Woman's Word*, Liza Potvin's *White Lies (for my mother)* and Fraser's *My Father's House*; later we could add *Crybaby!* to her list. The blurb of *Crybaby!* quotes Kim Echlin: 'Janice Williamson has told the truth [. . .] *Crybaby!* splits the world open', invoking Ellen Bass's declaration that 'The world has split open' at a conference on sexual abuse in 1993, in which she spoke out in passionate support of recovered memories. Recovered memories of sexual abuse and the importance of establishing 'truth' are underlying themes of Williamson's memoir, which knowingly inserts itself into a complex intertext of critical and popular discourses on sexual abuse, incorporating quotations from Freud, Lacan, poetry, feminist theory, Canadian women's magazines. This memoir foregrounds the question of how to bear witness to childhood memories of trauma in narrative through the recurring eponymous trope of the 'crybaby'. The memoir opens as follows:

> To cry is to address a listener. The crybaby's song goes not unheard but unheeded; not only the story of woe but the desire to be heard warrants condemnation [. . .] The wronged woman and the abused child speak out and are repudiated.
>
> (Williamson, 1998: 9)

The figure of the 'crybaby' embodies cultural conceptions of a child who performs suffering with no real justification, in a bid to be heard and recognized. The crybaby (both a derogatory and a childish term in itself) is despised and disregarded as one who makes illegitimate claims. Williamson links the 'wronged woman' and the 'abused child' as silenced figures of contempt whose testimonies are culturally dismissed. She recounts a public reading of a draft version of *Crybaby!*, when her listeners left in silent embarrassment without acknowledging her suffering and she recognizes the need to construct her testimony differently so as to move beyond the inevitable self-positioning as 'pitiful abject object' within her own story of abuse (1998: 9). The opening to *Crybaby!* is not a textual staging of self-pity, but a self-conscious admission that bearing witness to individual trauma can cast the witness into the position of object, constructed within his or her own testimony as either pitiful or self-pitying and, in either case, effectively silenced.

In an attempt to move beyond the position of victim/object, Williamson seeks strategies to construct a different model of testimony and narrative, one that does not fix sexual abuse as the single origin of all subsequent events and experiences. Williamson's narrative swings between different sources of trauma – her sexual abuse; her hysterectomy, ensuing infertility and marital breakdown; her father's suicide – without fixing a definitive cause. She admits of memories/fantasies of childhood abuse that are reconstructed: 'The more I think about it, the more my life appears retrospectively ordered by his disorder – as though each moment, gesture, conversation, lover, accomplishment or decision reverberates from the shock waves of incest' (1998: 69). She recognizes, however, that this organization of her life story is artificially imposed, partly because her memory is necessarily fallible, but mainly because it emerges from the demands of narrative. For Williamson, no memory exists outside narrative frameworks that reconstruct memories as they emerge. The pull of narrative is almost irresistible:

> Having recalled a scene, you begin to paint it, using the palette of the generic but retroactive description that came with the first intimations of memory . . . In real life the tighter the chain of causation . . . the better the narrative'.
>
> (1998: 76)

Williamson understands the seductive power of narrative, not just to shape memories, but also to construct them. The opposition in many theories of trauma between narrative and traumatic/bodily memory implies that memory and narrative can be separated. In *Crybaby!* they are inextricably woven together. 'Recovered memories', in this memoir, are indistinguishable from fantasy, dream or memories that have existed since childhood; they are all, to a certain extent, generated in and through narrative. Williamson's memoir certainly incorporates the 'variations on stories, half-memories and imagined reveries' that she calls for in her critical writing on sexual abuse; more, it shows how even half-memories, dreams, fantasy sequences are shaped around narrative templates.

Like Fraser, Williamson draws on family photographs from her childhood as a means to explore the past that remains partially inaccessible to her; unlike Fraser, she takes these photographs not as evidence of abuse, but as starting points for narrative experimentation. Williamson's memoir explicitly rejects the possibility of using photographs to discover 'what really happened' in her childhood:

> These photographs are not about finding 'the truth' of my childhood. They are a childhood. A possible account. Whether my father molested me will not be established. My memory has proven resilient in its ability to find an equilibrium somewhere between vision and articulation, a zone of possible plots, likely scenarios, blurred images. Gaps and fissures,

arguments and echoes make up what I know about this child who stands before me.

(1998: 26)

Where Fraser sees her story as unequivocally 'true', Williamson uses writing as a means to test different versions of her childhood, none of which will articulate an absolute 'truth'. The various narratives that she produces in *Crybaby!* do not, moreover, form a cohesive overarching story; instead, they are structured around 'gaps', 'fissures', 'echoes', that are never resolved or completed and form the very basis of Williamson's narrative testimony. Like Fraser, Williamson links traumatic memory to the body, but her method of articulating her bodily suffering is quite different. In her words:

> She does not want to expropriate her body's suffering but to distill its meaning and understand. Were she to read her crimped agonizing breaths through the I word, she could sound victim rather than subject of suffering [...] Cautious: she wants to tell a story with the I word, and won't.
>
> (1998: 127)

The testimony to Williamson's suffering is mediated via the body, yet to write via the body risks being cast into the position of victim/object, being unable to define herself (as embodied subject) as subject of her own story. Note that she speaks in the third person here, although elsewhere she uses the first person. These repeated shifts of position mark her resistance to piecing together the 'she' and the 'I' and her strategic adoption of the perspective of the fragmented subject. This fragmentation is never exclusively claimed as the consequence of abuse: indeed, abuse is shown to be bound up in other traumatic memories – the death of her father, her hysterectomy – that become inextricable from each other as points of rupture in her memory and past. 'Rooting in the dictionary, she finds her entrance to writing her body's suffering in the word: *ektomy*' ('cut'; p.126); this links her hysterectomy (and resulting infertility) with her father's suicide (which she experiences as an abrupt break) and with her fragmented memories of childhood. It is through this figure of a bodily cut – that itself represents a kind of loss[6] – that she can begin to find ways of recounting her past in and through rupture, rather than (as in Fraser's case) resolution and recovery. Like Danica's *Don't: A Woman's Word*, Williamson's memoir is itself structured in fragments and refuses the coherent, linear structure that Fraser's memoir adopts.

Like *My Father's House*, *Crybaby!* implicitly figures sexual abuse as bodily and psychic fragmentation. At one point, Williamson scans a childhood photograph of herself and her father and digitally manipulates it in order to eliminate firstly herself and then her father in order to separate them and to reaffirm her own bodily boundaries, blurred or ruptured by her sexual relationship with her father. In her words: 'Repossess my own. I want to make my boundaries that I longed for, the edges shirred or sharp' (p.33). The sexual relationship between father and daughter damages the daughter's sense of self. The father's literal penetration/invasion of her body is lived as a disruption of the parameters of her sense of self. When she cuts herself out of the image, however, 'she/I takes part of father with her. The girl's arm, now absent, cuts into her father's leg like a sword' (p.33). In her memory, the girl and her father are inextricably linked; to cut one out is akin to a bodily wounding, leaving one or the other incomplete.

Williamson concludes: 'The photograph is not documentary evidence, but a sign of the unsayable', adding that '*The impact of incest may be hidden from him*' (p.33). Where photographs have so often been taken as visual records of the past, here the photograph marks instead what cannot be said: that is, not so much the incest itself, which can be recounted, but the effect of incest on the daughter, which the father cannot know. The photograph reveals what the father cannot see and the daughter cannot say, but it fails to offer 'proof' of events. Instead, the photo marks the disjunction between the two witnesses' knowledge and interpretation of the past. Again, the image of rupture structures the narrator's quest to remember; she can recall her past only through conceiving of a fragmented body, a broken relationship between herself as a child and her father, as well as through discontinuous, disjointed memories that never allow certainty that her father did abuse her.

Fraser's narrative draws a sharp distinction between 'before' (when her self was divided and she had not recovered memories of abuse) and 'after' (a point of resolution and healing); Williamson's memoir unpicks that binary opposition. Where Fraser writes from the position of recovery and reconciliation, Williamson seems unable to move beyond fragmentation. This is shown even in the front cover of *Crybaby!* that features two photographs, both cropped and both action shots. The bottom image is quite conventional – if slightly blurred – showing a girl sitting on a swing and smiling as she is propelled forwards. This is a fairly typical photograph of a child at play. The upper image shows the underneath of the swing, the ropes holding it in place and the back of the child's legs as the swing moves past, with the child precariously swinging in the air. The double image of the abused child (smiling on the one hand as she strives for normality, terrified or tortured on the other) is familiar, yet the juxtaposition of photographs here is quite different. Neither shot captures abuse or its effects directly. The two photographs are not simple mirror images of each other; the image of the child smiling and swinging is not a direct opposition of the image of the underside of the swing in motion. Striking about the cover is the fragmentation of the images, the absence of overview, of a way of putting the pictures back together to create a composite image of the abused child. There is only the movement of the swing as the child moves forwards and backwards.

In *Crybaby!*, sexual abuse links physical/psychic ruptures with disjointed movement: the narrator never 'recovers' her childhood memories as such, but grasps at them fleetingly as they swing past. By contrast, Fraser's father's house is figured as a fixed space within which her traumatic memories are all located: in her words, 'I was lucky to find my family's dinosaur intact in one grave' (p.253), meaning that her father's abuse constituted her family history as simple and single origin. Fraser's individual story coheres neatly with the family history that she produces and that her mother and sister accept.

In *Crybaby!*, there is neither family history nor individual life story as such, only disparate narrative threads that the narrator cannot tie up and that remain open, reflecting her shifting relation with her family members. She admits that she cannot remember without the aid of her family, but that relations between them have been formed out of silence: 'Withholding, we waited for a response when silence had already spoken. *The border is a swing door*. Now in touch, we warm to each other' (p.120). The notion of the border as 'swing door' rather than barrier transforms her earlier quest to reinstate her bodily and psychic boundaries and to reaffirm herself as cohesive and bounded subject after her father's abuse. Here the border is reconfigured as a door that swings, rather than opens and closes; that is potentially in perpetual motion. This is an image of opening, rather than closure, of movement, rather than fixity; it is also an image of rupture, as the door cannot be closed completely.

My reading of *Crybaby!* suggests that the 'truth' of child sexual abuse lies in a fragmented, rather than coherent, narrative, and that any attempt to establish a definitive 'truth' or to construct a single narrative explanation works at the expense of other possible versions of the past. In the context of child sexual abuse, *Crybaby!* intimates, 'truth' is itself fragmentary, located in the (crucially shifting) disjunction between different potential stories and subjects. The very attempt to measure and define 'truth' is itself shaped by narrative; this does not mean abandoning the possibility of establishing 'what really happened', but taking on board narrative discontinuities and gaps, exploring narrative's capacity to invent and experiment, rather than reverting to a coherent and over-told story of villains and victims.

The discourses surrounding 'truth' versus fantasy in the recovered/false memory debate tend to imply that both the alleged abuser and accusing victim can be seen as single, coherent selves, either deliberately lying/telling the 'truth' or unable to distinguish between truth and fantasy. If this dichotomy is clearly over-simplified, it remains difficult to move beyond it without entering a post-modern impasse within which the past can only ever be invented, never recounted. The importance of at least attempting to know the 'truth' about child sexual abuse and to have that truth acknowledged is clear in *Crybaby!* Williamson describes frequent thwarted efforts to have her story heard and believed. Yet when elsewhere Williamson insists that we 'not misread' narratives of sexual abuse, this does not mean that we must believe them unquestioningly. Instead, we should attempt to develop and create alternative readings and narrative templates.

Conclusion: 'reading' narrative testimonies of sexual abuse

My readings of two memoirs of sexual abuse show that in order to move beyond prevailing narrative templates of sexual abuse and recovery – exemplified in Sylvia Fraser's *My Father's House* – we might focus on rethinking narrative, rather than memory, or rather, we should rethink memory as narrative. Typically the 'truth' of stories of sexual abuse is assessed in terms of coherence (does the story 'make sense'? are its characters' actions plausible?) that is in turn defined by narrative expectations of cohesive and integral selves. Individuals' stories of recovered memories of sexual abuse often work through opposing family histories, yet they also emerge from those family histories. Instead of rooting these histories in accepted notions of identity and resemblance, we ought to explore fragmented, shifting and plural aspects of those family histories (rather than the singular 'history').

Misreading, I suggest, means closing down and fixing single narrative versions of sexual abuse. Instead, the reader as witness should learn to open up different narrative possibilities. The figure of 'swing door' from *Crybaby!* marks a pivotal point where these stories can converge and diverge, a point of contact that is necessarily fleeting (as the door keeps swinging). Fraser insists that once she has told her story, 'I can close the coffin, truly close it', on her other self (1987: 242). This position is therapeutically important for her, allowing her psychic and narrative closure, but the closure that she requires is a narrative consequence of the story that she has chosen to tell. The reader can resist this closure and rework Fraser's self-depiction as coherent self, not in order to call her experiences into question, but to open up her story to new possible narrative outcomes.

What defines and plots a family history and a story of child sexual abuse is arguably less the past than the anticipated future that defines that past. Williamson ends her memoir as she prepares her father's cottage for the arrival of her newly adopted daughter, 'wash[ing] away fingerprints of another domestic life' (1998: 194), trying to erase the traces of her abusive childhood, not to forgive her father, resolve her past or recreate herself as healed, coherent subject, but to move her family history in a new direction. In order to move beyond the impasse that so often characterizes narratives of sexual abuse and their critical responses, we must explore these new directions, new versions of stories, not in order to discredit individuals' testimonies, but to expand and renegotiate the notions of 'truth', memory and narrative that both shape and restrict them.

Notes

1 For different sides of this debate, see Bass and Davis (1988), one of the key texts in the recovered memory movement, and Crews (1995), which criticizes the recovered memory movement quite sharply. Advocates of false memory syndrome often cite Elizabeth F. Loftus, who argues that memories can be 'recovered' by suggestion (see, for instance, Loftus and Ketcham, 1994).

2 This is clear in the high-profile conflict between the cognitive psychologist Jennifer Freyd, who claimed to recover memories of her father's childhood abuse as an adult, and her parents, who set up the False Memory Syndrome Foundation in a public attempt to disprove the possibility of recovered memories of sexual abuse. Both sides constructed compelling and clashing versions of a family history, but, as Jennifer Freyd pointed out, in the ensuing debate she was deemed less credible than her father. See Haaken (1998: 21–38) for discussion of this case in terms of authority, credibility, and parent/daughter dynamics.
3 As Gilmore writes, 'Something of a consensus has [...] developed that takes trauma as the unrepresentable to assert that trauma is beyond language in some crucial way' (2001: 6).
4 See Ahmed and Stacey (2001).
5 Fraser also describes herself as 'Sleeping Beauty' (1987: 252) and sees her mother 'dressed like the witch in Snow White' (p.226).
6 O'Dell (2003) shows how discourses on child sexual abuse often describe its effects in terms of loss – primarily a loss of innocence (p.137) – and argues that this works to position the abused child as definitively stigmatized and different (p.138). In *Crybaby!*, unlike in *My Father's House*, sexual abuse is not depicted as a loss of innocence, but as a possible sequence of experiences and memories that wound but do not define the child as victim.

References

Ahmed, S. and Stacey, J. (2001) 'Testimonial cultures: an introduction', *Cultural Values* 5(1): 1–7.
Bass, E. and Laura, D. (1988) *The Courage to Heal: A Guide for Women Survivors of Child Sexual Abuse*. New York: Harper and Row.
Caruth, C. (1996) *Unclaimed Experience: Trauma, Narrative and History*. London: Johns Hopkins University Press.
Clegg, C. (1999) 'Feminist recoveries in *My Father's House*', *Feminist Review* 61: 67–82.
Crews, F. (1995) *The Memory Wars: Freud's Legacy in Dispute*. New York: New York Review Books.
Danica, E. (1988) *Don't: A Woman's Word*. Charlottetown: Gynergy Books.
Fraser, S. (1987/1999) *My Father's House: A Memoir of Incest and of Healing*. London: Virago.
Gilmore, L. (2001) *The Limits of Autobiography: Trauma and Testimony*. London: Cornell University Press.
Haaken, J. (1998) *Pillar of Salt: Gender, Memory and the Perils of Looking Back*. London: Free Association Books.
Henke, S. (1998) *Shattered Subjects: Trauma and Testimony in Women's Life-Writing*. New York: St Martin's Press.
Herman, J. (1994) *Trauma and Recovery: From Domestic Abuse to Political Terror*. London: Pandora. (First published 1992.)
King, N. (2000) *Memory, Narrative and Identity: Remembering the Self*. Edinburgh: Edinburgh University Press.
Kirmayer, L. J. (1996) 'Landscapes of memory: trauma, narrative and dissociation', in P. Antze and M. Lambek (eds) *Tense Past: Cultural Essays in Trauma and Memory*. London/New York: Routledge.
Loftus, E. F. and Ketcham, K. (1994) *The Myth of Repressed Memory: False Memories and Allegations of Sexual Abuse*. New York: St Martin's Press.

O'Dell, L. (2003) 'The "harm" story in childhood sexual abuse: contested understandings, disputed knowledges', in P. Reavey and S. Warner (eds) *New Feminist Stories of Child Sexual Abuse: Sexual Scripts and Dangerous Dialogues*. London/New York: Routledge.

Potvin, L. (1992) *White Lies (for my mother)*. Edmonton: NeWest Press.

Showalter, E. (1997) *Hystories: Hysterical Epidemics and Modern Media*. New York: Columbia University Press.

Williamson, J. (1992) ' "I peel myself out of my own skin": reading *Don't: A Woman's Word*', in C. Potvin and J. Williamson (eds) *Women's Writing and the Literary Insititution/L'Écriture au féminin et l'insititution littéraire*. Alberta: Research Institute for Comparative Literature, University of Alberta, pp.219–35.

Williamson, J. (1994) 'Writing aversion: the proliferation of contemporary Canadian women's child sexual abuse narratives', in W. Waring (ed.) *By, For and About: Feminist Cultural Politics*. Toronto: Women's Press.

Williamson, J. (1998) *Crybaby!* Edmonton: NeWest Press.

9 Memory, sexual abuse and the politics of learning disability

Rachel Fyson and John Cromby

Introduction

Evening falls. In a neat house in a pleasant neighbourhood an elderly woman prepares for bed. As she changes into her nightdress and picks out fresh clothes for the morning, her demeanour changes. She begins to mutter, then shout. Her words are sometimes muffled, but include a man's name, followed by a string of self-directed obscenities, 'You slag; you bitch; you dirty whore; you fucking cunt', repeated over and over. As the litany continues she begins to hit out – striking walls, furniture and herself with equal ferocity. She punches her face with clenched fist, leaving bruises. As her voice rises higher, the bedroom door opens. A younger woman appears and stands in the doorway urging the older woman to quieten down and to come downstairs – to watch TV, drink cocoa, anything that will take her away from her memories and bring her back to the present. After a few minutes the older woman becomes calmer and does indeed come downstairs, joining the other residents and staff. But the same pattern is repeated night after night.

This is a description of 'Mary', one of the many people with learning disabilities with whom the first author worked during almost ten years as a support worker/residential social worker in group homes for adults with learning disabilities. Mary had previously lived for decades in a long-stay 'mental handicap' hospital, where it was believed that she had been serially sexually abused. Her night time terrors often included reference to the same man, although the hospital denied that they had ever employed anyone of that name. It was never possible to 'prove' that Mary had been sexually abused, but no-one who knew her well ever doubted that she had been. Since leaving hospital and moving 'into the community' considerable care had been taken to support Mary in many ways: support to learn self-care skills, support to participate in domestic chores such as cooking, cleaning and shopping, support to attend adult education classes and to participate in leisure activities. But there was *no* effective support to help with the burden of her past, to help her find a way of coping which did not involve self-harm. It was not that the staff were uncaring, they were not, but neither did they have the skills necessary to offer the kind of support which Mary needed. Moreover, because of her learning disability, the 'true' facts of her history remained unclear. Mary's only known relative was an elderly brother, with whom she had limited and infrequent contact. In many ways, other than the behavioural evidence of her abuse, Mary had no history – nobody to share her memories, good or bad, of her years in hospital; nobody who could ever know – let alone begin to understand – how the story of her life had been shaped.

Elements of Mary's experiences are typical of those of many people with learning disabilities. We will refer to her story throughout this chapter as we investigate the links between sexual abuse, memory and powerlessness in the lives of people with learning disabilities. Whether or not they have lived in institutional settings, people with learning disabilities are more likely than other children or adults to experience abuse of all kinds, including sexual abuse. At the same time, they are less likely to have their abusive experiences understood, believed or externally 'validated' in any way. Moreover, their own capacity to remember and make sense of histories of abuse is limited. This chapter will explore the reasons why memory in general and memories of sexual abuse in particular are problematic for people with learning disabilities. We will set out what is currently known about the sexual abuse of people with learning disabilities and relate this to the social and political circumstances in which most people with learning disabilities live. We use the term 'political' here to denote that the circumstances of this group of people have not been arrived at by chance, but are contingent upon particular social policies, laws and service provision.

Defining learning disability; exploring power relations

Learning disability is notoriously difficult to define with any degree of precision and, as a group, people with learning disabilities are extremely heterogeneous. They range from individuals who show no visible outward sign of disability, but whose limited cognitive abilities nevertheless restrict their educational achievement and social engagement, through to people with multiple physical and cognitive impairments who are unable to survive without 24-hour care. Between these two extremes are people whom the general public might recognise as typical of the 'mentally handicapped' – for example, people with Down's syndrome. The confusions arising from this heterogeneity are further compounded by rapid changes in nomenclature which, in recent years, have embraced and/or discarded terms including mental handicap, mental retardation, developmental disability and intellectual disability. Medical definitions of learning disability remain influential (e.g. Gillberg and Soderstrom, 2003) but standardised tests of intelligence quotient (IQ) are no longer regarded as a definitive diagnostic tool. Similarly, genetic causes can only be identified for a small proportion of people with learning disabilities. In the UK, the Department of Health offers the following definition, which has received general acceptance within services:

Learning disability includes the presence of: a significantly reduced ability to understand new or complex information, to learn new skills (impaired intelligence); with reduced ability to cope independently (impaired social functioning); which started before adulthood, with a lasting effect on development.

(Department of Health, 2001: 14)

This definition is broad enough to encompass people with learning disabilities with a wide spectrum of abilities ranging from relatively minor difficulties with abstract concepts and social norms of behaviour through to almost complete dependency on others. An alternative definition might therefore describe people with learning disabilities as individuals who are unable to live their lives without the ongoing assistance of family members and/or support services. In practice, it has been argued, this has created a *de facto* definition of learning disability as being any people who use specialist learning disability services (Simons, 2000).

These two ways of defining people with learning disabilities conceptualise their difference from other people by comparing their characteristics (intelligence; social functioning) to those of the general population or to the (ever-changing) eligibility criteria of public services. Neither adequately locates people with learning disabilities within the context of their ongoing individual and collective powerlessness, a powerlessness which is unthinkingly replicated by the definitions themselves – the first because it is a deficit model (it defines people by what they cannot do, rather than what they are or can do), the second because being defined in relation to public service provision would be unthinkable for almost any other group (imagine defining women as 'people who are eligible to receive gynaecology services'). Whilst thorough immersion in the debates surrounding the definition of 'learning disability' is beyond the scope (and unnecessary to the purpose) of this chapter, it is nevertheless worth emphasising that our understanding of learning disability accords broadly with Hughes and Paterson's (1997) proposed extension to the social model of disability. Hughes and Paterson argue that the social model can be extended to include embodiment by developing a 'sociology of impairment' which, instead of implicitly ceding the body and its abilities to medicine and biology, investigates the ways in which impairment itself is socially produced. In what follows we make the related argument that, with respect to memory, social and material conditions actually help constitute (rather than merely contextualise) learning disabled people's difficulties in remembering sexual abuse.

In terms of people's lived experience, the presence of a learning disability places individuals at the social, economic and geographic margins of society. Mild and moderate learning disabilities are associated with poverty and are more prevalent in deprived urban areas (Department of Health, 2001). More severe or profound learning disabilities are evenly distributed across socio-economic groups, but are associated with other disadvantages, including physical or sensory impairments and communication difficulties. Although there now exist substantial bodies of academic work concerning the individual or collective memories and histories of other socially and economically disadvantaged groups (e.g. working class people, women, people from black and minority ethnic communities) little has been written which systematically explores the disempowerment of people with learning disabilities. In fact, it is symptomatic of their disempowerment that people with learning disabilities have almost no historical voice, leading Ryan and Thomas (1987: 85) to comment that 'What history they do have is not so much theirs as the history of others acting either on their behalf or against them'. It is only recently that attempts have begun to be made to explore the individual and shared histories of people with learning disabilities *from their perspective* (Atkinson and Walmsley, 1999). Such work is important in broadening our understanding of people's lived experience, but may be of limited value to people with learning disabilities who are not themselves directly involved, since few have the literacy skills required to read the autobiographical accounts of others. If used to educate support staff such accounts could support collective remembering, but few services are designed to allow time for this kind of activity. Moreover, the rapid turnover of (low-paid) staff ensures that reminiscence work is sidelined and individual histories are limited to the duration of employment of the longest-serving staff member. This, then, is a group of people for whom history and remembering has been afforded little value. Notably, in the context of this chapter, although there are a number of academic studies which have looked at short-term memory in people with various degrees of learning disability, there is no corresponding body of literature examining their abilities or difficulties in relation to autobiographical memory.

We would argue that, over and above the impact of their cognitive impairments, individual abilities to remember have further been impeded by the manner in which most people with learning disabilities live out their lives. Historically, people like Mary were often placed in hospital from a young age. Such hospitals were usually found in the countryside on the edge of large conurbations and their locations ensured that only limited contact with the outside world was possible. Male and female 'patients' lived on segregated wards in dehumanising conditions: people were allowed few, if any, personal possessions – for example, clothes were provided from central stores rather than owned by individuals (May, 1994). These 'total institutions' provided the perfect environment in which abuse of all kinds could flourish, to the extent that acts which the outside world would construe as abusive interactions between individuals could come to be regarded not merely as commonplace but as part of the normative fabric of life (Goffman, 1968).

In the UK, the preferred model of service provision for people with learning disabilities has changed radically in the past half century, driven to a considerable extent by responses to abuse inquiries (Fyson *et al.*, 2004). Nowadays adults with learning disabilities who live outside the family home typically live in residential care homes or supported living services. However, the manner in which this change in provision was brought about is telling. Since 1969, more than 58,000 beds in 'mental handicap' hospitals have been closed and the former patients have been relocated 'into the community' (Department of Health, 2001). During the resettlement process, however, managerial and financial considerations often took precedence over individual wishes (Wing, 1989). For Mary and others this typically meant being separated from longstanding friendships groups and returned to the care of the local authority from which they had first been admitted to hospital, regardless of whether or not they still had any social or familial ties to the area.

Unlike the hospitals they replaced, current services generally purport to place great emphasis on supporting choice and independence for service users: indeed, they are required to do so (Department of Health, 2001). People living in such services are generally encouraged to make 'choices' about what to eat, what to wear, or whether or not to engage in a particular activity. However, it remains the case that few people with learning disabilities are given a say in the bigger choices which frame their lives – such as where and with whom to live, or from whom they receive support (Fyson *et al.*, 2007; Gorfin and McGlaughlin, 2003). Moreover, recent public inquiries have continued to demonstrate that, regardless of the size or organisational structure of the service in which they are supported, people with learning disabilities continue to suffer serious, and often systematic, abuse (Commission for Social Care Inspection and Healthcare Commission, 2006, 2007). The disempowerment and abuse of people with learning disabilities can therefore be seen to be something more enduring than service structures and it is naïve to assume that younger people in 'modern' services are necessarily less vulnerable than hospital residents (Fyson and Kitson, 2007).

In attempting to define learning disability within the context of power relations, and to relate this to vulnerability to abuse, it is also important to recognise the prevailing discourses which link disability and sexuality. Two powerful yet contradictory discourses dominate understandings of the sexuality of people with disabilities in general, and people with learning disabilities in particular (Brown, 1994; Craft, 1987; Priestly, 2003; Ryan and Thomas, 1987). The first discourse constructs adults with learning disabilities as asexual 'eternal children' who should be protected from sexual knowledge and prevented from engaging in sexual activity of any kind. This discourse can be traced back to early Christian beliefs about disabled children being 'holy innocents' or 'gifts from God' (Ryan and Thomas, 1987). It remains influential amongst some parents and carers, who erroneously believe that sexual ignorance can protect from sexual abuse. The second, equally enduring, discourse suggests the complete opposite and constructs people with learning disabilities as possessors of vast and unnatural sexual appetites, which must be suppressed. This idea was central to the eugenics movement, which flourished in the UK and elsewhere until after the Second World

War, and which actively campaigned to ensure the segregation of the 'feeble-minded' and 'moral defectives' from the rest of society. One earlier effect of this discourse was to facilitate the creation and maintenance of long-stay 'mental handicap' hospitals. Its ongoing legacy can be seen not only in the continuing social segregation of people with learning disabilities (Forrester-Jones *et al.*, 2006) but also in hate crimes against people with learning disabilities – for example the recent case in which a man was tortured and killed after being falsely accused by his tormentors of being a paedophile (Morris, 2007).

Sexual abuse in the lives of people with learning disabilities

Research now demonstrates beyond reasonable doubt that disabled children, including those with learning disabilities, are not only more likely to be abused than their non-disabled peers (NSPCC, 2003; Sullivan and Knutson, 1998, 2000; Westcott and Jones, 1999) but that their abuse is typically of longer duration (Westcott and Jones, 1999). Moreover, even after abuse is disclosed, statutory social services are less likely to intervene decisively or to offer therapeutic support (Cooke, 2000; Cooke and Standen, 2002). Indeed, the fact that disabled children are at greater risk of abuse is so well-established that it is now incorporated into UK child protection guidelines (HM Government, 2006). Studies which specifically identify the risk of sexual abuse for children with learning disabilities are less common, but Sobsey (1994) provides evidence of childhood sexual abuse prevalence rates amongst children with learning disabilities ranging from 39 to 68 per cent for girls and 16 to 32 per cent for boys, depending on the definition of sexual abuse and the sampling method used. More recently, in the UK, Balogh *et al.* (2001) reported on sexual abuse amongst a sample of children and adolescents with learning disabilities admitted to a psychiatric in-patient facility, finding that 37 out of 43 had been sexually abused.

However, unlike most other groups of people, vulnerability to sexual abuse for people with learning disabilities does not diminish once they enter adulthood (Brown and Turk, 1994). Studies of adults with learning disabilities continue to show high levels of sexual abuse, with prevalence rates ranging from 61 per cent for women and 25 per cent for men (McCarthy and Thompson, 1997) to 83 per cent for women and 32 per cent for men (Sobsey, 1994). Other studies, which have explored the characteristics of victim, offender and offence in cases of sexual abuse of adults with learning disabilities, confirm that both women and men with learning disabilities are at higher risk than those in the general population (Brown *et al.*, 1995; Sobsey, 1994); that the perpetrators of this abuse are most often men with learning disabilities, male family members, or paid staff (Brown *et al.*, 1995; McCarthy, 1993; McCarthy and Thompson, 1997; O'Callaghan *et al.*, 2003); and that severity of disability does not – as once believed – serve as a protective factor (O'Callaghan *et al.*, 2003).

Given the extent of their individual and collective disempowerment it is unsurprising that both children and adults with learning disabilities are subject to high levels of sexual abuse. As has been demonstrated, this vulnerability is created by a confluence of social and political factors. However, it is also further compounded by the nature of learning disability itself and the range of impairments with which it is commonly associated – including physical or sensory impairments and communication difficulties in addition to the intrinsic cognitive impairment. For example, a person with significant physical disabilities may quite literally be unable to escape their abuser, communication difficulties may prevent direct disclosure, and the need for help with intimate personal care may blur the boundary between caring and abusive touch (Cambridge and Carnaby, 2000). The last point is particularly important, not least because it is sometimes argued that the physical and sexual abuse of people with learning disabilities is unimportant because they do not know that they are being abused.

Whilst it may indeed be true that some people with learning disabilities remain unaware of the wider social context of their experiences, this does not mean that their experiences are not damaging. For example, in her description of the sexual experiences of women with learning disabilities, McCarthy (1993) notes that:

> ... they are largely unaware that things could be, and often are, very different for other women. Most people with learning disabilities find it very difficult to imagine how other people experience sex: people with learning disabilities generally find it hard to think in the abstract and have few avenues for finding out anything concrete about other people's sex lives.
>
> (Ibid.: 281)

She goes on to say that:

> This abuse by men with learning difficulties, with whom the women are often in close daily contact, is not usually perceived by the women themselves as abusive, but rather as 'normal' sex.
>
> (Ibid.: 283)

So abuse is not homogeneous, and those forcibly excluded from normative societal understandings may well fail to recognise their abuse as such when it is not accompanied by overt coercion, violence or pain. For such individuals, it may even be that ignorance of social norms partially insulates them from the shame, fear and anger typically experienced by non-disabled victims of sexual abuse. However, this certainly does not happen in all cases and there is compelling evidence that many people with learning disabilities, including those with severe and profound disabilities (who are unlikely to have concepts of 'abuse'), respond to sexual abuse in much the same way as other people

(O'Callaghan *et al.*, 2003; Sequeira and Hollins, 2003; Sequeira *et al.*, 2003). Indeed, the fact that some people who display symptoms of severe distress may be intellectually 'unaware' that they have been sexually abused may be indicative of the extent to which people with learning disabilities are already set apart from the rest of society. Amongst other influences, this separation is both mirrored, and partially created, by wider social and politico-legal structures. For example, in the UK prior to 2003 (when a new Sexual Offences Act was placed on statute) it was not legally possible for a woman with severe learning disabilities to be raped – her attacker could only be charged with the 'lesser' crime of 'sex with a defective' (Gunn, 1996).

One effect of the high prevalence of childhood sexual abuse amongst people with learning disabilities is that many people will carry personal histories of abuse into their adult years. For those who are unable to communicate verbally, or whose experiences are not believed or supported, memories of abuse may become externalised in ways that services regard as inappropriate. This could range from public masturbation to violent outbursts, or self-harm like Mary's – all of which are likely to result in the individual concerned being labelled as having 'challenging behaviours'. Given what is now known about the links between childhood abuse and adult mental health problems (Read *et al.*, 2005), this may be one of the many reasons for the higher prevalence of psychiatric diagnoses and 'challenging behaviours' amongst adults with learning disabilities. Recent literature on the impact of trauma in the lives of people with learning disabilities (Mitchell *et al.*, 2006; Sequeira and Hollins, 2003; Sequeira *et al.*, 2003) supports this hypothesis, which stands in stark contrast to the behaviourist approaches commonly adopted within many learning disability services in response to such outward signs of distress.

Memory and abuse in people with learning disabilities

Having established that sexual abuse is more common amongst people with learning disabilities than in other sectors of the population, we will now discuss some of the ways in which its recall may be more troublesome. Our discussion will show how the social and political influences upon the lives of people with learning disabilities that we have described are not merely contextual. Rather, these influences supply many of the mediating and facilitating factors by which memories of abuse are constituted. This is because they influence the availability and organisation of the various artefacts and practices by which such remembering is mediated and enabled. Our focus is not on some abstract notion of 'pure' remembering: rather, we are concerned with the kinds of remembering and forgetting that are actually, practically possible for people with learning disabilities in the social and material conditions of their lives.

Our discussion borrows concepts and analytic frames from the analyses of remembering and forgetting in Middleton and Brown (2005), who offer a range of strategies that make memory tractable from a social perspective.

Middleton and Brown draw upon authors including Deleuze and Guattari, Serres, Derrida and Latour; for example, they utilise notions of translation, mediation and 'punctualisation' to characterise the ways in which selected aspects of experience get collectively packaged, in networks of actors and objects, and made available as joint, composite memories. However, the core of their analytic frame is derived from the creative tension they set up between the work of Halbwachs and Bergson. Rejecting the troubling 'container' metaphors of memory frequently found in cognitive psychology, they follow Bergson (e.g. 1908, 1922) in postulating a notion of memory as 'always on', such that the past is continually both 'swelling' and 'gnawing into the present'. Bergson's is a process philosophy within which memory equates to 'duration' or the lived time of life (as opposed to the clock or calendar time of science and bureaucracy). Experience consists of perceptions or images 'thickened' by habit memories carried in the body, interspersed with recollection memories. These recollection memories are action-oriented 'actualisations' of the past, called out in the present in the service of a specific activity. They are extracted from the totality of prior experience, which therefore remains 'virtual' but nevertheless always potentially accessible – but in the process of extraction they get more-or-less subtly transformed, in line with the exigencies of present activity, Remembering, then, involves the actualisation or somewhat artificial 'cutting out' of aspects of prior experience, and their simultaneous reinsertion into the present. It is these processes of cutting out and reinsertion that transform the flow of experience from a ceaseless instantaneity, an eternal present, into a succession of sensible, graspable moments: in other words, it is memory that creates the lived time of duration.

In order to better understand how remembering is concretely achieved as the cutting out of aspects of experience, Middleton and Brown turn to Halbwachs (1925, 1950), whose sociological analyses of memory emphasised the importance of collective frameworks and the mediation of artefacts, bodily gestures and divisions of space. Halbwachs describes the sensitive interdependency of personal and collective memory, showing how what we might take to be entirely private memories – for example, recollections of a dream – are organised and bound up with familial, relational and social concerns and hence are already collective at the same time as they are also personal. This is not to claim that the personal is simply identical to the collective, but rather to recognise that what we regard as individual or personal is in fact a 'prior mode of sociality' that is already dependent upon and produced through the collective. People use collective frameworks – images of the past that are organised by its social relations – to lend substance and form to their memories. These frameworks are 'localised': rehearsed, and worked up jointly through the mediation of language, objects and spaces to provide the 'common sense mentality' of a group. Collective frameworks, then, are neither abstract nor individual, but are sustained by the complicated, mediated relations between humans and artefacts. Collective frameworks can 'territorialise' space, by apparently lending it their character;

moreover, by mediating activity they can inform the actual organisation of social space, a process Halbwachs calls *implacement*. Once an environment is thus shaped by a collective framework, reciprocally it 'supports and reinforces that framework to the point that it appears (erroneously) to be its very origin' (Middleton and Brown, 2005: 48).

Although the families and carers of people with learning disabilities figure only incidentally in Middleton and Brown's work, through their discussion of Hewitt's (1997) study of life story work with people with profound and multiple impairments, in which abuse is not discussed, their conceptual framework can usefully be applied to this group. We will now take up some of the analytical and conceptual strategies they supply, using them to identify difficulties that people with learning disabilities may encounter when remembering abuse. In so doing we will make frequent reference to Mary's story, in order to show how such troublesome consequences of abuse can be related directly to her material and social circumstances as well as to her embodied cognitive impairments.

Whilst Mary is a member of various groups or collectives, both these groups and her relationships to them differ in significant ways from those that non-disabled people take for granted. Collectively, people with learning disabilities are devalued and stigmatised (Szivos and Griffiths, 1990), and have relatively few shared or collective resources (whether material, or symbolic). Additionally, their access to each other is typically restricted by bureaucratic and organisational imperatives that determine, for example, the hours of day centre opening or the routines of the care home. Moreover, relationships and groups of friends may be changed as a consequence of policy or financial decisions taken elsewhere, such as mergers or closures of hospitals, day centres and other services. To the limited extent that people like Mary are allowed a voice in these decisions, cognitive and other impairments may make it difficult for them to articulate who their friends actually are. In any case, during the allocation of housing and other services, such preferences often take second place to medico-legal and related factors such as gender, degree of learning disability, the availability of suitably adapted accommodation, or more arbitrary indices of sociality and community such as place of birth. Already, then, we can see that opportunities for Mary to casually rehearse her memories with her peers are likely to be limited, arbitrarily available, and perhaps subject to unpredictable disruption over which she and her friends have no control. Whilst these factors alone may impede effective remembering, further insights may be gained by examining how social relations such as these give rise to collective frameworks for remembering with particular characteristics, and also by considering the intersection of the lived duration of people with learning disabilities with the durations and time frames of other people.

With regard to the collective frameworks for remembering that are available to someone like Mary, we can note three ways in which they may differ from those available to other groups. First, as we have seen, Mary's access to her peers is more routinised and less spontaneous than that typically enjoyed by non-disabled people; and second, the shared symbolic or cultural resources available to Mary and her peers are relatively restricted. Third, a significant proportion of Mary's relationships are professional ones – for example, with residential support workers, day centre staff, doctors, social workers and clinical psychologists. Such relationships are inevitably less than mutual, and are frequently dominated by the particular concerns of a specialist service or profession. Within such relationships Mary may struggle to establish the relevance of her memories (psychotherapeutic relationships are an exception here but, in the UK at least, relatively few people with learning disabilities gain access to such services – Arthur, 2003; Wilner, 2005). Because of these differences, the collective frameworks of remembering available to people like Mary are likely to be more fragile than those available to non-disabled people, and the symbolic resources from which they are constituted both more restricted and less equally distributed. Moreover, many of the significant social relations that order these frameworks will be unequal ones in which Mary is unable to direct her own activities and is positioned as comparatively incompetent or helpless. This is significant because self-directed activity is closely associated with effective learning and remembering, both generally and amongst people with learning disabilities (Cromby *et al.*, 1996).

Further insight can be gained by considering the extent to which these collective frameworks are effectively localised (mediated by language, objects and spaces) and implaced (able to influence the actual organisation of social space). Amongst non-disabled people the localisation of collective frameworks relies heavily on discourse, but many people with learning disabilities have impaired or even no ability with language. And whilst localisation is also mediated by objects and spaces, people with learning disabilities typically have little control over these aspects of their lives. For those who live in institutional settings, even personal spaces are subject to organisational constraints such as fire regulations and ease of access for cleaners. Moreover, people with learning disabilities have limited financial and other resources by which to purchase or obtain objects (photographs, souvenirs, etc.) that might mediate their memories, whilst their ability to place and display these objects in meaningful ways may be regulated by institutional or staff practices – for example, they may be discouraged from 'hoarding'. For many people, cognitive, sensory or mobility impairments will create further difficulties in both choosing and organising objects that could effectively mediate remembering. In these ways, then, localisation of collective frameworks for remembering in people with learning disabilities encounters a number of significant obstacles. The implacement of these collective frameworks may be similarly problematic, since the ability of groups of people with learning disabilities to materially shape and organise the spaces they occupy is significantly limited: by power relations and institutional strictures on the one hand, and by their cognitive, sensory or mobility impairments on the other.

The collective frameworks for remembering available to people with learning disabilities, mediated by their social relations, can thus be seen to be fragmentary, unstable, subject to arbitrary change and frequently imbued with unequal power relations, whilst their localisation and implacement is also problematic. To the extent that individual memories are constituted through such frameworks these features may impede successful remembering, lending it their properties of instability and fragmentariness. These impediments will influence remembering in general, but there will be further, specific consequences for memories of abuse because the social relations that mediate these frameworks are strongly shaped by institutional precedents (a smaller institution 'in the community' is still an institution, whatever advantages it may have over a large, isolated long-stay hospital; geographical integration does not necessarily result in social integration). The institutionalised processes of punctualisation that package up aspects of shared experience and render them memorable as composite shared events will, for obvious reasons, emphasise relatively banal occasions with an ostensibly positive affective tone: royal weddings, Christmas, the birthdays of staff members and service users. By contrast, incidents such as an abuse inquiry will not typically be formally punctualised: rendering them, and the abuse associated with them, collectively less accessible.

Further issues arise when we consider the duration or lived time of people with learning disabilities. Middleton and Brown (2005: 81) note that whilst our duration is always conjoined with those of others in 'an irreducible mix of co-existing planes of experience', it is when our own duration fails to coincide with others that we become most aware of its character. More so than the rest of us, the lives of people with learning disabilities are subject to temporal regimes over which they have little or no control: day centre opening hours, the schedules of institutional living, the timetables of training, working rotas, appointments with various professionals. Moreover, cognitive impairments may obstruct their comprehension of the relatively abstract patterns of clock and calendar time, and might even impair the ability to effectively partition experience into the dynamic categories of 'past' and 'present', 'then' and 'now'. Similarly, visual impairments and poor reading skills may make it difficult to use watches, clocks or calendars. The issue here is not that the lives of people with learning disabilities are not experienced as duration, as lived time. Rather, their facility for sensibly relating this lived time to other frames may be limited because the ways in which their prior experience is 'cut out' and reinserted into the present may be somewhat unconventional, frequently driven by affects, or by the partially-known temporal regimes of others. An interview study of trauma in people with mild intellectual disabilities found that questions involving judgements about time and age were particularly difficult for participants (Mitchell *et al.*, 2006), and clinical experience shows that trauma can be re-experienced by people with learning disabilities as flashbacks and incomplete memories (Hollins and Sinason, 2000).

Clearly these features will impact upon successful remembering generally, but may have particular consequences for memories of abuse. One possibility is that the enforced precedence of institutional time may mean that memories of abuse more readily get tied to elements of the institutional schedule than the lived experience of the person concerned. In Mary's case, for example, it did not seem that being alone in her bedroom prompted her self-harm, nor getting undressed: rather, it seemed to be the institutional routine of 'getting ready for bed' that occasioned her difficulty. However, an alternative possibility is that lived time gets thoroughly disconnected from institutional time, which may mean that memories of abuse play themselves out apparently randomly, inappropriately, with no obvious connection to the circumstances and situations the person occupies. In such circumstances the effects of abuse may more readily get construed as 'challenging behaviours' than meaningful, if somewhat obscure, responses to life events: people with learning disabilities who have been abused are significantly more likely to be described as having challenging behaviours than matched, non-abused controls (Sequeira *et al.*, 2003).

Of course, these social and material influences are not the only impediments to people with learning disabilities remembering incidents of abuse in coherent ways. We have emphasised these factors in our discussion so far because they are more-or-less generally applicable, and because they draw attention to influences upon remembering that are both rarely considered and, in many cases, potentially capable of transformation. However, as Middleton and Brown acknowledge, memories also have an affective or felt dimension. This means they can get enrolled in emotional dynamics which may further problematise them, although the particular ways in which this occurs for people with learning disabilities are poorly understood. Indeed, Arthur (2003) claims that the emotional lives of people with learning disabilities have generally been neglected, despite their having significantly higher levels of emotional difficulties and disturbance than the general population. What research there is frequently characterises the social relations and emotional lives of people with learning disabilities using such terms as loss, grieving, mourning, bonding and attachment difficulties (Bicknell, 1983; Clegg and Lansdall-Welfare, 1995). Psychiatric research suggests that rates of emotional disturbance are higher in people with learning disabilities, both generally and amongst those who have been abused (Sequeira and Hollins, 2003; Sequeira *et al.*, 2003). Stokes and Sinason (1992) suggest that people with learning disabilities may be highly emotionally responsive despite their cognitive impairments, and that this sensitivity can render them painfully subject to the damaging responses of parents and others. Parental failures of separation, their grief responses for the 'normal' child they did not have, and familial tendencies to attribute their problems to the learning disabled member, all provide a potentially toxic affective dynamic within which children with learning disabilities develop. In conjunction with the prejudice and discrimination of the wider world, it is claimed that such dynamics may foster the development of 'secondary handicaps', the defensive adoption of a stance of relative stupidity in order to avoid engagement with a difficult reality.

Secondary handicaps may be particularly common amongst people with learning disabilities who have been abused (Sinason, 1986) since 'if knowing and seeing involve knowing and seeing terrible things, it is not surprising that not-knowing, becoming stupid, becomes a defence' (Stokes and Sinason, 1992: 52). And abuse is indeed damaging, associated with challenging behaviours, relationship difficulties, sexualised behaviour, psychiatric diagnosis, self-harm, social withdrawal, aggression and low self-esteem (Sequeira and Hollins, 2003). However, despite such behavioural manifestations (and as we noted earlier), not all people with learning disabilities actually recognise their abuse as abuse. Moreover, the emotional reactions of people with learning disabilities to abuse occur both in tandem and in response to those of their parents and/or paid carers, who may themselves experience strong mixtures of conflicting emotions (see Brown *et al.*, 1994; O'Callaghan *et al.*, 2003). Additionally, the abilities to recognise abuse, recall abuse and deploy defensive emotional strategies of disavowal or denial that would impede remembering are not only productive of secondary handicaps, but also already dependent upon pre-existing levels of cognitive impairment. So, for people with learning disabilities, remembering abuse is mediated by the social, relational and material factors we have described above, and simultaneously interpenetrated by affective dynamics that may serve both to invest memories with salience and force, and to render them less accessible because they are too threatening. Furthermore, as we have tried to show, these complex mixtures of social, material and affective influences are related to cognitive impairment in ways that not only interact with, but are also constitutive of, difficulties in recall.

Conclusion

In superficial ways the lives of people with learning disabilities, both in the UK and in many other developed nations, have changed dramatically over the past half century. In particular, the closure of long-stay hospitals has enabled people to become geographically, if not socially or economically, part of the mainstream. What has not changed, however, is their ongoing vulnerability to sexual abuse – a vulnerability which may derive in part from their cognitive impairments, but which is compounded and magnified by their devalued social position.

In the past decade there have been concerted efforts in the UK to enable people with learning disabilities to obtain justice following abuse. Considerable progress has been made on many fronts, including a requirement that all local authorities develop and implement adult protection procedures (Department of Health and Home Office, 2000), revised guidance on how to support vulnerable witnesses throughout the court process (Home Office,

1998, 2002) and a new Sexual Offences Act (2003). This Act not only rescinded the law (mentioned earlier) relating to 'sex with a defective', but also introduced a new sexual crime of 'abuse of a position of trust', which makes it an offence for any carer to have sexual relations with someone they are caring for. However, while such legal and policy initiatives are to be welcomed, they are unlikely to be of immediate benefit to most people with learning disabilities – not least because they are concerned with intervening *following* abuse, rather than with the more difficult task of preventing abuse from occurring in the first place.

Profound changes, both within services and across society more broadly, are needed in order to both prevent and respond effectively to the abuse of people with learning disabilities. Current rhetoric, which in the UK (and elsewhere) emphasises the need for people with learning disabilities to be supported to achieve rights, independence, choice and social inclusion (Department of Health, 2001), is not of itself sufficient to challenge deeply enculturated social attitudes and practices. Moreover, a simplistic interpretation of complex notions such as 'choice' and 'independence' may lead to some already vulnerable people being made even more vulnerable (Fyson and Kitson, 2007). For example, remaining in an abusive or otherwise damaging situation can be presented as the 'choice' of a person with learning disabilities, with no recognition of how such a choice will already have been informed by previous life experiences and (lack of) knowledge about how things could be different. Moreover, structural or economic barriers, including limited financial and social capital or lack of availability of alternative support services, currently render meaningful choices of any kind difficult or impossible for most people with learning disabilities.

Those who plan and deliver services for people with learning disabilities have yet to develop an approach that takes into account the implications of working with a population that experiences such a high prevalence of abuse and for whom memories of abuse are so seldom validated or supported. There remains scant therapeutic support for individuals who have been abused in either hospital or community-based settings. At present, for many people with learning disabilities, this can result in a double jeopardy: first when they experience abuse and again when their memories of abuse are ignored, or when its behavioural manifestations are misinterpreted as irrational 'challenging behaviour' rather than as a rational response to a hostile world. In such circumstances, it is difficult to say precisely what it would mean for people with learning disabilities to successfully integrate their memories of abuse such that they no longer cause ongoing distress. Nevertheless, our analysis suggests that services which actively seek to validate and support individuals' life histories, and which provide suitable material, relational and (where appropriate) therapeutic support to do so, would be beneficial.

References

Arthur, A. (2003) 'The emotional lives of people with learning disability', *British Journal of Learning Disabilities* 31: 25–30.

Atkinson, D. and Walmsley, J. (1999) 'Using autobiographical approaches with people with learning difficulties', *Disability and Society* 14(2): 203–16.

Balogh, R., Bretherton, K., Whibley, S., Berney, T., Graham, S., Richold, P., et al. (2001) 'Sexual abuse in children and adolescents with intellectual disability', *Journal of Intellectual Disability Research* 45(3): 194–201.

Bergson, H. (1908/1991) *Matter and Memory*. New York: Zone.

Bergson, H. (1922/1999) *Duration and Simultaneity* (edited by R. Durie). Manchester: Clinamen.

Bicknell, J. (1983) 'The psychopathology of handicap', *British Journal of Medical Psychology* 56: 167–78.

Brown, H. (1994) ' "An ordinary sexual life?": a review of the normalisation principle as it applies to the sexual options of people with learning disabilities', *Disability and Society* 9(2): 123–44.

Brown, H. and Turk, V. (1994) 'Sexual abuse in adulthood: ongoing risks for people with learning disabilities', *Child Abuse Review* 3: 26–35.

Brown, H., Hunt, N. and Stein, J. (1994) ' "Alarming but very necessary": working with staff groups around the sexual abuse of adults with learning disabilities', *Journal of Intellectual Disability Research* 38: 393–412.

Brown, H., Stein, J. and Turk, V. (1995) 'The sexual abuse of adults with learning disabilities: report of a second two-year incidence survey', *Mental Handicap Research* 8(1): 3–24.

Cambridge, P. and Carnaby, S. (2000) 'A personal touch: managing the risks of abuse during intimate and personal care', *Journal of Adult Protection* 2: 4–16.

Clegg, J. and Lansdall-Welfare, R. (1995) 'Attachment and learning disability: a theoretical review informing three clinical interventions', *Journal of Intellectual Disability Research* 39(4): 295–305.

Commission for Social Care Inspection, and Healthcare Commission (2006) *Joint Investigation into the Provision of Services for People with Learning Disabilities at Cornwall Partnership NHS Trust*. London: Commission for Healthcare Audit and Inspection.

Commission for Social Care Inspection, and Healthcare Commission (2007) *Investigation into the Service for People with Learning Disabilities Provided by Sutton and Merton Primary Care Trust*. London: Commission for Healthcare Audit and Inspection.

Cooke, P. (2000) *Disabled Children and Abuse*. Nottingham: Ann Craft Trust.

Cooke, P. and Standen, P. (2002) 'Abuse and disabled children: hidden needs?', *Child Abuse Review* 11: 1–18.

Craft, A. (1987) 'Mental handicap and sexuality: issues for individuals with a mental handicap, their parents and professionals' in A. Craft (ed.) *Mental Handicap and Sexuality: Issues and Perspectives*. Tunbridge Wells: Costello, pp. 13–34.

Cromby, J., Standen, P. and Brown, D. (1996) 'The potentials of virtual environments in the education and training of people with learning disabilities', *Journal of Intellectual Disability Research* 40(6): 489–501.

Department of Health (2001) *Valuing People: A New Strategy for Learning Disability for the 21st Century (CM 5086)*. London: The Stationery Office.

Department of Health and Home Office (2000) *No Secrets*. London: The Stationery Office.
Forrester-Jones, R., Carpenter, J., Coolen-Schrijner, Cambridge, P., Tate, A., Beecham, J., et al. (2006) 'The social networks of people with intellectual disability living in the community 12 years after resettlement from long-stay hospitals', *Journal of Applied Research in Intellectual Disabilities* 19: 285–95.
Fyson, R. and Kitson, D. (2007) 'Independence or protection – does it have to be a choice? Reflections on the abuse of people with learning disabilities in Cornwall', *Critical Social Policy* 27(3): 426–36.
Fyson, R., Kitson, D. and Corbett, A. (2004) 'Learning disability, abuse and inquiry', in N. Stanley and J. Manthorpe (eds) *The Age of the Inquiry: Learning and Blaming in Health and Social Care*. London: Routledge.
Fyson, R., Tarleton, B. and Ward, L. (2007) *Support for Living? The Impact of the Supporting People Programme on Housing and Support for Adults with Learning Disabilities*. Bristol: Policy Press.
Gillberg, C. and Soderstrom, H. (2003) 'Learning disability', *Lancet* 362: 811–21.
Goffman, E. (1968) *Asylums: Essays on the Social Situation of Mental Patients and Other Inmates*. London: Penguin.
Gorfin, L. and McGlaughlin, A. (2003) 'Housing for adults with a learning disability: "I want to choose, but they won't listen" ', *Housing, Care and Support* 6: 4–8.
Gunn, M. J. (1996) *Sex and the Law: A Brief Guide for Staff Working with People with Learning Difficulties*, 4th edn. London: Family Planning Association.
Halbwachs, M. (1925/1992) *On Collective Memory* (edited, translated and with an Introduction by L. A. Coser). Chicago, IL: University of Chicago Press.
Halbwachs, M. (1950/1980) *The Collective Memory* (trans. F. J. Didder Jr and V. Y. Didder, Introduction by M. Douglas). New York: Harper Row.
Hewitt, H. (1997) *Identities in transition: formulating care for people with profound learning difficulties*. Unpublished PhD, Loughborough University, UK.
HM Government (2006) *Working Together to Safeguard Children: A Guide to Inter-agency Working to Safeguard and Promote the Welfare of the Child*. London: The Stationery Office.
Hollins, S. and Sinason, V. (2000) 'Psychotherapy, learning disabilities and trauma: new perspectives', *British Journal of Psychiatry* 176: 32–6.
Home Office (1998) *Speaking Up For Justice*. London: Home Office.
Home Office (2002) *Achieving Best Evidence*. London: Home Office.
Hughes, B. and Paterson, K. (1997) 'The social model of disability and the disappearing body: towards a sociology of impairment', *Disability and Society* 12(3): 325–40.
May, M. (1994) 'A personal story (Foreword)', in D. Sobsey (ed.) *Violence and Abuse in the Lives of People with Disabilities: The End of Silent Acceptance?* Baltimore: Paul H Brooks.
McCarthy, M. (1993) 'Sexual experiences of women with learning difficulties in long-stay hospitals', *Sexuality and Disability* 11(4): 277–86.
McCarthy, M. and Thompson, D. (1997) 'A prevalence study of sexual abuse of adults with intellectual disabilities referred for sex education', *Journal of Applied Research in Intellectual Disabilities* 10(2): 105–24.
Middleton, D. and Brown, S. D. (2005) *The Social Psychology of Experience: Studies in Remembering and Forgetting*. London: Sage Publications.
Mitchell, A., Clegg, J. and Furniss, F. (2006) 'Exploring the meaning of trauma with

adults with intellectual disabilities', *Journal of Applied Research in Intellectual Disabilities* 19: 131–42.
Morris, S. (2007, Saturday 4 August) 'Tortured, drugged and killed a month after care visits were stopped', *The Guardian*, pp. 8–9.
NSPCC (2003) *'It doesn't happen to disabled children'. Child Protection and Disabled Children. Report of the National Working Group on Child Protection and Disability*. London: NSPCC.
O'Callaghan, A., Murphy, G. and Clare, I. (2003) 'The impact of abuse on men and women with severe learning disabilities and their families', *British Journal of Learning Disabilities* 31: 175–80.
Priestly, M. (2003) *Disability: A Life Course Approach*. Cambridge: Polity.
Read, J., van Os, J., Morrison, A. P. and Ross, C. A. (2005) 'Childhood trauma, psychosis and schizophrenia: a literature review with theoretical and clinical implications', *Acta Psychiatrica Scandinavica* 112: 330–50.
Ryan, J. and Thomas, F. (1987) *The Politics of Mental Handicap*, revised edn. London: Free Association Books.
Sequeira, H. and Hollins, S. (2003) 'Clinical effects of sexual abuse on people with learning disability', *British Journal of Psychiatry* 182: 13–19.
Sequeira, H., Howlin, P. and Hollins, S. (2003) 'Psychological disturbance associated with sexual abuse in people with learning disabilities', *British Journal of Psychiatry* 183: 451–6.
Simons, K. (2000) *Life on the Edge: The Experience of People with a Learning Disability Who Do Not Use Specialist Services*. Brighton: Pavillion.
Sinason, V. (1986) 'Secondary mental handicap and its relation to trauma', *Psychoanalytic Psychotherapy* 2(2): 131–54.
Sobsey, D. (1994) *Violence and Abuse in the Lives of People with Disabilities: The End of Silent Acceptance?* Baltimore: Paul H. Brooks.
Stokes, J. and Sinason, V. (1992) 'Secondary mental handicap as a defence', in A. Waitman and S. Conboy-Hill (eds) *Psychotherapy and Mental Handicap*. London: Sage Publications, pp. 46–58.
Sullivan, P. and Knutson, J. (1998) 'The association between child maltreatment and disabilities in a hospital-based epidemiological study', *Child Abuse and Neglect* 22: 271–88.
Sullivan, P. and Knutson, J. (2000) 'Maltreatment and disabilities: a population-based epidemiological study', *Child Abuse and Neglect* 24: 1257–74.
Szivos, S. and Griffiths, E. (1990) 'Group processes involved in coming to terms with a mentally retarded identity', *Mental Retardation* 28(6): 333–41.
Westcott, H. and Jones, P. (1999) 'Annotation: the abuse of disabled children', *Journal of Child Psychology and Psychiatry* 40: 497–506.
Wilner, P. (2005) 'The effectiveness of psychotherapeutic interventions for people with learning disabilities: a critical overview', *Journal of Intellectual Disability Research* 49(1): 73–85.
Wing, L. (1989) *Hospital Closure and the Resettlement of Residents*. Aldershot: Avebury.

10 Memory, truth, and the search for an authentic past

Sue Campbell

In a reflection on the rapid emergence of memory studies as an interdiscipline, Susan Radstone identifies three linked aspects of contemporary memory research that place it at the heart of many political debates: 'Its urgent and committed engagement with various instances of contemporary and historical harm, its close ties with questions of identity – and, relatedly, with identity politics – and its bridging of the domains of the personal and the public, the individual and the social' (2008: 32). This thematic configuration requires renewed attention to the epistemic value of memory claims – their status as true or accurate. Expressed memory of harm often demands a political response, especially so when the harm is linked to membership in a vulnerable or marginalized group. Yet recognition of the multiplicity of social influences on our changing experience of the past can cast significant doubt on the reliability of persons' claims to have been harmed, and on the very integrity of selves formed, in part, through remembered experience of harm. Such doubt became intense during the 'false memory debates' of the 1980s and 1990s when many women's claims to have remembered child sexual abuse came under intense public, legal, and theoretical scrutiny. It was alleged that the inappropriate suggestions of therapists caused vulnerable women clients to reinterpret their childhoods through a narrative of repressed abuse, searching for its signs. This quest was said to have resulted in widespread false memories of abuse where no such abuse had occurred, and in self-concepts shaped by illusion.[1]

This chapter does not re-enter these debates but engages their legacy. We scrutinized memory in a context of public alarm about potential false accusations of serious harm. Our distrust of the social dimensions of memory, of how others influence the ways in which we re-experience our pasts, may not have been remedied by changes to therapists' practice, and may continue to threaten inappropriately the credibility of those vulnerable to harm.[2] I challenge memory theorists to recognize that we have not yet bridged the individual and the social in ways that deal adequately with excessive skepticism about memory. There are obviously many occasions on which it is sensible to distrust the reliability of our recollections. Nevertheless, in order to avoid a destructive skepticism about a fundamental source of knowledge, we also need ways to understand the basic compatibility of our memories being true to the past and often shifting interpretations of this past.

In what follows I examine and support a recent attempt by Paula Reavey and Steven Brown (2006) to develop a framework that can credit both the reality and interpretative dimensions of child abuse recollections. The theoretical approach advanced by Reavey and Brown (2006), supported by a close reading of survivor narrative, is important for two reasons. First, while the authors work in psychology, they make use of theory from a variety of perspectives and disciplinary orientations, including work on social remembering, feminist writing on gender and power, and philosophical reflection on the nature of time. They offer an exemplary text in memory studies that displays the importance of interdisciplinary facility to new ways of conceiving epistemological questions about memory. Second, Reavey and Brown attempt to dissolve the purported tension between truth and interpretation in memory through a complex and sophisticated account of the dynamics of our self-constitution as agents. Their work suggests that bridging the individual and social requires rethinking the nature of the self.

I argue that Reavey and Brown's framework would be further enriched by incorporating philosophical work on truth and accuracy. As I show below, memory theorists have often adopted an instrumental attitude towards truth in memory. That is they have regarded truth as only important given the goals of specific recollective contexts; they have, moreover, sometimes suggested that truth easily gives way in identity projects. This chapter attempts to fortify Reavey and Brown's account of the self with Michael Lynch's critique of instrumentalism about truth. Lynch examines the role of truth in autobiographical contexts, arguing that a commitment to knowing the truth about our lives is a necessary part of the other values that we strive for in self-constitution (Lynch, 2005). His work supports Reavey and Brown's own attempt to explore the compatibility between the reality and interpretability of the past via a more complex and adequate model of the self. These authors direct our attention to the ethical dimensions of self-constitution, and challenge us to grasp the necessary interdependence of epistemic and ethical values in our attempts to move forward through a remembered past. I propose that neglect of this value interdependence can lead to a destructive skepticism about memory – one with troubling political implications.

I first present Reavey and Brown's account of the contemporary tension between truth and the kinds of interpretive activity that signal autobiographical memory and trace a compelling articulation of this tension in key writings from the false memory debates. I then move to a discussion of the nature of truth as a value, its place in memory research, and its relation to our autobiographical projects.

Deconstructing the forensic self

Reavey and Brown offer a reading of survivor narratives that seeks to illuminate how a survivor of child sexual abuse negotiates memories of abuse and victimization in the context of shaping her ongoing identity as an agent. They consider how this identity project registers on a contemporary tension in our conceptualizations of memory. The tension is now a familiar one. The shift to a social reconstructive model of remembering stresses the multiple interpretability of the past. This interpretability seems hard to reconcile with the idea of true or accurate memory that is linked to an older model. Western theorists, arguably since the time of Plato, have tended to conceive of memory as the storehouse of an individual's experience, preserved as durable and discrete representations, 'experiences ... laid away for later retrieval in their original form' (Schechtman, 1994: 6). I am interested in how Reavey and Brown frame the tension in terms of an underlying view about the indeterminacy or determinacy of the past, and the ramifications of this framing for an account of the self.

A social reconstructivist approach to memory emphasizes that we often remember with others in complex relational settings, causing the project of clearly demarcating individual from social memory to give way (Halbwachs, 1992/1925; Middleton and Brown, 2006; Mitzal, 2003: ch. 4; Prager, 1998; Sutton, 2008). As children, we learn to remember through activities of joint reminiscing with our caretakers that foster close relationships through encouraging shared perspectives on the past (Fivish, 1994; Hoerl and McCormack, 2005; Waites, 1997). As adults, we continue to co-construct autobiographical memory. Those with whom we have shared experience add details to our narratives; friends, colleagues, or therapists offer interpretations of our actions that reshape our experience of the past; we often use resources for constructing a personal history made socially available in the very context of recollecting; and we inevitably use social narrative schemas that impute a certain causal structure to the events we relate (Campbell, 2003; Engel, 1999; Haaken, 1998; Hacking, 1995; Middleton and Brown, 2005; Middleton and Edwards, 1990; Schacter, 1996). Because of the various and repeated ways in which we might revisit an occasion, the 'past is not given once and for all in a particular memory, but may be manifested in multiple and often contradictory recollections' (Reavey and Brown, 2006: 180). Reavey and Brown note that 'this relative indeterminacy of the past,' our multiple and contradictory recollections of it, has led many theorists to contemplate that 'the question of the true accuracy of recollections' is 'less important than understanding the effects that a given version of events has on the present' (ibid.).[3]

Yet Reavey and Brown point out that the reconstructive model remains uncomfortably positioned against the older storehouse model of memory. The storehouse model remains entrenched in key institutions that can aid the survivor in managing a traumatic history, in part because they credit the reality and impact of abuse as evidenced through her memory (Reavey and

Brown, 2006: 180). Law and some approaches to therapy assume there is a determinate meaning to the past, a true or accurate representation of what really happened, credentialed as such by the fact that memories are impressed directly on our consciousness by our experience of the events remembered; they are not constituted, even partly, by post-event influence. Put somewhat differently, Reavey and Brown see both projects as committed to what they term 'the forensic self' (2006: 183) – the idea inherited from John Locke that memories are caused by our experience of the past and constitute a continuous self, conscious of and thus responsible for its past actions, a 'forensic' self capable of law (Locke, 1961/1706: 171). David Middleton and Steven Brown comment that on Locke's account, 'to be a person is to be endowed with a chain of successive memories that map out what we have seen, what we have done, what we are' (Middleton and Brown, 2005: 180). One consequence of this view of the self is that, provided we speak sincerely, the accurate representations of the past recorded in memory allow others to trust our accounts of this past. The forensic self seems one apt for disclosing the nature of the past to others.

We need further explanation, however, of why the past should not allow of multiple descriptions through memory that are all nonetheless true. Reavey and Brown locate the key point of conflict in memory models as one of determinacy/indeterminacy that seems to correspond to conflicting possibilities for truth in memory, and it is worth pausing to ask about this connection. Why might we think that the idea of a determinate past, contrasted to a multiply interpretable one, supports truth in memory? Determinacy is a complex and ambiguous notion. The idea of a determined state directs our attention backwards to cause. But when applied to representations, the idea of 'determinate' always carried implications for meaning, implying that meaning is fixed and will not change. I take Reavey and Brown's understanding of determinacy in the context of discussing memory models to carry both these senses. The storehouse model represents memories as not only caused by the past, but as singular and stable in meaning as a reflection of what we assume to be the nature of the past itself. If the past has a singular meaning, the mere fact that I might remember it in many different ways seems to jeopardize truth in memory. We might otherwise consider that there are several true readings of a past event.

Legal systems have the task of assigning liability and penalty for actions that fall under determinate categories of harm, like sexual assault. It is at least understandable that law would rely on a determinate meaning to the past, and on memory testimony as its direct and transparent representation.[4] It seems odd that the interpretive project of therapy would be similarly committed to determinacy rather than encouraging a range of perspectives on one's past. Reavey and Brown note that in the case of the trauma survivor, in particular, therapists have often assumed that the singular truth of the past, the pain of trauma as given in memory, whether or not this memory is accessible to consciousness or dissociated or repressed, determines the identity of the survivor in the present (2006: 180–1). Fundamentally, however, it is the forensic self – both supporting and supported by the storehouse view of memory – that requires our memories to have stable meaning. If we just *are* the memories that our past delivers, the coherence and stability of the self must be found in the character of our memory. Historically, unstable, shifting, gappy, or contradictory memories have been taken to indicate the presence of a disturbed self, of fragmentation, dissociation, or other psychopathology (Hacking, 1995).

The tension between the interpretability of the past and our seeming need for its determinate meaning, as reflected in long-standing commitments to the forensic self, reached a point of crisis during the false memory debates. The identity of someone who has survived traumatic harm may present as extraordinarily fixed and marked by the memory of trauma – identity as a seeming testament to the forensic self. And as Reavey and Brown point out, therapy may reinforce this sense of determined identity. But it was, in fact, the very investigation of survivor memory that gave considerable theoretical impetus to a cross-disciplinary consensus about the reconstructive nature of memory (Sutton, 2002).

Two particularly powerful and influential texts, devastating for the forensic self, were Janice Haaken's *Pillar of Salt: Gender, Memory, and the Perils of Looking Back* (1998) and Ian Hacking's *Rewriting the Soul: Multiple Personality and the Sciences of Memory* (1995). These texts deconstruct the forensic self as expression and evidence of interpretive dynamics of memory. Haaken argues that the seeming singularity and determinate meaning of memory manifest in some survivor narratives is in fact evidence of a particular reconstructive process at work. She elaborates a theory of *transformative remembering* as a process in which certain social narratives – for example, a feminist narrative of the devastating impact of child sexual abuse – come to have 'superordinate explanatory power' (1999: 16) in our reinterpretations of a personal past.

Hacking offers a history of multiple personality disorder (MPD) as a diagnostic category that supports Haaken's insights about the power of social narrative. For many years, MPD was regarded as a severe dissociative response to child sexual abuse. A significant number of therapists contended that those who suffered from MPD would only become reintegrated as continuous, coherent selves by recovering their memories of the trauma, that 'memories of early cruelties are hidden and must be recalled to effect a true integration and cure' (Hacking, 1995: 20). They assumed a forensic self as the model of self stability. Hacking argues compellingly that because we remember human actions through concepts and narrative schemas supplied by our present, recall is always as much redescription as recovery of the past:

> The multiple sees or finds the cause of her condition in what she comes to remember of her childhood and is thereby helped. This is passed off as a specific etiology, but what is happening is more extraordinary than that.

> It is a way of explaining oneself, not by recovering the past, but by redescribing it . . .
>
> The past becomes rewritten in memory, with new kinds of descriptions, new words, new ways of feeling, such as those grouped under the general heading of child sexual abuse. The events as described, which the multiple in therapy comes to feel as the cause of her illness, did not produce her present state. Instead, redescriptions of the past are caused by the present.
>
> (1995: 94)

On Hacking's account, memories are not the key to the self by virtue of being caused by the past. Rather memory gains meaning through acts of interpretive self-creation in the present that often misunderstand their own character.

Haaken's and Hacking's analyses stress the illusion of the forensic self[5] involved in autobiographical projects, problematizing the extent to which our ways of remembering are compatible with self and social knowledge. Yet both their projects are guided by ethical/political concerns that direct us to the importance of such knowledge. Haaken's critique of the hegemonic edge to abuse narratives is deeply political: she believes that the kinds of transformative rememberings of victimization that have sometimes characterized feminist consciousness-raising projects can oversimplify aspects of women's choice and agency that are required in a libratory politics. Hacking's account extols the value self-honesty as a part of our 'best vision of what it is to be a human being' (1995: 267), even if he is skeptical and pessimistic about its attainment. The tension between true and reconstructive memory recurs as an internal point of difficulty in reconstructive approaches motivated by the ethical/political imperative of adequate self-knowledge. I contend that our response to this imperative requires confrontation with skepticism about truth in memory.

Whatever one's assessment of some of the very complex dimensions of the false memory debates, one of their effects was to fortify a theoretical consensus about the reconstructive nature of remembering in the context of a growing social skepticism about the epistemic fidelity of women's projects of self-constitution. Some of the most publicly influential voices in these debates, for example forensic psychologist Elizabeth Loftus and sociologist Richard Ofshe, explicitly encouraged this skepticism (Loftus and Ketcham, 1994; Ofshe and Watters, 1994), and women who suffered sexual abuse have certainly felt its effects, in, for example, the increased legal scrutiny of their therapy relationships (Busby, 1997; Bowman and Mertz, 1996; Campbell, 2002), and in responses to their disclosures of suspicions of abuse (Brownlie, 1999; Williamson, 1998).

Lynch describes skepticism as the 'Janus face' of a concern for truth (Lynch, 2005: 29), provoked in part by the very critical practices in which we engage in trying to ascertain the truth (see also Williams, 2002). There is no easy remedy to a skepticism that comes from a deep suspicion about the reliability of a core area of knowledge and our knowledge of the past is especially vulnerable. The past is beyond the reach of our perceptual checking and it requires no great effort to find inaccurate histories or autobiographies. The false memory debates gave impetus to interdisciplinary collaboration on memory. Theorists came together, theorists from neurobiology, psychology, the social sciences and humanities, and many turned attention to issues of suggestibility and memory distortion.[6] Critical as these concerns are, an equally important legacy of the debates will be our ability to develop epistemic approaches to memory that are sensitive to the momentum of skepticism, and can respond effectively to unwarranted doubt.

Reavey and Brown suggest two possible courses of response to the tension they isolate, each of which answers skepticism in a different way. The first strategy, which they reject, affirms the importance of interpretation over truth in autobiographical memory, mollifying skeptical anxiety by downplaying the importance of truth in self-constitution. Though I shall argue that this response is both unstable and inimical to our projects of self-constitution, examining its role in the memory research yields important insights about models of truth in memory. The second strategy contends that reconstructive remembering is compatible with truth, self-honesty, and self-knowledge. I take Reavey and Brown to be exploring this strategy and I argue that we can think about truth in ways that fortify this response. It is important to note that both strategies reject the forensic self: the claim that we are the memories that our past delivers. Our choice is not whether to reject the forensic self but how.

Truth in memory research

In the last chapter of *Rewriting the Soul*, Hacking asks if we can simply be utilitarian about the importance of truth in autobiographical memory: 'What is wrong with mistaken memories that do no harm?' (1995: 258). Mistaken memories might after all serve our goals as well as or better than true memories. The former might bring us happiness or self-stability. Hacking is made deeply uncomfortable by the suggestion that we should only care about true memories when there is an instrumental reason to do so; that is, when true memories would serve our goals better than mistaken memories or fantasies. What is perhaps surprising is how reasonable and unremarkable this instrumental lens on truth is for many memory theorists. The idea that we should be modest about epistemic demands on memory is not simply the consequence of recent reflection on issues of indeterminacy, but has a broader base in the traditions of memory research, its division of labor and discourse of function.

I note that the discussion of epistemic value of memory typically takes place not in terms of truth but rather the associated value of accuracy. There seems to have been little direct attention to the differences in these terms, and they are most often simply used interchangeably. Adam Morton suggests that we typically use 'accuracy' to describe representations that are both true and *precise* (Morton, 2002), where what counts as precise will depend on the context in which the representation is being assessed.[7] It is a natural vocabulary for a science of memory where the amount of detail to recall is often an important part of how good memory is assessed. The contrasts offered for accurate memory – memory as false, distorted, or a good story – show that memory theorists take accuracy to presuppose truth, and for the purposes of this chapter, I follow most theorists in using the terms interchangeably.

James Wertsch contends that 'a major divide in memory studies' (2002: 31) is marked by an interest in different functions that correspond to different criteria for good remembering. Individualist studies of memory in empirical and cognitive psychology have tended to focus on accurate representation as the function of memory, 'the standard against which empirical results are measured' (p. 32). Scholars in the humanities and social sciences have been more concerned with theories of memory 'in rhetorical or political processes concerned with identity and a usable past' (p. 32). Wertsch warns against a simple opposing of functions, saying they tend to operate in tandem 'vying for position in any particular instance of remembering' (p. 31). Yet, although theorists of social memory may not believe that accuracy is completely unimportant, Wertsch notes that they do 'view memory as being sufficiently committed to an identity project that the notion of accuracy can be downplayed or sacrificed in the service of producing a usable past' (p. 33).

The tendency to affirm the importance of one kind of value over another given different functions of memory is common in our current interdisciplinary conversations. For example, at a 2006 symposium on the conceptual foundations of individual and collective memory, the participants were asked to provide preliminary statements on a number of issues, including the importance of accuracy in studying memory. Most tied the importance of accuracy to memory function. Here is a sample of the response: 'This depends on which type of memory performance we study. For some memory tasks in daily life, accuracy is crucial (e.g. Where did I put my keys? When does my plane leave?). For other tasks, it is much less important whereas aesthetic, symbolic and other communicative values of memory may be central and cause memory distortions at the level of accuracy [sic].' 'The answer here is unequivocally ambiguous: It depends ... Accuracy matters in many contexts. A good story matters more in other contexts.' 'It depends on the situation, particularly the person's goal.' 'Accuracy matters if accuracy helps individuals and social groups deal with current life circumstances. Otherwise it is not so important.'[8] I want to highlight three contestable assumptions that help diagnose this functional approach.

The first is that accurate memory is of only instrumental value. Accuracy is important, for example, when the function of memory is to represent past actions, events, and places in ways that make possible our negotiations of present environments. The relevant contexts are often exampled through our ongoing daily quotidian needs to remember names, dates, directions, tasks, and the location of objects (Where are my keys? What time does my plane leave?). Other functions of memory may not require true and detailed representations of the past, but, rather, a good story. We might reinforce group cohesion and identity by misremembering the rain, the bugs, and the petty resentments of our recent trip, co-affirming instead that for all of us, every moment was enjoyed. Lynch writes that 'we care about [instrumental goods] for what they can do for us' (2005: 10). When Wertsch and most symposium participants easily contemplate that whether memories are true or accurate can be downplayed given our objectives, they treat truth as an instrumental good. Instrumentalism about truth is not our only option. Lynch, who I discuss below, regards truth in our representations as a non-dispensable value 'worth caring about for its own sake' (2005: 16).

The second assumption is that we can understand accuracy by isolating it as a value and researching it in a context sealed against the complicating nature of interpretive projects. To note that memories can be subject to different standards of functional assessment may seem to place our interest in truth and accuracy in the context of a broader discussion of the value of memory. This seeming placement is illusory. The history of empirical memory research has fragmented our inquiry into value through narrowing the context of investigation so as to exclude the interpretative dimensions of rememberings and the values that might be at stake in such contexts. According to Haaken, classic positivist memory research assumes 'that there is an objective reality that can be established and consensually verified, independently of the subjectivity of the observer' (1998: 43). This assumption is enacted in the experiments by minimizing interpretability – the past is rendered objective and verifiable through a list of what is to be remembered. The significance to people of the events remembered, and the contested interpretations that attend this significance, are rendered irrelevant to the study of accurate memory through the structure of these experiments (Neisser, 1981).

Third, the development of classic memory science has failed to dislodge an assumption about how memories come to be true that is at the core of our discourses of memory legitimacy. It is common for theorists to hold that we form true perceptual beliefs through causal interaction with the objects of our environment, as long as conditions are present for our perceptual mechanism to operate reliably (Lynch, 2005). For example, we must be near enough to objects to see them clearly. Memory has often been understood on analogy with perception (Warnock, 1987), and classic memory experiments encode this understanding. Namely, memories are made reliably true by our causal interaction with a piece of the world – words on a page, for example – as long as we are in the right conditions for that process to be reliable, as long as we minimize interpretability. The experiment presents what is to be remembered not only as fixed and stable but as available for perceptual checking. There is little space for engagement over what the past was really like or about whether we can ever ascertain what it was like. The classic empirical study of memory has ceded theory of interpretation to the humanities and social sciences while commandeering truth. At the same time it has entrenched a picture of how memories come to be true that is inadequate to interpretive contexts, and makes it difficult to talk about true and interpretive memory.

The symposium answers illustrate that although memory research is increasingly sophisticated and interdisciplinary, the indexing of truth or accuracy to function continues to be offered as an accommodation to the complexity of memory. But when we use a functional approach to memory as the ground for a discussion of value, we need to recognize that remembering in ordinary contexts is a complex and multidimensional activity. A remembering may, all at once, help me to negotiate my environment, contribute to an ongoing self-narrative, and be an act of identification with others, supporting a particular social identity as my own. I may add to or contest a social grasp of events, either intentionally or accidentally. Moreover, my expressing memory typically licenses others to take what I say as a source of testimony about the past. The multi-functionality of memory, its unstable potentiality as testimony and history, makes the willingness to downplay truth in interpretive contexts a problematical resolution: 'There is no way of sticking to everyday truths and no more' (Williams, 2002: 12).

I believe that the commitment to truth or accuracy as of merely instrumental value too easily licenses the thought that these are unimportant values in many memory contexts. This thought is reinforced by a research history that isolates truth through its methods of testing and so fails to see truth's interconnectedness to other values. But at most I seem to have argued that because memory is unpredictably multi-functional in ways that implicate truth, truth is an instrumental value of memory in most or all contexts; it is instrumental but indispensable. In the next sections I read Reavey and Brown's rapprochement between truth and interpretation through the lens of Lynch's defence of truth as a non-instrumental value to show that witnessing our respect for truth enriches an account of self-constitution.

Truth and self-constitution

Reavey and Brown ask whether the 'truth of an event (i.e. child sexual abuse) can be positioned alongside its transformation in the present' (2006: 183). Their exploration of the compatibility of truth and interpretation rightly argues that our memories do not have to be fixed and singular in meaning, as is suggested by the storehouse model, to bear witness to the reality of the past. This section will support their contention. The theorists invoke Henri Bergson's model of the continuous flow and progression of our experience as an option to thinking of lived time as a linear series of time phases each of which can bear meaning independently of those that follow. Instead, a past event will gain its meaning and character in the context of a continuously evolving life, and will have complex significance within that life: 'a given recollection is always partial ... it fails to exhaust the manifold sets of relations it can potentially bear on the totality of ongoing experience' (2006: 190). The past, then, is not determinate.

Hacking points out that our most significant memories are of what we or others do, and that it is in the nature of action to be interpretable (1995: ch. 17). How we might describe an action may change given the context of description (Haaken, 1998), the accumulation of effects, or the evolution of our conceptual frameworks. Yet Hacking worries that the indeterminacy of action complicates our accounts of agency and responsibility. Reavey and Brown contend that acknowledging indeterminacy is a necessary enrichment of our grasp of agency. Bergson's account directs attention to how explicit recollection can 'extract' a partial and contextually relevant perspective on the past from the flow of duration. A child sexual abuse survivor must cope with the harm in her past in ways that allow her to go forward as an agent. In analysing a survivor's narration of this process, her attempts to understand her present agency through reflection on past responsibilities and choices, Reavey and Brown exemplify strategies through which we 'tame' the past through recollection (2006: 190). At the same time, the narrative shows how the very indeterminacy of the past, its legitimate interpretability, can form the heart of intelligent self-reflection.

In the first excerpt, taken from interviews with women survivors of child sexual abuse, the narrator, Sara, uses spatial features of the environment of abuse to construct and consider dilemmas of choice she may have faced as a child:

> I used to go and stay with my grandma, for most weekends, because my mother was having a hard time with my two brothers, and she used to cross me over the road, for me to go and visit these people who lived across the road, and it gave my grandmother a break in the afternoon. Er, and it was at this house where it happened.
> (Reavey and Brown, 2006: 191)

As the narrative progresses, crossing the road comes to symbolize the complex issue of whether a child has choice and responsibility. Sara describes how important it was for her to give her grandmother a break although she didn't want to cross the road and be subject to abuse. Sara could proceed to the playground angering her mother and frightening her grandmother, or she could 'cross the road:'

> But at 6 years old, it, do you think all those things, I don't know, I mean I think children are quite responsible, aren't they, in many ways, they feel they're responsible for choices, and things, they do ask questions, but you know, I didn't want to be a naughty girl, really I wanted to do the right thing.
> (Reavey and Brown, 2006: 192)

Reavey and Brown comment that 'the working up of choice ... through the spatial distribution of objects is a significant feature of establishing coherence in retrospect' (2006: 193). In more recent work, Reavey and Brown (2007), and Reavey (Chapter 7 this volume) have continued to explore the material environments through which people articulate memory in order to forefront the complex and ambivalent ways in which sexual abuse survivors understand their own past agency. My own use of Sara's narrative, in the discussion that follows, focuses on the specific issue of her struggle for integrity, and what that struggle might tell about the nature of truth as a value.

The complicated issue of how to understand a child's agency is by no means resolved through the coherence that Sara establishes, which rather structures the past as an occasion for self-reflection. In the second excerpt, Sara pursues the issue of child agency and responsibility by imagining what different groups (i.e. men and women) might say about a sexually abused child who later becomes promiscuous and sexually active. Though Sara wants to know 'that the child had no choice' (Reavey and Brown, 2006: 195), she imagines that men's and women's perspectives on this will differ. Men will be more likely than women to straightforwardly affirm that the child had no choice. Here again, now through use of different social perspectives, Sara renders her past intelligible and apt for self-reflection in a way that highlights rather than forecloses the interpretability of action.

It may be that Sara comes to a quite definite resolution about her degree of agency as a child. What I take Reavey and Brown to be encouraging is our recognition that memory does not transparently deliver the meaning of behavior or desire. Self-reflection is the hard work of interpreting our own and others' behaviors and of apportioning responsibilities. Our status and self-conception as agents is vested in this capacity. Moreover, the agentic project of reflection on responsibilities involves much more than determining whether we could be blamed, praised, or excused for particular choices. Although it is common to think of responsibility as a backward-looking issue of praise or blame, many theorists have pointed out that there are equally important forward-looking senses that involve *taking responsibility* for people and situations (Card, 1996; Walker, 1998). I can choose to be the person who takes care of particular others, or who makes myself accountable for how the people around me are faring. In reflecting on her mother's and grandmother's needs and burdens, and in saying that children feel responsible not only for choices but for 'things,' Sara engages the issue of the responsibilities to her mother and grandmother that she may have undertaken. *She wants to know what was true*, not only of those choices for which others might hold her accountable, but also of her own commitments.

Bergson's model of experience eliminates the idea of an originary memory impression that acts as the stable, singular meaning of a time or event. The significance of the past is multiply and diversely constructed through the dynamics of recollection. Lynch would argue that the multiplicity of perspectives is in itself no threat to accurate memory. He points out that our descriptions of the world are context responsive and utilize many different kinds of conceptual resources depending on the context (2005: 41). Memories represent different maps for the same area of the past. Allowing multiple diverse descriptions of an event is no concession to a destructive relativism about truth as long as we acknowledge 'that not every story of the world is true' (p. 41). 'It is the way the world is that matters for truth' (p. 11).[9] I will return to a more specific concern about moving the vocabulary of truth into highly interpretive contexts that I find in Reavey and Brown's text. I first consider how Lynch makes room for the importance of truth in self-interpretive projects through challenging our assumptions about this value.

Sara is committed to grasping what's true of her past as required for self-understanding. For Lynch, her narration exemplifies one of the key projects for which our need to know what's true is of more than instrumental value: the very project of self-constitution. 'One of the things that makes you plausibly the kind of person you are is the nexus of commitments, beliefs, principles, and so on that constitute what you care about. This nexus of commitments might be called yourself, in a certain sense of that word' (2005: 145). The narrator's knowledge of what she cares about is partly constitutive of her sense of self. To have an intelligible sense of self is a fundamental good, the ground of our other projects, and Lynch stresses that knowing what one cares about is not simply *one means* of attaining a sense of self, it is an important part of what it is to have one. Seeking what's true about one's own commitment is thus of more than instrumental value (2005: 124). Further, Lynch goes on to propose that having a sense of self is itself a constitutive part of other deep values. It is 'essential for a certain network of attitudes we need to have towards ourselves' (2005: 123). Lynch's account investigates the relation of truth to self-respect and authenticity. My own interest is in the narrator's struggle for integrity.

Recent feminist accounts of integrity have stressed that it is both a personal and social value, formed in how we narrate our lives and commitments to others (Calhoun, 1995; Walker, 1998). Margaret Urban Walker, for example, argues that it is both for moral purposes and 'purposes of intelligibility over time that we read and reread actions and other events backwards and forwards, weaving them into lives that are anything more than just one damn thing after another' (1998: 110). Walker hypothesizes that we interweave three types of stories – stories of relationship, identity, and value – in order to shape a self that can live 'responsibly a life of one's own' (ibid.), in other words a life that has integrity. Each story line is evident in the narrative that Reavey and Brown discuss. To understand her commitments, the narrator must, for example, reread and reflect on her relationships with her mother and grandmother, their 'developed expectations, [their] basis and type of trust' (Walker, 1998: 111). Her interpretation is imbricated with reflection on her own identity, on 'what she cares for, responds to, and takes care of' (1998: 112). Narratives of relationship and identity inform each other:

> The narratives of relationships I sustain, the way I combine and order them, the continuations I find more valuable than others, the losses I am willing to accept or impose, are controlling structures of the moral life that is specifically mine, even when its matter includes an unpredictable lot of demands that originate with others with whom I'm connected by history or occasion.
>
> (Walker, 1998: 112)

Finally, Walker contends that these two kinds of narrative thread require the support of a third, a story of our shared understandings of 'the moral terms themselves' (p. 110). The narrator's reflections on the notion of responsibility 'span and support' the relational self she reads into her past (p. 113).

In Reavey and Brown's analysis, Sara interprets her childhood through memory to help determine her present agency. The sense of self and the moral understandings described, though nascent and tentative, are important to the narrator's capacity to make her life her own in a fashion that sustains a central virtue of agency: integrity. Such integrity consists in the ability to shape a self-constituting narrative that integrates who one is in particular with one's accountability to others (Walker, 1998: 115–20). Lynch and Walker would emphasize, moreover, that our shared moral understandings of integrity require our commitment to truth: that we do not deceive ourselves or others about who we are and what we stand for.

My argument has not been that the narrator holds an accurate memory of her past. I cannot know that she does. Rather the way she rereads her past can help us see that seeking the truth of one's past is importantly interrelated to other values in the very kind of interpretive identity context in which many memory theorists are willing to downplay the importance of getting the past right. To understand truth in these contexts, we must also move away from a simple perceptual model of how our memories come to be true.

In countering skepticism about the possibility of truth, Lynch contends that we must give up not only the idea that truth is a merely instrumental value, but also the assumption that all beliefs come to be true in the same way. 'When it comes to beliefs about the physical world around us . . . it is likely that the truth of [a] belief is realized by its being causally responsive to some bit of the concrete world . . . But even so, this doesn't mean the job always gets done in the same way' (2005: 99). The truth about what we care about is, for Lynch, an illustration of why we need a more complex account of how certain beliefs come to be true.

First, in clarifying what we care about, the concepts and standards that we use in interpreting action and types of responsibility will be social ones. The objectivity of our self-interpretations will be answerable to how our communities apply social and moral concepts such as responsibility. While standards will be contestable, there will be clear applications and clear misuses of the terms. Second, how I represent myself is never simply an act of description but is always creative of who I am: 'the self that answers questions about who a person is . . . is both expressed and created by the process of self-representation' (Flanagan, 1996: 69–70. Quoted in Lynch, 2005: 145–6). Lynch remarks that the creative aspects of self-constitution do not mean that we can make our identity 'out of whole cloth' (p. 146). There are many constraints on what we can truly say of ourselves that range from verifiable facts about us to our ability to respond to others' challenges to our self-perceptions; we can make mistakes about what we care about, what we are committed to (p. 146). I agree with Lynch but want to make a more particular point about memory.

We cannot make our memories out of whole cloth. It is a condition of my remembering an event that I experienced that event. Yet, the articulation of the self, including its expression in memory, is always forwards looking and our self-representations are made true partly by how we go on to act. The narrator's memories of the nature of her relationship with her grandmother at a certain time – that she cared about her grandmother's need for a break or that she wanted to be a good girl and not a naughty one – are responsive for their truth to ways in which she acted subsequent to the time remembered. In this way, what we remember about our actions, commitments, and responsibilities can never simply be caused to be true by interactions with the world at that time and in the absence of post-event influence. How we determine what commitments we have had and have now reinforces Reavey and Brown's Bergsonian approach to lived time, where 'the character of a given region of the past becomes reconfigured by the ongoing expansion and extension of experience' (2006: 189). To remember an action or event is to be carried beyond that time, and to be shaping a sense of self that is as much commitment as description.

Our self-constituting memory narratives may involve plural perspectives on our past; our accounts and moral understandings will be contestable by others; and our self-perceptions will be forward-looking, tentative truths seeking further confirmation in how we go on to act. Nevertheless, Lynch insists that if we give up thinking that truth is merely instrumental, singular, free-standing as a value, caused in one way, representing a mind-independent reality, or requiring certainty, we will have gone a long way towards making room for truth in these narratives. Moreover, we will see that indifference to truth is not compatible with our care for the integrity of the self.

Our responsibilities to rememberers

Lynch's expansive and complex defence of the importance of truth to our projects of self-constitution is a powerful challenge to skepticism about its possibility. Lynch requires us to systematically isolate and interrogate the assumptions that seem to render truth unattainable, rather than complex and contestable. I have attempted to mark assumptions in the history of memory theory that block truth from a place in interpretive contexts. I want to conclude by briefly taking up two challenges to my own optimism about the compatibility of truth and interpretation in memory. I respond to both by noting the responsibilities we may have as witnesses and interpreters of others' memories.

The first challenge involves my promissory note to address what I read as Reavey and Brown's concern with moving the vocabulary of truth into interpretive contexts. In considering survivor narratives, the theorists acknowledge our concern about the facts of the past but allow that the resources we use to shape its significance can compromise the literality of memories. For example, recognizing the narrator's symbolic use of the road should lead us to accept that the physical environment may have been slightly reorganized to give expression to her dilemma of choice. Reavey and Brown's negotiation of the tension between our need for literality and our ability to grasp the symbolic use of representations is contextual and nuanced. How we remember reflects the influence both of present needs and of discursive contexts. They thus propose that a survivor might express memory with a high degree of determinacy and literality in the context of a forensic inquiry; 'however, on other occasions ... it is perfectly plausible that the same experience might be reconfigured and extracted in a less determinate manner' (2006: 190). I believe they are right to stress our willingness and ability to credit the distinction between occasions. But Reavey and Brown carefully shift from talk of *truth* on the latter kinds of occasion to that of our license to assume the *reality* of the events described. I want to firmly keep truth for interpretive contexts, in part because I have insisted that remembering is a multidimensional activity that may always contribute to a social grasp of the past. We need to collectively shape, respond to, and judge the social and moral significance of past events. We must thus take responsibility for the hermeneutical skills that allow us to epistemically assess memory without always insisting on its literal presentation.[10]

I do not think that Reavey and Brown would reject the above suggestion. But it may lead to a deeper worry: namely, that the hermeneutical skills that we have have led reasonably to the skepticism I resist. As Bernard Williams reminds us, skepticism is provoked by the critical practices that help constitute our concern for truth (2002). We might take the analysis of narrative remembering in Haaken and Hacking, for example, as evidence of the power of the social narratives to inevitably compromise our integrity as rememberers, compelling us to remain skeptics about the compatibility of truth with interpretation. I do not read Haaken's argument in this way, and will indicate why as a way to return to my initial dictum that we should think about *how* we want to give up the forensic self. Do we downplay the importance of truth in autobiographical contexts suspecting it is unattainable, or insist that reconstructive remembering is compatible with self and social knowledge?

I have argued in previous writing that a number of theorists during the false memory debates presented women sexual abuse survivors as having little regard for the truth of their memories (see Campbell, 2003).[11] I was particularly disturbed by some representations of women during these debates as so suggestible as to be incapable of a commitment to truth. I contended that we cannot hope to arrive at a reasonable view of memory if we start with a distorted view of rememberers. Lynch's account requires us to interrogate the assumptions that make us skeptical about the possibility of truth, including assumptions about the moral character of rememberers. The narrator in Reavey and Brown's text may be wrong about her past, but unless we assume that she cares about the truth we cannot credit her with aiming at self-knowledge or integrity. We are not always willing to credit particular individuals with caring about self-knowledge or integrity. But it was this kind of failure of credit to women as a group, I contended, that helped fuel a destructive skepticism about memory in autobiographical contexts. Our respect for others requires that we credit them with a sense of integrity about their pasts, even when we recognize the difficulties of achieving self-knowledge. I thus reject the strategy of downplaying the importance of truth. I believe that unless we recognize its importance to people, we will not understand the difficulties they may face in their projects of self-knowledge and self-constitution.

Haaken's analysis positions women as struggling to articulate what's true of their experience within particular political circumstances. Her work resituates some of the difficulties of self-knowledge as an issue of social responsibility tied to the fact of oppression. Haaken writes that 'for all oppressed groups, emancipation involves struggling to achieve a more authentic account of the past, out from under the dominant, repressive accounts of the powerful' (1999: 14). In other words, oppressed groups find themselves in circumstances of a kind of epistemic injustice: 'the injustice of having . . . significant area[s] of one's own experience obscured from collective understanding' and from self-understanding (Fricker, 2006: 100). Haaken's account is concerned, for example, with the daily intrusions and violations that women have lacked a vocabulary to articulate, and to which, she argues, incest narratives powerfully respond.

Such circumstances of epistemic injustice give rise to certain moral risks for oppressed groups, including the risk of developing narrative resources that oversimplify the past and compromise the integrity of self-constitution. Haaken's analysis of narratives makes these risks clear and calls on oppressed groups to give them more attention. But for the argument of this chapter, what is also important to see is that we cannot even get a grip on this distinctive kind of injustice, and our responsibilities to help ameliorate it, unless we believe that those who are oppressed are trying to get at the truth of their experience.[12]

Notes

1 For a range of different perspectives on these debates see Brown *et al.* (1998), Campbell (2003), Haaken (1998), Hacking (1995), Loftus and Ketcham (1994),

Ofshe and Watters (1994), Pope (1996), and Schacter (1996). For an extensive list of resources, see the web bibliography maintained by John Sutton: http://www.phil.mq.edu.au/staff/jsutton/Recoveredmemory.htm

2 Although I cannot prove this assertion, it seems to me a plausible one. The assumption that social dimensions of remembering are sufficient in themselves to raise strong concerns about memory reliability was still problematically evident in the mid to late 1990s. For example, in the first international war crimes prosecution that focused solely on rape and sexual assault (The Prosecutor v. Anto Furundzija), the Defense charged several reasons that Witness A's memory was unreliable, including that 'her recall of events and identification were reconstructions for postwar political activists and investigators' (Campbell, 2002: 162). Noting that memory is reconstructive is offered here as sufficient reason that it should be judged unreliable. In a quite different context, Indigenous Canadians' reports of their traumatic experiences in government sponsored Indian Residential Schools were often suspected to have been the result of picking up exaggerated ways of describing their experience from sharing memories with other students. As these experiences were difficult for students to talk about, and many said they were doing so for the first time, there were no compelling grounds for this concern. The kind of skepticism about influence generated by controversy over women's purported abuse memories seemed easily transferable to this different context. See Donnelly (1998).

3 In this chapter, I focus on multiplicity. I believe that genuinely contradictory recollections are quite rare and that when assertions really are contradictory, only one can be true.

4 Legal theorists, however, have certainty turned attention to reconstructive views. See, for example, Campbell (2002) and Sarat (2003).

5 As far as I can determine, neither Haaken nor Hacking uses the words 'forensic self' in their texts.

6 The topic of distortion, for example, was chosen for the first sponsored conference of the interdisciplinary Harvard Center for the Study of Mind, Brain, and Behavior in order to encourage academics to contribute to public debate. Contributions are in Schacter (1997).

7 For example, remembering truly that I left my glasses somewhere last week may be sufficiently precise to be accurate if I am deciding whether to keep searching my office, but hopelessly vague if my objective is to actually recover them.

8 The symposium was 'Individual and Collective Memory: Conceptual Foundations,' May 12–14 2006, Washington University in St Louis. The remarks on accuracy are, respectively, by Dorthe Berntsen, Roddy Roediger, Larry Jacoby, and Michael Ross.

9 Lynch grants that truth is difficult to define partly because it is such a contested concept. However, he believes that we all share a fundamental understanding of it, and have since the time of Aristotle, as an interest in trying to make sure our representations of the world correspond to what the world is really like. Aristotle famously remarked that 'to say of that which is, that it is, and of that which is not, that it is not, is true' (quoted in Lynch, 2005: 11).

10 I should not be read as suggesting that we enlist different ideas of truth, for example forensic versus personal truth or historical versus narrative truth (Spence, 1984). Adverting to varieties of truth often sets up a situation in which so-called personal or narrative truth becomes, politically at least, the devalued side of a dichotomy – not really truth at all. See Loftus and Ketcham (1994) for this devaluing, and Waites (1997) for an articulation of concerns like mine. Lynch's account does not offer different kinds of truth, and asks us to take on the complex task of assessing the truth of different kinds of representations. I believe that this view puts complexity and responsibility in the right place.

11 I was particularly critical of the writings of Loftus (Loftus and Ketcham, 1994), Ofshe (Ofshe and Watters, 1994) in this regard, and some members of the False Memory Syndrome Foundation. I also raised concerns about the representation of women in Hacking's account (Hacking, 1995). Chapter 5, in particular, develops the argument that both historically, and at present, our theories of memory reflect our beliefs about the character of rememberers. I recognize that many people read these particular debates differently than I did. For a range of views, see note 1, above. My concern about respect is a general one that has application to a broad range of political contexts in which group vulnerability to harm is at issue.

12 I am grateful to the editors and to Jan Sutherland for many useful comments on earlier drafts of the chapter.

References

Bowman, C. G. and Mertz, E. (1996) 'A dangerous direction: legal intervention in sexual abuse survivor therapy', *Harvard Law Review* 109(3): 551–639.

Brown, D. P., Scheflin, A. W. and Corydon Hammond, D. (1998) *Memory, Trauma Treatment and the Law*. New York: W.W. Norton and Co.

Brownlie, E. B. (1999) 'Lies, secrets and silence: substantiated memories of child sexual abuse', in M. Rivera (ed.) *Fragment by Fragment: Feminist Perspectives on Memory and Child Sexual Abuse*. Charlottetown: PEI: gynergy books.

Busby, K. (1997) 'Discriminatory uses of personal records in sexual assault cases', *Canadian Journal of Women and the Law* 9:148–77.

Calhoun, C. (1995) 'Standing for something', *Journal of Philosophy* 92(5): 235–60.

Campbell, K. (2002) 'Legal memories: sexual assault, memory and international humanitarian law', *Signs: Journal of Women in Culture and Society* 28(1): 149–78.

Campbell, S. (2003) *Relational Remembering: Rethinking the Memory Wars*. Lanham, MD: Rowman and Littlefield.

Card, C. (1996) *The Unnatural Lottery: Character and Moral Luck*. Philadelphia: Temple University Press.

Donnelley, P. (1998) 'Scapegoating the Indian residential schools', *Western Report* 12(52): 6–11.

Engel, G. (1999) *Context is Everything. The Nature of Memory*. New York: W. H. Freeman.

Fivish, R. (1994) 'Constructing narrative, emotion and self in parent-child conversations about the past', in U. Neisser and R. Fivish (eds) *The Remembering Self: Construction and Accuracy in Self-Narrative*. Cambridge: Cambridge University Press.

Flanagan, O. (1996) *Self-expressions*. Oxford: Oxford University Press.

Fricker, M. (2006) 'Powerlessness and social interpretation', *Episteme. Journal of Social Epistemology* 3(1–2): 96–108.

Haaken, J. (1998) *Pillar of Salt: Gender, Memory, and the Perils of Looking Back*. Piscataway, NJ: Rutgers University Press.

Haaken, J. (1999) 'Heretical texts: *The Courage to Heal* and the Incest Survivor Movement', in S. Lamb (ed.) *New Versions of Victims: Feminists Struggle with the Concept*. New York: New York University Press.

Hacking, I. (1995) *Rewriting the Soul: Multiple Personality and the Sciences of Memory*. Princeton: Princeton University Press.

Halbwachs, M. (1992/1925) *On Collective Memory*. Louis Coser, trans. Chicago: University of Chicago Press.

Hoerl, C. and McCormack, T. (2005) 'Joint reminiscing as joint attention to the past', in N. Eilan, C. Hoerl, T. McCormack and J Roessler (eds) *Joint Attention, Communication, and Other Minds*. Oxford: Oxford University Press.

Individual and Collective Memory: Conceptual Foundations. http://artsci.wustl.edu/%7Epboyer/MemoryWorkshop/Statements.html (accessed 24 June 2007).

Locke, J. (1961/1706) *An Essay Concerning Human Understanding* (abridged). Selected and edited by John W. Yolton. London: Dent (Everyman's Library).

Loftus, E. and Ketcham, K. (1994) *The Myth of Repressed Memory: False Memories and Allegations of Sexual Abuse*. New York: St Martin's Press.

Lynch, M. (2005) *True to Life: Why Truth Matters*. Cambridge, MA: MIT Press.

Middleton, D. and Brown, S. D. (2005) *The Social Psychology of Experience: Studies in Remembering and Forgetting*. London: Sage Publications.

Middleton, D. and Edwards, D. (1990) 'Conversational remembering: a social psychological approach', in D. Middleton and D. Edwards (eds) *Collective Remembering*. London: Sage Publications.

Mitzal, B. A. (2003) *Theories of Social Remembering*. Philadelphia: Open University Press.

Morton, A. (2002) 'Emotional truth: emotional accuracy', *Supplement to Proceedings of the Aristotelian Society* 76(1): 265–75.

Neisser, U. (1981) 'John Dean's memory: a case study', *Cognition* 9: 1–22.

Ofshe, R. and Watters, E. (1994) *Making Monsters: False Memories, Psychotherapy, and Sexual Hysteria*. New York: Charles Scribner's Sons.

Pope, K. S. (1996) 'Memory, abuse, and science: questioning claims about the false memory syndrome epidemic', *American Psychologist* 51(9): 957–74.

Prager, J. (1998) *Presenting the Past: Psychoanalysis and the Sociology of Misremembering*. Cambridge, MA: Harvard University Press.

Radstone, S. (2008) 'Memory studies: for and against', *Memory Studies* 1(1): 31–40.

Reavey, P. and Brown, S. D. (2006) 'Transforming past action and agency in the present: time, social remembering, and child sexual abuse', *Theory and Psychology* 16(2): 179–202.

Reavey, P. and Brown, S. D. (2007) 'The embodiment and spaces of memory: child sexual abuse and the construction of agency', *Journal of Social Work Practice* 21(4): 5–21.

Sarat, A. (2003) 'When memory speaks: remembrance and revenge in *Unforgiven*', in M. Minow and N. Rosenblum (eds) *Breaking the Cycles of Hatred: Memory, Law and Repair*. Princeton: Princeton University Press.

Schacter, D. L. (1996) *Searching for Memory: The Brain, the Mind, and the Past*. New York: Harper Collins.

Schacter, D. L. (ed.) (1997) *Memory Distortion: How Minds, Brains, and Societies Reconstruct the Past*. Cambridge, MA: Harvard University Press.

Schechtman, M. (1994) 'The truth about memory', *Philosophical Psychology* 7: 3–18.

Spence, D. (1984) *Narrative Truth and Historical Truth: Meaning and Interpretation in Psychoanalysis*. New York: W.W. Norton.

Sutton, J. (2002) 'Representation, reduction and interdisciplinarity in the sciences of memory', in H. Clapin, P. Staines, and P. Slezak (eds) *Representation in Mind: New Approaches to Mental Representation*. Boston: Elsevier.

Sutton, J. (2008) 'Remembering', in P. Robbins and M. Aydede (eds) *Cambridge Handbook of Situated Cognition*. Cambridge: Cambridge University Press.

Waites, E. A. (1997) *Memory Quest: Trauma and the Search for a Personal History*. New York: W.W. Norton
Walker, M. (1998) *Moral Understandings: A Feminist Study in Ethics*. New York: Routledge.
Warnock, M. (1987) *Memory*. London: Faber and Faber.
Wertsch, J. (2002) *Voices of Collective Remembering*. Cambridge: Cambridge University Press.
Williams, B. (2002) *Truth and Truthfulness: An Essay in Genealogy*. Princeton: Princeton University Press.
Williamson, J. (1998). *Crybaby!* Edmonton, AB: NeWest Press.

11 Therapy as memory-work
Dilemmas of discovery, recovery and construction

Erica Burman

> The analyst . . . has to enable the patient to know what he already knows – to refind a talent as it were. After all, the patient has only forgotten himself. And the analyst is an expert in the forms of ignorance – in the forms ignorance can take in the service of self-protection.
>
> (Phillips, 1995: 5)

The initial furore over the 'false memory' debates has subsided, although the consequences reverberate on (Frankland and Cohen, 1999). In this chapter I go beyond the polarisations of truth and falsehood that continue – of legal versus psychotherapeutic truth, and professional competencies versus disciplinary procedures[1] – to discuss a set of dilemmas that remain concerning clinical practice. In this chapter, I draw upon my positions as an academic developmental psychologist and a psychotherapist to comment on these dilemmas and the particular configuration of their relations within current socio-political contexts. First, I consider some key political features the crisis threatens to obscure, as well as the specific conditions that made such contests around memory so prominent. Second, I suggest how such analyses may function in useful ways, not only to tighten up and strengthen therapeutic practices, but to promote reflection upon the place and space of therapy in memory-making – including (crucially) therapists' own memorial practices. Third, I suggest that these reflective approaches intimate connections with other more explicitly political projects of recalling and transforming histories. Fourth, I draw out connections between psychotherapy training and the institutional dynamics around scientific 'evidence' and accountability that these debates set in motion. And finally, I attempt to reconfigure the current preoccupation with putting psychotherapy and psychoanalysis in the courtroom to broader social contexts concerning memorial practices and the culturally repressed histories of women, in particular of violence against refugee and minoritised women.

High anxiety

The immediate issues that generated scrutiny of therapeutic technique concerning retrieval of childhood memories of sexual abuse are well-known. These include accusations that therapists were imposing or implanting memories rather than facilitating the client's own memorial account. The debates extended to a questioning of the entire project of psychotherapy, with one side of the debate charging that therapists create fictions out of people's lives in the process of exploring previously forgotten or dismissed material. The notion of unconscious processes, central to any variety of psychoanalytic thinking, was a key site of this controversy.

These are serious questions of model and technique, the gravity of which was deepened by the seriousness of the issue around which general questions about therapeutic practice arose – namely recovery in therapy by adults (mainly women) of memories of sexual abuse in childhood. Whatever else may be justified about the extensive scrutiny to which psychotherapeutic practice was subjected, this scrutiny did seem to be a case of punishing the bearer of unpopular news. Many feminists charged that the debate involved a refusal to face up to that news. Indeed, the entire debate over credibility and suggestibility was transferred from supposedly vulnerable or manipulative women patients to their apparently equivalently gullible, or alternatively, incompetent or dogmatic, therapists. A further significant circumstance in which this debate arose centred on misconduct within therapy, as a specific arena of professional practice also affected by the cases of murderous or otherwise exploitative therapeutic and medical professionals. The public suspicion of professional accountability was perhaps exemplified for Britons (although the case was reported worldwide) by the case of Harold Shipman, the Manchester general medical practitioner who was found in 2003 to have murdered perhaps hundreds – the exact number is still undetermined – of his elderly female patients. But the crisis of confidence in therapeutic authority began earlier in the 1990s, with the false/recovered memory debates.

Many lay people, academics, therapists, practitioners, and professionals of all kinds (feminist and non-feminist), were very exercised by these discussions. Laura Brown – a feminist therapist based in the US – and I co-edited a Special Feature of the journal *Feminism and Psychology* that was published in 1997, presenting seven very different feminist responses to what we called 'the delayed memory debate' (precisely to illustrate the diversity of feminist positions that the debate incited). As our editorial introduction commented:

> So to the extent that FMS exposes issues of exploitation in therapy, including feminist therapy, and feminist (psychologists') collusion with the depoliticization of political problems in therapy, it may even be helpful. But to the extent that it invalidates and silences women, and bolsters a culture that chooses to ignore the violence and abuse perpetrated in 'happy families', it is clearly dangerous.
>
> (Brown and Burman, 1997: 11)

Therapists in general are concerned, perhaps over-anxiously so, with working appropriately with their clients and with challenges to their professional identities. The institutional response (of the United Kingdom Council of Psychotherapists, the Royal College of Psychiatrists and the British Psychological Society, for example) was to develop guidelines and codes of practice, in an attempt to specify standards concerning therapeutic probing of memory. It is perhaps significant that no such guidelines existed previously. Such documents on professional norms and standards can be helpful in that they indicate what other professionals and clients should be able to expect of psychologists and psychotherapists (and other health professionals). However, they also function to differentiate between and demarcate different professional groups, as in the different positions adopted by psychiatrists and psychologists for example (British Psychological Society, 1995; Brandon et al., 1998), suggestive of additional professional boundary-setting interests.

Yet these same guidelines acknowledge the limits of codes of conduct and offer caveats. The UKCP document 'Notes for Practitioners: On Legal Issues Connected to the Practice of Psychotherapy' developed in the late 1990s acknowledges (in point 6) that 'leading questions' are unavoidable in therapy. This arises because 'many empathic responses can be regarded as leading questions if they put some thought of the therapist into the client's mind'. But they also point out that 'any link between the past and the present, or any comment that goes beyond what the client has said is a form of suggestion'. The Notes continue: 'Clearly without it [suggestion] there would be very few forms of therapy that could survive, but therapists need to be aware of what we are doing' (1996: 2).

Negotiating the boundary between reflection and suggestion, that is, interpreting what lies behind or beyond the client's words, is not only at the centre of therapeutic exploration but also requires attentiveness to power relations between the conversational partners in therapy. In therapeutic work with vulnerable individuals, it is undoubtedly possible – inadvertently as well as wilfully – to offer comments which introduce new material in often startling ways. Such interventions serve as powerful reminders of how contingent and arbitrary that distinction between reflection and construction can be.

Rather than breathing a sigh of relief at warding off the legal threat to clinical practice (expressed through diligent subscription to these guidelines), thus protecting the sanctity of the consultation room, many psychotherapists responded with increased anxiety. It is worth recalling, however, that recourse to litigation has always been central to the whole process of societal recognition of individual trauma. This was especially evident in the area of psychiatric diagnosis. Indeed the emergence of the category of post-traumatic stress disorder was directly related to the compensation claims of Holocaust survivors and Vietnam war veterans seeking 'reparation' for their physical and psychic injuries (Antze and Lambek, 1996). Hence the prototypical US TV drama of the courtroom scene has long figured within the imaginary (and practice) of therapeutic work, from the early Hitchcock films that popularised psychoanalysis to *The Sopranos*, as indeed have notions of resisting oppression and injustice via legal challenge, and rightfully so.

So notwithstanding the distinctions made between psychotherapeutic and legal means of accessing memory, or historical and narrative versions of truth (cf. Spence, 1982), it is worth bearing in mind that the two conceptions of truth have been mutually involved in the very elaboration of such distinctions. Yet just as professional guidelines may generate excessive therapeutic anxiety concerning litigation, they also may inhibit therapeutic training. However helpful codes of conduct may be in containing institutional and personal anxieties, they are not nearly as easily interpreted or applied as they might seem. Perhaps this is obvious, yet it remains worth saying, given that ethical codes can become terrorising for trainee psychotherapists and psychologists who are trying to learn the trade and get it right. It is all too easy to 'forget' just how complex and difficult adhering to such guidelines can be.

Take, for example, the requirement specified in the section on 'Ethical Issues' within the UKCP guidelines on recovered memories to 'be aware of research and knowledge in relevant areas such as memory and repression', or that psychotherapists have a 'duty to inform themselves of current theory and knowledge' (UKCP, 1997). These requirements have been taken forward in Continuing Professional Development agendas, yet are quite difficult to implement or assess in practice.

As Phillips notes, 'Belief, as Freud shows, domesticates desire. Experts keep us on their best behaviour' (1995: 15). What he is drawing attention to is how the 'desire' to be ethical comes to be limited to (or domesticated by) technocratic 'expert' criteria. In thinking about ethical desire and expertise, we may ask: what knowledge, and which experts? Who owns the expertise, and by whose authority? Such questions take on acute relevance in relation to memorial processes.

Contexts and contests for memory

> Acts of remembering often take on performative meaning within a charged field of contested moral and political claims. They do so, moreover, in ways that reflect specific beliefs about the nature of memory and its relationship to identity.
>
> (Antze and Lambek, 1996: vii–viii)

We cannot adequately engage the complexities of the memory debates without asking what is at stake. Alongside therapeutic models and techniques in working with accounts of abuse, there are important cultural-political questions over how the debates arose in the first place. Antze and Lambek open their important collection, *Tense Past*, with the comment: 'memories are never simply records of the past but are interpretive reconstructions that bear the imprint of local narrative conventions, cultural assumptions, discursive formations and practices and social contexts of recall and commemoration' (1996: vii). Just as in psychotherapy, we must ask: why this, and why at this specific historical moment? Clearly the abuse of children, including sexual abuse, is a longstanding problem in all societies. So it is relevant to consider why the issue (belatedly) generated so much public attention at a particular moment in the late twentieth century. Moreover, why did the focus lie on women's previously forgotten accounts of abuse in childhood, often emerging in therapy? At the same time, it is important to remember that these recovered memories of childhood sexual abuse account for only a small fraction of work around abuse in therapy, since most women retain some memory of their abuse (see Contratto and Gutfreund, 1996).

First, we need to situate the debate in the broad crisis in gender relations in contemporary industrialised societies in the second half of the twentieth century, coalescing around the changing position of women, and the challenge to normative family arrangements. Alongside these shifts in the position of women, there was the emergence of a general climate of disaffection and alienation. Broader societal and economic transformations in the late twentieth century generated desires for certainty and nostalgia for securely fixed images of past traditions. The search for an identity rooted firmly in the past extended to inventing heritages that never existed, for example in the marketing of Scottish tartans as emblems of 'authentic' lineage (Hobsbawm and Ranger, 1978).

In a sense we could see the rise of 'false memory' implantation claims as a measure of the impact of, as well as the significant backlash to, feminism in general, including a backlash to the success of women within the psychotherapy professions. Janice Haaken (1998) concludes her landmark analysis of gender, therapy and memory by commenting on the social symbolic loadings of the current debate:

> The incest survivor is Every Woman in that her sexual awakening confronts the prior presence of patriarchal authority and her story chronicles an emerging awareness that the Law of the Father circumscribes female desire. The traditional fate of female development has involved the transfer of feminine attractions from one father figure to another. Feminism has intervened in this ancient, cultural transfer, refusing both literal and symbolic father their traditional right to sexually control daughters.
>
> (Ibid.: 273)

Another modern romantic myth that was at the centre of the crisis, in addition to that of the idyllic nuclear family, concerned the innocence of children. Indeed the very distinction between child and adult was elaborated alongside the separation within modernity between public and private, and between work and play. These spaces and statuses are, by definition, covertly culturally gender-coded and age-related. The great paternalistic gesture of 'women and children first' speaks to a general cultural and legal infantilisation of women, and a corresponding feminisation of childhood (Burman, 2008).

But children, including girl children, work, are sexually active, and are on the streets – that is, engaged in activities outside normative understandings of what children (should) do. Indeed, key cases of children murdering, abusing and bullying other children in the 1990s severely challenged Western cultural assumptions about the innocence of children. Such cases can be reconciled with dominant norms of childhood only by either lamenting the childhood 'lost' or 'stolen' from them (as in the 2004 children's charity Barnardo's campaign against child prostitution) or by expelling the child perpetrators from the category of childhood – or indeed even humanity – as in the attributions of monstrosity accorded the two (significantly working class, Liverpudlian) British boy murderers of two-year-old Jamie Bulger in 1993 which so gripped the world stage.

Nevertheless, approaches to childhood – at least in the UK – do appear to be shifting in response to broader societal changes. Indeed Franklin (2002) charts the course of the second half of the twentieth century as one of increasingly punitive approaches to youth distress and disorder, particularly in Britain, while late 2006 Britain was preoccupied with debates about 'toxic childhood' – with the 'toxicity' shifting from the conditions for childhood to the children themselves. Such punitive responses to juveniles can perhaps be seen as registering some effort to contain social anxieties concerning children's status following international and national legislation confirming children's rights.

It was in the context of shifting roles and positions for both women and children that current debates over the recovery of women's memories of childhood abuse in therapy arose. Moreover, amid such flux and challenge there were further overdetermining cultural factors centred on the slippage between the categories 'child' and 'woman'. For within the Western cultural imaginary, the child came to signify the self, the innermost, precious core of subjectivity, within us all. Carolyn Steedman's (1995) historical analysis traces the emergence of the child as quintessential modern Western subject:

> The idea of the child was the figure that provided the largest number of people living in the recent past of Western societies with the means for thinking about and creating a self: something grasped and understood: a shape, moving in the body . . . something inside: an interiority.
>
> (Ibid.: 20)

From Goethe onward, across Europe there was a longstanding cultural preoccupation with the motif of the enigmatic and suffering female child, named Mignonne in the original folktale. Her sexuality and knowledge, as well as her uncertain origins, were a source of fascination for Victorian audiences. Hence the child came to represent the model of authentic selfhood that formed the focus of psychotherapeutic intervention, a model that shows no sign of abating. Indeed if anything the discourse of inner childhood has proliferated since the 1990s and gained a wider circulation outside 'new age' contexts.

External evidence

As the metaphorical trope of the child becomes further embedded in the Western cultural imaginary, and as the conditions of children's lives depart ever further from it, the demands to prove the efficacy of therapy have become ever more tied to the scientistic 'evidence-based practice' agenda (see Freshwater and Rolfe, 2004; Lambert, 2006). The crisis in psychoanalysis and associated psychotherapeutic legitimacy is driven by state funding priorities that in turn reflect a renewed faith in science – especially neuroscience – in the era of the mapping of the human genome. The false/recovered memory debates broke at the moment when a new anxiety arose over the credibility of psychoanalysis and therapy, linked to notions of scientific evidence. There is a cultural-historical dimension to the resources we might draw upon in discussions of scientific evidence Ian Hacking (1996) has argued that current knowledge about memory arose as 'surrogate sciences of the soul', that is, as modern successors to much older European ideas about self-knowledge that link notions of self-enlightenment to moral philosophy. He opens his historical analysis with the comment that 'If we address only the surface facts about memory, the politicisation of memory will seem only a curious accident. But if we think of how the very idea of such facts came into being, the battles may seem inevitable' (1996: 70). He depicts this 'memoro-politics' as a power struggle around the status of a psychodynamic 'depth knowledge' claiming to offer underlying truths about memory. Yet the 'surface knowledge' was provided by several other memory sciences that emerged at the same time. These began with neurological studies which locate different types of memory, begun by Broca in the 1860s; and, secondly, with experimental studies of recall, conducted by Ebbinghaus from 1885 as the forerunner of modern experimental psychology.

Hacking draws attention to two key points. First, he identifies the paradox that despite our deep societal commitment to the unity of science, these different disciplinary sciences of memory have little in common. Second, although it is the neurological (rather than the psychological) research that has significantly advanced with the development of new technologies, nevertheless the psychodynamics of memory has had the most profound impact on Western culture. Arguably, at least until the late twentieth century, models of subjectivity were so suffused with psychoanalytic notions that we have become unable to think about ourselves without them (Parker, 1997), and these include psychoanalytic notions of remembering and forgetting.

A longstanding battle has been raging, therefore, between empirical and interpretive sciences of memory. Some psychiatrists, psychologists and psychotherapists have argued that we cannot know from inside therapy – through therapeutic practices and procedures – whether a reported memory of abuse is 'true', and that 'external evidence' is needed (Brandon *et al.*, 1998). Yet empirical work from neurology and psychology is enlisted as privileged or primary 'evidence' in addressing psychotherapeutic issues of memory. For example, the recent rapprochement between psychoanalysis and neurophysiology draws heavily on the technology of functional magnetic resonance imaging and other technologies (which are nevertheless still interpretive, Rutter, 2002). Peter Fonagy and his associates have been leading the way in attempts to reconcile psychoanalysis and the neurosciences, and rescuing psychoanalysis from its crisis of scientific credibility in the era of evidence-based practice (see especially Fonagy, 2004; but also Fonagy and Target, 2004; Fonagy *et al.*, 2004). Yet this form of reliability requires triangulation across radically different paradigms and knowledge bases. Notwithstanding the recent convergence between experimental cognitive psychology and psychotherapeutic analysis of unconscious processes, this triangulation runs the risk of misconstruing key concepts in each of the paradigms (Burman, 1998).

There has been a century of contest between psychoanalysis and psychology over methodological and theoretical commitments. But this long-standing contest is being suppressed through an alliance forged between professionals claiming to protect the public from, and so exclude, designated mal-practitioners. Indeed, moves toward state regulation have largely been prompted by these protectionist concerns, although officially presented as a response to both the 'false memory' controversy and the lofty aim of international harmonisation or standardisation of psychotherapy qualifications. Not only does it appear that such rumours (of harmonisation of legislation) were groundless, in the sense that international regulation was not initially on the EU agenda, but moreover it seems that this concern was retroactively constitutive, in calling into being the central regulatory bodies in the process. Far from protecting the public from abusive practice, the new movements to regulate psychotherapy appear to be dominated by concern to protect the status and legitimacy of the profession. It also appears that the discipline of psychology is set to assume a privileged position within newly emerging 'health professions' regulating bodies, as the most 'scientific' of the 'psy' disciplines (Parker and Revelli, 2008).

However we might weigh tactical alliances among professionals, we need to think about collective defensive processes that have been instituted. In the context of sexual abuse investigations, we know that 'evidence' is subject to many constraints on its articulation, outside, as well as inside, the consulting room. There are widely documented contextual limits on the production of such 'evidence', including (1) the underreporting of sexual assaults, (2) the pressures of cross-examination in the courtroom, (3) the disclosures of adult women's sexual histories in court and their impact on jury evaluations (see e.g. Hanmer and Itzin, 2000), and (4) the ethical difficulties around the interrogation of children and the possibilities of reproducing aspects of their abuse – either in their being forced to tell, or to keep, secrets in that process (Burman, 1997).

As someone with an academic background in developmental psychology, as well as being a qualified psychotherapist, I have been particularly struck by the recourse to empirical developmental research in debates about both the psychology of memory and psychotherapy. Although many look to the field of academic psychology, and developmental psychology in particular, to settle disputes over evidence (for key studies that are cited see Ceci and Bruck, 1993; Lindsay and Read, 1994; Poole and White, 1993; Saywitz *et al.*, 1991), evidence in the research field of psychology is no less subject to the effects of construction than in psychotherapy.

The role of cultural dynamics in blurring boundaries between the categories of woman and child also is important to remember. For it is this blurring that affords the elision in discussions of therapy between the child the woman was – or, rather, narrates about – and actual, real children's memory reports and their susceptibility to influence (Burman, 1996/7). Accounts of childhood spoken about in therapy are clearly not the same as current, chronological children's reports of their memories for recent events. While such blurring in the developmental psychology literature between woman and child is bolstered by popular notions of regression and discourses of 'the child within'/'inner child', and between real children and idealised/sentimentalised (and therefore fictional) cultural models of childhood, it is the empirical psychological research that is called upon as evidence in the psychotherapy literature. Indeed even this empirical research is far less 'reliable' in practice than it often appears. Motzkau (2006; in press a, b) has traced the circularity of reasoning between commonsense/naturalised and 'technical' renderings of scientific/psychological research on children and memorial accounting processes, which leads judges and other legal experts to a position where they can only acknowledge, at the end of the process of reasoning, the limits of what they know about children.

Historical versus narrative truth

Just as past debates are being recreated anew within developmental psychology, or reorganised according to current concerns, so, too, discussions of construction of memory have a long history within psychoanalysis. While Freud subscribed to archaeological metaphors in describing the uncovering of the past, and in his earlier work pursued this in a very literal way, his later reflections on analytic process go to some lengths to acknowledge what we would now call the intersubjective and interactive character of memorial accounts produced in psychotherapy. Indeed archaeology is as much a process of inferred and creative construction as careful uncovering and analysis of scant remains. In his 1937 paper 'Constructions in Analysis' Freud uses the terms reconstruction and construction synonymously: 'His [the analyst's] task is to make out what has been forgotten from the traces it has left behind or more properly to construct it' (Freud, 1937: 259). Hence the analyst's process of construction is an ongoing and necessary part of the thinking process, only some of which might be communicated to the patient as interpretation. Freud thus acknowledged the interplay between transference and suggestion, regarding the general process of interpretation as more properly termed construction.

Within contemporary psychoanalysis the notion of reconstruction is regarded as a major and inevitable aspect of interpretation within the analytic process, one that intersects with and potentiates transference. The process of building a picture of a patient's early life history is a key part of the therapeutic process, even if that picture is constantly undergoing revision. The US psychoanalyst Harold Blum (1994) describes it well:

> The reconstructed past as obtained in analysis has been retrieved, recreated, and created ... The analytically determined past is history evolving, co-determined by fantasy and reality. It is a past of multiple perspectives and many dimensions, brought into a cohesive and coherent fit that offers the most meaning and comprehensive integration ... This construction of the past, whether of childhood seduction, illness, loss or special identification, is more like a developing, ever more detailed and documented life study than a palpable, static archaeological relic.
>
> (Ibid.: 36)

Thus a psychoanalytic approach recognises that the analysand perceives the past differently at different times – both within the course of an analysis and within one's lifecourse more generally. Hence '[r]econstruction gains in clarity and objectivity as the analytic process proceeds but is never "what really happened" as might be proposed by external observers or historians' (ibid.: p. 37). Similarly the British psychoanalyst Christopher Bollas considers the past that is constructed in psychotherapy one that undergoes continuous transformation. The past moves 'from debris into meaningful presence' (Bollas, 1995: 114). Bollas draws attention not only to the transience and flexibility of memory-making, but also to its self-confirming character. He explains how memorial accounts oscillate between being generated and dismantled, whereby 'historical texts of reconstruction give birth to other ideas and contrary reflective theories, which destroy the placid aim of creating commemorative plaques to one's new discoveries' (p. 145).

By contrast, key participants in the 'false memory' debate set up an opposition between believing the whole account offered by women and regarding it as a meaningless (according to Brandon *et al.*, 1998), or, alternatively, a metaphorically meaningful, potential fabrication (UKCP, BPS). One of the ways psychotherapists attempted to protect their knowledge claims was to distinguish between historical truth and narrative truth. That is, they claimed that therapists work with the meanings conveyed by what is being said rather than with verification of facts. This distinction between narrative and historical truth emerged as the key struggle in arguing for the different status of accounts within legal and therapeutic arenas.

Holding too tightly to this distinction may underestimate, however, the extent to which historical accounts are far from literal representations of past events, As Harold Blum argues: 'the narrative aspect of psychoanalysis is not a substitute for historical truth, but is presumed to be the form in which history exists' (Blum, 1994: 140). Moreover therapy deals with recollections of the past which analysands have played a part in producing; they are actors as well as self-observers and accounters: 'Reconstruction is not concerned with simple historical or factual events of the past but rather with the inner meaning and consequences of that past as it was also shaped by the patient' (Blum, 1994: 32). We must, as Gardner (1996) put it, be 'open to all possibilities'.

Transformative remembering and clinical training

Far from being undermined in acknowledging the mobile and provisional character of the therapeutically constructed accounts of the past, psychoanalytic therapies are strengthened by them. Psychoanalytic therapies focus on the interpersonal processes through which the past is produced, and stress power dynamics associated with representing the past. In particular, psychoanalytic methods for attending to the construction of memory bring into focus precisely those issues of power and authority that memorial records all too often obscure. Moreover, such methods extend to the construction of the very material available for thinking about therapeutic work.

Once again, this understanding of therapeutic processes links with the memory debates. For public concern over 'false/recovered memories' also reflects wider dangers of 'false memories' in everyday life and the 'self-protections' that arise on all sides of this debate (see Phillips, 1995: 5). To take a specific example, I have been struck by how little discussion there is in the UK of forms of therapeutic records or personal process notes, except in terms of client and legal access prompted by legislation concerned with data protection and human rights (see Swartz, 2006; Burman, 2006). But if structures of thinking arise to deal with thoughts, rather than vice versa, as Bion (1967) suggests, the construction of therapists' own memorial accounts of work with clients may be subject to all kinds of selective remembering and forgetting, including what gets discussed in therapeutic supervision.

Part and parcel of the work of supervision as well as therapy is something akin to the process of transformative remembering, a notion Haaken (1998) introduced to describe the active and instigated character of remembering, spanning a continuum from continuous to discontinuous representations of the past. She proposed that '[n]ew understanding is attached to a previously remembered experience in such a way that it may feel like a new memory' (p. 18), while other memories 'take on the character of a conversion experience, with the subjective sense of a radical disjuncture between prior and present knowledge of one's personal history' (p. 18). The process of training as a psychotherapist seems to rely on just such dynamic continua. Supervision plays a key role as a site of elaboration for interpersonal structures fostering the toleration of, and thereby access to, thoughts that were previously unavailable (Sharpe, 1995; Moro, 2007).

Memory-work

Once we admit the work of remembering as a socially mediated activity (Middleton and Edwards, 1990; Middleton and Brown, 2005), as a storytelling relationship with (imagined or real) others, additional political possibilities arise. Frigga Haug's feminist 'memory-work' began as a writing collective in Berlin in the 1960s. In this project, a group of women worked on writing stories of their everyday lives for a two-year period (Haug *et al.*, 1987). As feminists, they shared the aim of analysing the ways political structures entered into the fine grain of their subjectivities via the sexualisation of their bodies.

The method involves generating written accounts, often of childhood experiences, with a focus on everyday detail and small things – avoiding soliciting the 'well-worked up memories' that readily spring to mind and are already the product of much analysis. Instead, they wanted to explore women's own participation within oppressive social and psychological structures (see also Haug, 1998). This concentration on the specific helped free them from the determining narrative of autobiographical histories, which unifies subjects, obscures ruptures, and subordinates the past to a passive position as mere cause or condition of the present. As she describes the process,

> We considered it important to uncover points of disjuncture between our stories of childhood and the way of life we mark out for ourselves today. Our inhibitions about active intervention, fear of conflict, cowardice, evasiveness, debilitating melancholy; all of these may be connected with breaks in our biographies that we continue to live unconsciously. If we allow ourselves to subject our past to dispassionate scrutiny, we may perhaps be able to effect some change in the present.
> (Haug *et al.*, 1987: 51)

The aim was not simply to provoke empathy between women, which they regarded as often oriented toward sustaining each other in exploitative relationships. Instead their project was centred on equipping each other to reflect on their shared biographies and to challenge one another, so as to provoke new vantage points on the past. They sought to generate analyses of how they could have responded differently, including assuming positions of political resistance. Haug outlines theses aims:

> Our initial aim was to use collective discussions to make it possible to uncover new relations and important traces of evidence within the chosen field of study ... Once we began to note down exactly even the most inconsequential detail, we came to recognise the enormous

constraints hitherto placed on us by the use of criteria of 'relevance', censoring and restricting our imagination and our memory. In subjecting this and other criteria to newly-conscious scrutiny we began to see how we could criticize dominant orthodoxies on socialization processes, mother-child relations and so on.

(Ibid.: 49)

From these written accounts, new ways of understanding and of theorising each woman's socialisation process were elaborated. Indeed it is this focus on theorisation that made the project very different from many women's self-help groups, for at issue was not the expression or validation of 'experience', but rather an interrogation of the dominant narratives that structure how women construct their gendered subjectivities and identities. For example, the accounts women generated concerned the construction of women's bodies as *fetishised commodities* for display and service, including stories of wearing ankle socks or wanting a middle parting in one's hair, extending to investigating broader social structural analyses of the role of the church and state in the regulation of power and in the construction of their sexualities.

Memory-work generated many possibilities as both an educational method and a therapeutic approach that takes the political construction of the individual and their gendered identities as its topic (see e.g. Stephenson and Kippax, 1999). Indeed Haug (2000) relates this approach specifically to problematise the condition of anxiety that surrounds women's relationship with bodily movement in public spaces, specifically through a sensibility of vulnerability engendered by prevailing discourses of femininity.

As a form of group-work, this method bears resemblance to group analysis (Foulkes, 1986; Burman, 2002) and is clearly informed by psychoanalytic ideas (Haug, 1992). But part of what is interesting and challenging about the method, particularly for therapists, is that the accounts are written in the third person. This third person narrative is explicitly advocated both to ward off conventional moral judgement and to initiate a process of looking anew at oneself as another; that is, as another tactic of estrangement distancing the narrator from the narrative resolutions of the autobiographical genre. Insofar as the autobiographical frame is always vulnerable to the compulsion to repeat (to re-member oneself as one is), memory-work explicitly attempts to disrupt this self-confirmatory process. In this sense the psychoanalytic move of interrogating one's own meaning-making from the position of not-knowing, of the opacity (rather than the transparency) of the speaking subject to itself, is linked to a project of empowerment.

However important it may be for women to speak and write of themselves as 'I' and thereby to register a protest against the pressures on them to leave their own selves out of account – to attempt, that is, to find a place for themselves within the categories of abstract and impersonal thinking – we believe that it is nonetheless essential to use the third person in memory-work. Writing about past events is almost impossible, unless we have some way of distancing ourselves. . . . By translating our own experiences into the third person, we were enabled to be more attentive to our selves. Thus the gaze we cast today on our selves of yesterday becomes the gaze cast by one stranger on another.

(Haug *et al.*, 1987: 45–6)

A further (and perhaps more controversial) feature of the method, taken up by other practitioners of memory-work (Crawford *et al.*, 1992), centres on the rewriting of memories. For once the stories were written and presented to the group, the group discussed them and on that basis, each woman rewrote her story. The social process of analysis and reconstruction also was used as an explicit tool to generate possibilities for political transformation – for imagining alternative realities. In this form of memory-work, the political project of emancipation and the therapeutic project of self-exploration converge in attending to the textual generation of memorial accounts (see also Haug, 1998).

Forgotten histories and some lessons

The 'memory wars' of the late 1990s suggest a broader public desire in patriarchal societies to forget the extent of child sexual abuse and domestic violence as social problems. But as uncertainties over how to fortify the boundary between true and false recollections linger on, the memory wars also register anxieties over the crisis of national memory and the 'war against terror' of the late twentieth and early twenty-first centuries (Thobani, 2007). In the twenty-first century, post-colonial liberation movements have been undermined, and neo-colonialism has taken the form of relentless economic globalisation. Political destabilisation and corresponding massive dislocation and migration of peoples across and between nation states enters popular media and national awareness through obsessive and conservative discourses on immigration quotas and asylum statistics.

It seems that legal and psychological discourses of memory continue to converge, although the targets (and casualties/beneficiaries) of such convergences are no longer the privileged middle class women recovering memories of abuse in privately paid for therapies; nor even the male survivors of institutional church care, whose court cases for child abuse are now bankrupting the Catholic church in the US, UK, Italy and Ireland (to name just a few countries) as well as inspiring dedicated therapeutic services to cater for them. What are the lessons, apart from the 'empire strikes back' argument of the return of the repressed (of colonialism and patriarchy)?

There are immense pressures to hide these current as well as historical abuses so that they are not admitted to public consciousness. Feminist theory and practice engaged early on with the debates surrounding questions of credibility, suggestibility and evidence to generate more rigorous empirical, therapeutic and pedagogical practices. At the level of research, this work has intersected with the discursive turn which has shifted the focus from author to text, and from discourses of authenticity, 'voice' and empowerment to positioning, situated provisionality and claims-making (see e.g. Burman *et al.*, 1996; Burman, 2001; Bondi *et al.*, 2002). Beyond this, it is worth making another connection that concerns the cultural and legal framing of the admission of memory. As Ahmed's (2004) analysis of the *Cultural Politics of Emotion* highlights, in the first decade of the twenty-first century, the candidates for the status of abjection (or most derided and disowned subject positions, who fail to inspire identification) are immigrant men and women whose presence arises from forgotten historical connections (of trade and culture, Gilroy, 1995) as well as past and current traumatic appropriation and exploitation (including slavery).

Significantly, in these contexts therapeutic and other support services are not deemed relevant – since women (or men) whose immigration status defines them as having 'no recourse to public funds' are disallowed access to such services. Their insecure immigration status means they have no entitlement to access such services (that would be accorded those with residency or citizenship status), so that the services can recover no state funds for tending to them and so cannot afford to provide. Hence uncertainties over memorial accountability become coalesced into a legal judgment that either accords 'leave to stay' or calls for compulsory deportation (Chantler, 2006). This arena reveals significant state imperatives at stake in the evaluation of specific memorial accounts.

'Psychological mindedness' and amenability to therapeutic intervention are thus overdetermined by structures of racialisation as well as class and gender (Burman *et al.*, 2004; Tuckwell, 2006; Isaac, 2006). For while under neoliberalism some women have shifted position from 'victim' to 'beneficiary' (in the sense of being economically empowered or gaining access to some features of power and privilege hitherto reserved for men) (Burman, 2004), other less privileged women are effectively denied therapeutic support that would render their memories more intelligible, and their distress amenable to treatment. In research exploring approaches to the legal and other support services for Pakistani women asylum seekers, for example, whose asylum claims arose from domestic violence, advocacy workers reported that judges dismissed some women's accounts of longstanding captivity, torture and abuse at the hands of their husbands and families, because they could not believe a woman could survive such experiences (Siddiqui *et al.*, 2008). This wider context informs debates about credibility and memorial accountability. For in its broadest sense, memory-work (inside and outside therapeutic contexts) is thus both cultural and individual; its conditions of possibility are historically shaped, but its practices very much oriented to contemporary agendas (see also Clare, 2006).

Two kinds of detective

I want to conclude by drawing together the themes of memory, (auto)-biography, textuality (or attention to narrative form) and legislation around some commonalities elaborated within the structure of psychotherapy training. In *Looking Awry*, Žižek (1991) takes up the longstanding preoccupation within psychoanalytic commentaries between the work of the detective and the analyst. Both face the same formal problem of 'the impossibility of telling a story in a linear, consistent way', i.e. of rendering the 'realistic' continuity of events (p. 49). It is well-known that Freud considered such parallels, reading Sherlock Holmes stories and so on, and that Lacan's *Écrits* begins with a detailed (and celebrated) analysis of Edgar Allen Poe's story of 'The Purloined Letter'.

The analyst, like the detective, has to uncover the clue or key element that speaks to the latent meaning of the dream/crime scene. This clue, or disruption within the manifest content, betrays traces of what has been disguised. Thus the detective, like the analyst, occupies the position of the subject who is supposed to know (*le sujet supposé savoir*). His or her role is 'to catch the murderer in his deception ... [so that] The very deceit the murderer invests to save him is the cause of his downfall' (Žižek, 1991: 57). (Psychoanalysis, also, is concerned with exposing the unconscious crime!)

In the classical detective novel of Conan Doyle or Agatha Christie the detective retains a dispassionate distance, and his thoughts (and typically it is a 'he') remain obscure until the end of the novel when he tells some admiring minion (like Watson) how he arrived at his conclusions. This inscrutability is both a condition and effect of transference (in the deference and attraction to the power of the analyst, as the repetition of past dynamics of authority), with the reasoning concealed until the final denouement (like the mutative, transformative, interpretation). By contrast, Žižek points out how the contemporary genre of 'hard-boiled' detective novels is narrated in the first person, elaborating an entirely different set of relationships between the dialectic of truth and deception than those described earlier in Haug's memory-work.

> By means of his initial decision to accept a case, the hard-boiled detective gets mixed up in a course of events that he is unable to dominate; all of a sudden it becomes evident that he has been 'played for a sucker' ... The 'truth' at which he attempts to arrive at is not just a challenge to his reason but concerns him ethically and often painfully ... In short, the dialectic of deception in the hard-boiled novel is the dialectic of an active hero caught in a nightmarish game whose stakes escape him. His acts acquire an unforeseen dimension, he can hurt someone unknowingly. In this case, then, it is the detective himself – not the terrified members of the 'group of suspects' – who undergoes a kind of 'loss of reality', who

finds himself in a dreamlike world where it is never quite clear who is playing what game.

(Žižek, 1991: 62–3)

Žižek goes on to offer a Lacanian analysis of this shift towards the involved, 'hard-boiled' detective novel as an index of contemporary forms of subjectivity. But this different interpellation, this call to narrate within the first person and thereby to become a psychotherapeutic subject, as also required by the structure of any psychotherapy training, sets up similar effects. There is an 'ethical' and 'painful' character to engaging in therapeutic work – as a practitioner as well as a patient – with corresponding challenges to personal identities. As Žižek's description of such 'unforeseen dimensions' suggests, there is an awareness of the possibilities of 'hurting someone unknowingly.' Moreover, the process and structure of training requires us to write about our work as therapists and researchers in the first as well as the third person. These personal narrative forms, prompted by the institutional imperative towards accountability, inevitably usher in forms of self-scrutiny of the level of one's own self-deception. As Žižek describes the dilemma of the detective, this means 'clarifying the contours of the trap into which he has fallen'.

Perhaps part of the completion of a psychotherapy training, as with all claims to professional identity, includes the sense of being able to move from a first to a third person narrative. But what the memory debates underscore is that such positions of objectivity and identification can only ever be transitory. So, if nothing else, recent controversies around memories teach us that it is only at our peril that we ignore the multiple agencies operating in the construction, reconstruction and recovery of memories of – and in – therapy, and remind us of the wider political contexts in which claims to memory-making take place.

Note

1 A first version of this paper was presented to the North West Institute for Dynamic Psychotherapy at their graduation event, in March 1999.

References

Ahmed, S. (2004) *The Cultural Politics of Emotion*. Edinburgh: Edinburgh University Press.
Antze, P. and Lambek, M. (eds) (1996) *Tense Past: Cultural Essays in Trauma and Memory*. London: Routledge.
Bion, W. R. (1967) *Second Thoughts*. London: Heinemann.
Blum, H. (1994) *Reconstruction in Psychoanalysis: Childhood Revisited and Recreated*. Madison, CT: International Universities Press.
Bollas, C. (1995) *Cracking Up*. London: Routledge.
Bondi, L., Avis, H., Bankey, R., Bingley, B., Davidson, J., Duffy, R., Einagel, V.,

Green, A., Johnston, L., Lilley, S., Listerborn, C., Marshy, M., McEwan, S., O'Connor, N., Rose, G., Vivat, B. and Wood, N. (2002) *Subjectivities, Knowledges and Feminist Geographies: The Subjects and Ethics of Social Research.* Boston: Rowman and Littlefield.

Brandon, S., Boakes, J., Glaser, D. and Green, R. (1998) 'Recovered memories of childhood abuse: implications for clinical practice', *British Journal of Psychiatry* 172: 296–307.

British Psychological Society (1995) *Recovered Memories.* Leicester: BPS.

Brown, L. and Burman, E. (1997) 'The delayed memory debate: why feminist voices matter' (Editorial Introduction to 'Feminist Responses to the "False Memory" Debate', Special Feature of), *Feminism and Psychology* 7(1): 7–16.

Burman, E. (1996/7) 'False memories, true hopes and the angelic: revenge of the postmodern on therapy', *New Formations* 30: 122–34.

Burman, E. (1997) 'Telling stories: psychologists, children and the production of "false memories" ', *Theory and Psychology* 7(3): 291–309.

Burman, E. (1998) 'Children, false memories and disciplinary alliances: tensions between developmental psychology and psychoanalysis', *Psychoanalysis and Contemporary Thought* 21(3): 307–33.

Burman, E. (2001) 'Emotions in the classroom: and the institutional politics of knowledge', *Psychoanalytic Studies* 3(3–4): 313–24.

Burman, E. (2002) 'Erinnerungsarbeit als feministische Gruppenarbeit: therapeutische Beziehungen in der Lehre', in J. Meyer-Siebert, A. Merkens, I. Novak and V. Rego Diaz (eds) *Die Unruhe des Denkens nutzen: Emanzipatorische Stanpunkte in Neoliberalismus.* Frankfurt: Argument Verlag, pp. 89–98.

Burman, E. (2004) 'Taking women's voices: the psychological politics of feminisation', *Psychology of Women Section Review* 6(1): 3–21.

Burman, E. (2006) 'Analytic third or law? Reflections on regulation in psychotherapy case-notes', *Feminism and Psychology* 16(4): 445–50.

Burman, E. (2008) *Developments: Child, Image, Nation.* London and New York: Brunner-Routledge.

Burman, E., Aitken, G., Alldred, P., Allwood, R., Billington, T., Goldberg, B., Gordo López, A., Heenan, C., Marks, D. and Warner, S. (1996) *Psychology Discourse Practice: From Regulation to Resistance.* London: Taylor and Francis.

Burman, E., Smailes, S. and Chantler, K. (2004) ' "Culture" as a barrier to domestic violence services for minoritised women', *Critical Social Policy* 24(3): 358–84.

Ceci, M. and Bruck, M. (1993) 'Suggestibility of the child witness: a historical review and synthesis', *Psychological Bulletin* 113: 403–39.

Chantler, K. (2006) 'Independence, dependency and interdependence: struggles and resistances of minoritized women within and on leaving violent relationships', *Feminist Review* 82: 27–50.

Clare, M. (2006) 'Psychodynamic context, knowledge and the social context', in S. Wheeler (ed.) *Difference and Diversity in Counselling: Contemporary Psychodynamic Perspectives.* London: Palgrave, pp. 20–33.

Contratto, S. and Gutfreund, M. (eds) (1996) *A Feminist Clinician's Guide to the Memory Debate.* New York and London: Harrington Park Press.

Crawford, S., Kippax, S., Oxyx, J., Gault, U. and Benton, P. (1992) *Emotion and Gender: Constructing Meaning from Memory.* London: Sage.

Fonagy, P. (2004) 'Psychotherapy meets neuroscience: a more focused future for psychotherapy research', *Psychiatric Bulletin* 28: 357–9.

Fonagy, P. and Target, M. (2004) 'What can developmental psychopathology tell psychoanalysts about the mind?', in A. Casement (ed.) *Who Owns Psychoanalysis?* London: Karnac, pp. 307–42.

Fonagy, P., Gergely, G., Jurist, E. and Target, M. (2004) *Affect Regulation, Mentalization and the Development of the Self.* London: Karnac Books.

Foulkes, S. (1986) *Group Analytic Psychotherapy: Method and Principles.* London: Karnac Books.

Frankland, A. and Cohen, L. (1999) 'Draft guidelines for psychologists working with clients in which issues related to recovered memories may arise', *The Psychologist* 12(2): 82–3.

Franklin, B. (2002) 'Children's rights and media wrongs: changing representations of children and the developing rights agenda', in B. Franklin (ed.) *The New Handbook of Children's Rights.* Oxford: Routledge, pp. 15–42.

Freshwater, D. and Rolfe, G. (2004) *Deconstructing Evidence-Based Practice.* London: Routledge.

Freud, S. (1937) 'Constructions in analysis', in J. Strachey (ed.) (1966) *Standard Edition* 23: 255–69. London: Hogarth Press

Gardner, F. (1996) 'Open to all possibilities', *British Journal of Psychotherapy* 12(3): 343–9.

Gilroy, P. (1995) *The Black Atlantic.* London: Verso.

Haaken, J. (1998) *Pillar of Salt: Gender, Memory and the Perils of Looking Back.* London: Free Association Books.

Hacking, I. (1996) 'Memory sciences, memory politics', in P. Antze and M. Lambek (eds) *Tense Past: Cultural Essays in Trauma and Memory.* London: Routledge, pp. 67–88.

Hanmer, J. and Itzin, C. (2000) *Home Truths About Domestic Violence: A Feminist Reader.* London: Routledge.

Haug, F. (1992) *Beyond Female Masochism: Memory-work and Politics.* London: Verso.

Haug, F. (1998) 'Questions concerning method in feminist research', in E. Burman (ed.) *Deconstructing Feminist Psychology.* London and Thousand Oaks: Sage, pp. 115–39.

Haug, F. (2000) 'Memory work: the key to women's anxiety', in S. Radstone (ed.) *Memory and Methodology.* Oxford and New York: Berg, pp. 155–79.

Haug, F. and others (1987) *Female Sexualisation.* London: Verso.

Hobsbawm, E. and Ranger, T. (eds) (1978) *The Invention of Tradition.* Cambridge: Cambridge University Press.

Isaac, M. (2006) 'Psychodynamic counselling and class', in S. Wheeler (ed.) *Difference and Diversity in Counselling: Contemporary Psychodynamic Perspectives.* London: Palgrave, pp. 156–66.

Lambert, H. (2006) 'Accounting for EBM: notions of evidence in medicine', *Social Science and Medicine* 62: 2633–45.

Lindsay, D. and Read, J. (1994) 'Psychotherapy and memories of childhood abuse: a cognitive perspective', *Applied Cognitive Psychology* 8: 281–338.

Middleton, D. and Brown, S. D. (2005) *The Social Psychology of Experience: Studies in Remembering and Forgetting.* London: Sage.

Middleton, D. and Edwards, D. (eds) (1990) *Collective Remembering.* London: Sage.

Moro, L. (2007) 'The role of supervision in training psychotherapists', *Group Analysis* 40(2): 178–88.

Motzkau, J. F. (2006) *Cross-examining suggestibility: memory, childhood, expertise*. Unpublished PhD thesis, Loughborough University.

Motzkau, J. F. (in press a). 'Speaking up against justice: children's rights, suspended testimonies and development free spaces', *International Journal of Critical Psychology*.

Motzkau, J. F. (in press b) 'The semiotic of accusation: reconsidering the language of deconstruction in the case of developmental critique – taking a pragmatic step back towards critical impact', *Forum Qualitative Social Research* (online journal).

Parker, I. (1997) *Psychoanalytic Culture: Psychoanalytic Discourse in Western Society*. London: Sage.

Parker, I. and Revelli, S. (eds) (2008) *Psychoanalytic Practice and State Regulation*. London: Karnac.

Phillips, A. (1995) *Terrors and Experts*. London: Faber and Faber.

Poole, D. and White, L. (1993) 'Two years later: effects of question repetition and retention interval on the eye-witness testimony of children and adults', *Developmental Psychology* 29: 844–53.

Rutter, M. (2002) 'Nature, nurture, and development: from evangelism through science policy and practice', *Child Development* January/February, 73(1): 1–21.

Saywitz, K., Goodman, G., Nicholas, E. and Moan, S. (1991) 'Children's memories of a physical examination involving genital touch: implications for reports of child sexual abuse', *Journal of Consulting and Clinical Psychology* 59: 682–91.

Sharpe, M. (ed.) (1995) *The Third Eye*. London: Routledge.

Siddiqui, N., Ismail, S. and Allen, M. (2008) *Safe to Return? Pakistani women, domestic violence and access to refugee protection – A report of a trans-national research project conducted in the UK and Pakistan*. Manchester: South Manchester Law Centre/Women's Studies Research Centre, Manchester Metropolitan University.

Spence, D. (1982) *Narrative Truth and Historical Truth*. New York: W.W. Norton.

Steedman, C. (1995) *Strange Dislocations: Childhood and the Idea of Human Interiority, 1780–1930*. London: Virago.

Stephenson, N. and Kippax, S. (1999) 'Minding the gap: subjectivity and sexuality research', in W. Maiers, B. Bayer, B. Duarte Esgalhado, R. Jorna and E. Schraube (eds) *Challenges to Theoretical Psychology*. Ontario: Captus University Publications, pp. 383–92.

Swartz, S. (2006) 'The third voice: writing casenotes', *Feminism and Psychology* 16(4): 427–44.

Thobani, S. (2007) 'White wars: western feminisms and the "War on Terror"', *Feminist Theory* 8(2): 169–85.

Tuckwell, G. (2006) 'Psychodynamic counselling, "race" and culture', in S. Wheeler (ed.) *Difference and Diversity in Counselling: Contemporary Psychodynamic Perspectives*. London: Palgrave, pp. 135–55.

United Kingdom Council for Psychotherapy (1996) *Notes for Practitioners: On Legal Issues Connected to the Practice of Psychotherapy*.

United Kingdom Council for Psychotherapy (1997) *Notes for Practitioners: Recovered Memories of Abuse*.

Žižek, S. (1991) *Looking Awry: An Introduction to Jacques Lacan through Popular Culture*. Cambridge, MA: MIT Press.

12 Transformative remembering
Feminism, psychoanalysis, and recollections of abuse

Janice Haaken

One of the organizing principles of psychoanalytic therapy is that the best road from a problem to its source is often indirect and, further, that important truths reside at the periphery of what is most readily noticed. The fixation throughout the 'memory wars' of the late 1990s on dramatic encounters and absolute claims and counter-claims narrowed possibilities for divergent routes into the uncertainties of remembering (Hacking, 1995). And as clinical memories of sexual abuse became increasingly gothic, migrating from scenes of incest to tales of children tortured by robed Satan-worshippers, the more mundane sources of female suffering fell below the threshold of public sympathies. In writing *Pillar of Salt: Gender, Memory and the Perils of Looking Back* (1998) in the late 1990s, my aim was to find alternative portals of entry into the recovered memory debate, primarily through the critical lens of feminist psychoanalytic theory.

One of the psychoanalytic ideas advanced in *Pillar of Salt* involves what I term *transformative remembering* – how the emergence of memories that depart from previous autobiographical accounts may register shifts in the organization of the self, as well as shifts in the historical and cultural grounding of the self. This concept builds on research and clinical findings suggesting that current states of mind and self-representations influence processes of memory retrieval, whether in the affective tone of the memory or in the specific events recalled (Bower, 1981; Spence, 1982; Lindsay, 1994; Schacter, 1996). As the patient tells his or her life story, particular events emerge as prototypical of later conflicts. Transformative remembering also is affiliated with social approaches to autobiographical recall, both in emphasizing the relational constellations of memory that constitute the internal world and in attending to the cultural materials available in structuring stories about the past (Middleton and Brown, 2005).

Feminist theory is enlisted here as a critical framework for the psychoanalytic exploration of remembering, and for understanding how cultural dynamics shape the versions of the past recovered (Minsky, 1998). After introducing the psychoanalytic concept of the unconscious and feminist employment of the unconscious in the trauma recovery movement, I present a case from my clinical practice to show how sexual scenes from childhood may shift over time in their psychodynamic significance. I show how culture and history shape processes of looking back in psychotherapy, and how childhood sexual scenes register a broad range of disturbing experiences and boundary violations.

Feminism and discourses of the unconscious

As a psychology of secrets – a theory of hidden knowledge revealed through narratives – psychoanalysis creates a more hospitable audience for female storytelling than does the highly operationalized world of scientific psychology (Haaken, 1998). In contradistinction to cognitive theories of memory that stress the encoding and retrieval of memory, psychoanalysis asserts a narrative coherence to mental life (Kihlstrom *et al.*, 1992). From a psychoanalytic perspective, repression is not simply understood as interference in the mental retrieval of information but, rather, signifies human conflict over self-knowledge (Ellenburger, 1970; Hilgard, 1977; Eagle, 1987; Singer, 1990; Elder, 1994).

Many feminists position women – and the oppressed generally – as guardians of repressed truths, possessors of a language silenced but not destroyed. Adrienne Rich (1979), for example, insists that 'whatever is . . . is buried in the memory by the collapse of meaning under an inadequate or lying language – this will become, not merely unspoken, but unspeakable' (p. 199). There is a certain affinity between feminism and beliefs in 'occult' psychological processes because women have themselves been hidden from history, operating behind a screen of masculine assumptions and fantasies (Doanne, 1989; Toronto, 1991; Haaken, 1998). Beyond this affinity between the unconscious and the female position of holding rejected social knowledge, there is also a subversive dimension to discourses on the unconscious (Rose, 1985; Benjamin, 1988). Any project of progressive social change requires a capacity to transcend mundane reality, to probe for deeper meanings, and to uncover hidden potentialities.

The concept of the unconscious also may be used in mystifying or intrusive ways, particularly as therapists become over-invested in exposing hidden parts of the patient's interior world. In bridging the distance between the private and the public, between fantasy and reality, many clinicians in the burgeoning field of trauma therapy in the late twentieth century sought to decipher the origins of female disturbances in concealed memories of sexual abuse. Further, therapists assumed that fragments of trauma memory tended to leak into consciousness in the form of dream-like imagery (Herman, 1992; van der Kolk and Fisler, 1995).

Throughout the recovered memory debates, feminists tended to be aligned with the trauma model and with the position that women's memories must be validated, whatever the conditions under which they were produced (see Bass and Davis, 1988; Herman, 1992; Freyd, 1996). As a corrective to the history of silencing women, or of labeling angry women as hysterics, this stance of 'believing women' acquired the force of a moral mandate. One cost of the mandate to 'believe' women, however, was to adopt a literalist view of memory that stripped women's stories of complexity. Further, this literalist view downplayed how official translators on the scene (including therapists) shape the transformation of inchoate, unstoried experience into narrative accounts (Haaken, 1998; Burman, 1996/7; Middleton and Brown, 2005).

The genre of memories that came to dominate public discourse and divide the mental health community in the late twentieth century departed in key respects from earlier descriptions of clinically facilitated recollections. First, there was a dramatic disjuncture between prior autobiographical recollections and the recovered memories reported in the trauma therapy literature during the 1980s and 1990s. Women had begun to speak more openly about incest and other forms of sexual abuse during the 1970s, but their narratives generally stressed the prohibition to speak rather than the failures of memory (see Bass and Davis, 1988; Herman, 1992).

Most critics of trauma therapy and recovered memory drew a line between incest survivors who held continuous knowledge of having been abused, cases thought to be non-problematic, and those women who 'found' their memory through a therapy or recovery group experience. The scientific critiques generally focused on these latter cases, where hypnosis or other social influences were thought to account for the emergence of memories of abuse (Loftus and Klinger, 1994; Pendergrast, 1996). Critics also relied heavily on the distinction between continuous and new memories to defend against charges that they were denying the scope and traumatic impact of childhood sexual abuse. Fixated on the factual veracity of recovered memories, many of these critics overlooked the more unsettling question of why large numbers of women were experiencing such a deep disjuncture in autobiographical recall.

Trauma theorists argue that childhood sexual abuse leads to extreme forms of dissociation, including alternating experiences of identity, alter ego states, and feelings of unreality or emotional detachment (Freyd, 1996; Herman, 1992). These distancing defenses serve to protect consciousness from knowledge of the abuse. Trauma therapists also advanced the concept of *body memories* (see also Robson, Chapter 8 and Woodiwiss, Chapter 6, this volume) – that the body remembers what the mind attempts to forget (van der Kolk and Fisler, 1995).

There are everyday clinical examples of dissociated mental states, however, that do not necessarily involve trauma: the woman who pulls her wedding ring on and off as she describes impassively some recent effort to appease her husband; or the man who describes with an air of emotional detachment a recent episode of being humiliated by a colleague, as though it were happening to someone else. But the joining of the concepts of dissociation and trauma produced a clinical tendency to register a wide range of dissociated states as indicators of trauma.

Transference and countertransfrence

Beyond the dynamics of the patient that structure the revisiting of the past, the therapeutic relationship provides its own complex prompts for engaging early history. The questions asked, the responsivity evoked in relation to particular themes, the co-constructed memories of the patient's past, all mediate the knowledge that is gained. Much like the concept of priming, therapeutic interpretations sensitize the patient to subsequent meanings and associations in looking back on an unfolding personal history.

Ongoing relationships, particularly those originating in early dependency ties, are generative of complex, divergent meanings encompassing a wider scope of self/other configurations than are relationships of a more limited nature. Out of the contours of these more ambiguous yet determinative vistas of self/other images, efforts to identify an original cause, the source of selfhood as it is presently constituted, becomes a creative act as well as one of self-discovery.

A central difference between psychoanalytic therapy and various competing approaches that emphasize mental processes, such as cognitive-behaviorism, lies in its focus on the dynamic flux between past and present, and how painful or conflicted relational experiences may be reactivated at a later time and re-emerge in a disguised form. The concepts of transference and countertransference refer to the misrecognition that inheres in the unconscious reliving of some past association, which becomes the focus of analytic exploration in psychotherapy. Just as the patient's relational conflicts and defenses are unconsciously evoked in the clinical encounter, so, too, are those of the therapist. And just as feelings and conflicts originating in relational struggles of the past may be transferred onto the person of the therapist, the therapist may experience a parallel process. A key difference, ideally, lies in the therapist's knowledge of her/his own inner world and emotional reactions, and in the therapist's ability to make use of this self-knowledge in helping the patient to gain new self-understanding. For the therapist, listening to memories requires attentiveness to multiple meanings and to the position of self in relation to the Other embedded in the memory narrative.

The following case from my psychotherapy practice illustrates some of the critical problems in the clinical interpretation of abuse memories and dissociative states. The woman I present is not a survivor of father/daughter incest but does meet the current criteria as a sexual abuse survivor in that she reported during the course of therapy having had sexual experiences with adults in childhood. Through the discussion of my work with this patient over two years of psychodynamic therapy, I hope to illustrate and make salient three points: (1) the ambiguities in clinically differentiating the effects of sexual abuse from other traumatic childhood events; (2) the shifting meanings attached to abuse experiences in the course of treatment; and (3) the variable meanings of dissociation in the patient's intrapsychic and interpersonal worlds.

The case of Lana

'Lana' is a Vietnamese woman who was in her thirties at the time I initially saw her. Born in Vietnam, she had arrived with the first boat lift in 1975 during early adolescence. A slight, soft-spoken woman with large expressive eyes, she sat quite motionless during our first session. There was a tremendous sense of suffering about her, as well as palpable tenseness. She was still except for her hands, and I noticed her graceful, long fingers, circling the air to assist her in her efforts to speak. She described herself as very shy. At the same time, she dressed in a flamboyant style that suggested another side to her that co-existed with her timidity.

Lana sought psychotherapy because of a deteriorating relationship with her husband 'Jack,' a European-American man with whom she had lived for about five years. She also wondered if she might have been sexually abused as a child, adding that she recognized herself in many of the self-help portraits of sexual abuse survivors. While she initially reported having no memories of sexual abuse, this 'wondering' introduced an important vector into our subsequent therapeutic exploration of the past.

Most immediately distressing to Lana was her sense of emotional numbness and her lack of sexual feeling for her husband. Jack had very high standards, she informed me, and he was 'always helping me to improve myself, particularly my English.' She overtly welcomed his tutoring and agreed with his assessment that she needed 'self-improvement,' yet she was less able over time to make use of his many suggestions. Lana was in agreement with Jack's observation that she was not improving but, rather, worsening in her professed desire for greater social independence and cultural literacy.

I was aware during this first session of my hostility toward her husband and the sympathy I felt for this terribly oppressed woman. I felt the impulse to protect her and to invoke in her some rage toward this man who seemed to be so undermining of her capabilities. At the same time, I knew that Jack might represent some aspect of Lana's own ego ideal, so that my impulse to attack him was also directed at a part of her.

Many of the elements of Lana's experience – the depressive symptoms and sadomasochistic flavor of her relationship with her husband – were familiar clinically. But my initial feeling was that I would not be able to understand Lana. It was not her English, which was quite fluent, but rather her cultural world that left me uncertain. I was keenly aware of the limitations of my background, as a European-American, and my impulse was to retreat in the face of the cultural divide between us. I wondered whether the range of affect or integrative capacities that I assume to be normative could be applied to another culture, and how to think about the difference between cultural labeling and therapeutic diagnostics. Do categories such as depression, dissociation, or dependent personality – an even more problematic label – really apply? So the problems that are always latent in clinical work – the various assumptions we bring in order to structure and organize the material – intruded on my consciousness, stirring feelings of uncertainty and inadequacy.

Part of this sense of wanting to withdraw, of feeling inadequate to the task, was in response to Lana's own sense of helplessness and emotional isolation. Just as she often lapsed into dissociative distance in her relationships with others, I had, over the course of the hour, experienced some aspects of this emotional retreat.

Over the early months, Lana spoke more and more freely even as she cried softly during most of the sessions. We talked about crying and what she was aware of as she cried. She confessed that crying felt extremely shameful, and associated with submission and defeat. At the same time, as we probed the meaning of her crying, she began to understand her tears as not simply an expression of her mute and humiliated state, but as an effort to feel something and to evoke a feeling within me. The fights with Jack always left her in tears, followed by an inconsolable sense of isolation. As she cried with me, I felt a vague sense of guilt, of feeling implicated in her suffering.

We began to explore what these fights and numbing tears evoked historically. Lana talked of growing up in a family where there was a tremendous amount of fighting and warfare, not only in the cultural backdrop of her early childhood but at home between her mother and father. The dissociated states that she connected with the fighting, where she could imagine herself as having vacated her body or as being somewhere else, also evoked the memory of frantic efforts to escape the aggressively charged atmosphere of her early world.

Lana began to construct a picture out of fragments of the past. Her early experience in Vietnam was very hazy and not very accessible to her. There were glimmerings of the war, as a vague backdrop, with fighting at home recalled more vividly. Lana's move to the United States during the first boat lift was associated with confusion. Most of what she remembered was her mother crying. She described her mother as a joyless woman whose hopelessness and grief were deeply inscribed in Lana's memory of emigration. This crossing of the ocean also came to serve as a metaphor for the traumatic loss of childhood – and of her entry into adolescence without a sense of emotional protection. Her crying mother felt useless to her, as she felt useless to herself in alleviating emotional distress in the present.

Memories of her early years also included recollections of criminal dealings. Lana's parents had been involved in some kind of illegal activity in Vietnam that was carried over to the United States. There was a vague memory of her parents being away in jail – one of the parents, maybe both, she wasn't sure. There also was a hazy sense of something having happened when she was little – during the time when someone was in jail. The parents also traveled, and their various comings and goings were cloaked in secrecy. She also remembered relatives and friends taking care of her during these mysterious parental absences, providing a vital sense of belonging and emotional warmth.

Some therapists would stress the importance of recovering more fully these disturbing early memories out of the clinical assumption that Lana's emotional numbness was a dissociative response to early trauma. While this formulation may be correct, my psychodynamic approach focused on understanding how this patient was making use of memory, and what she was communicating of her relational world through emerging memory fragments.

I commented, at this point, on the coming and going of people, of her own struggle, even now, to find something to hold on to in these frightening moments when her world seemed like it was falling apart. She responded by telling me of how she comforted herself when she was little by making doll clothes, dressing and undressing her dolls, over and over.

As Lana told this story, I privately wondered whether the 'something that happened' involved sexual abuse. Since dissociation may take the form of unconscious acting out of a conflict, the ritual of dressing and undressing the doll may have been her own way of attempting to gain control over things that had happened to her. I asked what she could recall, and about her own associations with dressing and undressing dolls. She remembered that as a young girl she had wanted to be someone else, and that going to America meant that she could transform herself. Looking back, she felt this doll play centered on remaking herself, a private, ritualized act of transfiguration.

While early images of the parents centered on their criminal activity and the experience of emotional abandonment, memories then turned to her mother's powerful temper, particularly aroused during Lana's adolescence. She recalled that her mother would become enraged, and that she, as the oldest daughter in the family, would be the primary object of the mother's fury. Lana experienced her mother as weak and helpless in her frequent fights with the father, but as frighteningly powerful when she turned on her daughter. As Lana moved into adolescence – and American culture – she began to defy her mother and the two of them were in a state of continual escalating combat with one another.

This imago of the defiant, aggressive daughter initially struck me as surprising, six months into therapy, and conflict between her passive, submissive side and her aggression and rage became a central motif in psychotherapy. She recalled a fight with her mother when she had 'talked back.' Her mother yelled at her and hit her, and Lana recalled giving her mother a wooden spoon, the instrument of her own punishment. In this sense, she aided her mother's aggression – engaging her in a relational struggle that signified an effort to break through her state of helplessness and numbing isolation.

In working with this kind of material – memories of childhood abuse – the therapist's readiness to impose an interpretation or particular moral cast on the events inhibits exploration of other potential meanings, including how the patient may be making use of a particular memory. Lana was very conscious of her hostility and contempt toward both her parents, and particularly toward her mother. She had some sense of her own entitlement, and of superiority over her mother that she had felt from an early age. We discussed what it felt like to give her mother the spoon, and her own associations with this active engagement with her tormentor. She described her sense of moral triumph over her mother in this act, of feeling the victor even in this moment of defeat.

As the imago of the monstrous mother became more vivid, I wondered if Lana's own infantile rage had infused these memories of the mother. Over time, we returned to this prototypical struggle with the mother in different ways, with the shifting valencies of our therapeutic relationship allowing new uses of this formative scene. What came to feel particularly troubling to Lana was her discovery, through her own defiance, of some weakness and desperation in her mother. As we explored her feelings of hatred toward her mother, a deeper concern emerged that she had destroyed a vital maternal connection through her own rage. In looking back, this act of aiding in her own punishment seemed to be a way of reasserting the corporeal reality of the maternal object, of resuscitating the defeated mother. Lana recognized a form of atonement in the beating and in later sadomasochistic engagements, a strangely comforting sense of being held, of feeling terrifyingly connected.

Sexuality emerged early on as a concern for Lana, initially expressed through sexual problems with her husband. She described his sexual withdrawal from her and his complaint that she merely wanted a father-figure – that she was using sex to be held. He had noticed – unlike other men with whom she had been sexual – that she did not derive much pleasure from sex in the genital sense. Her sexuality was organized around a pre-genital longing for bodily contact with a holding presence. Yet Jack's recognition of her made her feel more exposed and unable to protect herself from the shamefulness of his discovery. Sex with Jack left her feeling empty and alone.

Lana's early sexual awakenings were against the backdrop of her father's sexuality. She recalled that her father and mother mainly fought about his infidelity. He apparently had lovers and occasionally saw prostitutes. The mother would find out about his sexual exploits and they would fight. Lana's maternal grandfather had abandoned Lana's mother when she was a young girl and Lana recognized her mother's tremendous sadness over this loss, while at the same time despising her for her helplessness. Lana guiltily recalled admiring her father and envying his capacity to escape the torment of the family's enforced dependency. The father both caused the mother pain through his infidelity, but, at the same time, he embodied the prized, masculine other, the one who possessed the freedom to act on his own desires.

Early on in therapy, Lana recalled an experience, during early childhood, when she was fondled and undressed by an older brother. She began to talk about this memory as we explored her early sexual experiences and feelings. She remembered being quite stimulated by this experience with the brother and a sense of 'doing what daddy was doing.' There was some forbidden pleasure in this association with what daddy had done, and of a sibling enactment of childish awareness of paternal transgressions. This may very well have been a later reconstruction of the experience, but the shame she described was that she was like the prostitutes whom daddy saw. So the incestuous relationship with the brother seemed to evoke less an awareness of his intrusiveness than it did a sense of a forbidden discovery.

During early adolescence, Lana became sexually involved with a much older man. Her discovery of her own sexuality at this time was for her a very important bridge out of her mother's world. She recalled her parents having card parties where she would serve the guests and felt herself in the position of servant. Her responsiveness to this older man, who was a frequent guest at these parties and a kind of avuncular presence in the family, represented a violation of both incest and age taboos. At the same time, her eager interest in him was a flagrant and defiant protest against her own position as servant. She warmed to this man's overtures and they began a sexual affair.

While the age difference did make this relationship a form of sexual abuse, Lana's initial memory of it was that this man did care for her. To characterize these experiences as traumatic or abusive, prior to her own explorations of their meanings, would be to rob her of her initial insight: that this man provided a bridge, a kind of transitional object, out of a very depressed state.

Lana's mother found out about the secret affair and this discovery marked a new period of warfare between them. The mother/daughter feuds culminated in Lana leaving her family when she went to live with relatives in another state. Before she moved away, Lana and her mother battled over her sexual behavior. Lana persisted in seeing this man, sneaking out of the house, and engaging in furtive phone calls in defiance of her mother's insistence that she stop.

Lana's final expulsion from the family was precipitated by her call to the police after her mother had beaten her. She had some understanding by then of the concept of child abuse and of her own legal rights. To call the police represented both an assertion of her rights and, at the same time, a violation of a cultural taboo. She had shown the ultimate disrespect of her parents by calling in the authorities – white people – to rescue her from her torture. This was a very painful conflict for her, one that led her to flee Vietnamese culture entirely. Her intrapsychic experience was one of having killed her culture, which carried the memory of stable, maternal objects even as it evoked more destructive ones.

Lana was intent on becoming Americanized as she took flight from her family and community. She saw Vietnamese culture as destructive and as repressive of women. 'You are a slave,' she said, 'and if you are a daughter you are more of a slave. Children obey their parents, no matter what.'

Over the first six months of therapy, much of her aggression was directed toward her culture, which she cast as the enemy of her own emotional survival. I began to be aware of my own uneasiness as this hostility mounted. I felt that this warfare against her culture was an effort to free herself from her own harsh, cruel superego. On the other hand, I felt that the devaluing of her 'mother culture' was part of the Americanization experience, the demand of enculturation itself that had left her vulnerable to new forms of oppression in the dominant culture she had entered.

About nine months into therapy, Lana suddenly changed her name, from Lana to 'Lan,' reporting matter of factly, 'I've gone back to my Vietnamese name,' the name she had given up when she had left home as an adolescent. This seemed to signal a form of rapprochement with the cultural world she had rejected. At the same time, she began to express a longing for a deeper closeness with me, a desire for something more. She wanted to know more about me and felt resentful of my reserve, asking to hug me at times at the end of sessions. She alternated between idealizing me, as her first woman friend, and feeling an unbearable sense of insufficiency in the relationship. She joined a women's group which both was a way of recognizing the limits of what I could give her, and of acting out her rage toward me. (She would compare my approach to the group, often finding me lacking.) At the same time, joining the women's group represented a very progressive effort toward knowing women in a more vital and intimate way than in the past.

As she began to express more criticism of me, Lan expressed the suspicion that I held some secret knowledge, privately triumphing over her (as she had over her mother). At the same time, she began to demand that I tell her what to do, and she seemed to be provoking me to become more 'Jack-like.' Her sense of failing to find the gratifying, maternal object mobilized aggressive engagement. But she was no longer in the passive, masochistic position but, rather, in open defiance, even as she wanted to be held and controlled.

With this more openly aggressive engagement, Lan began to describe her fear that she was really like her father, that she used sex the way he used it, and that sex was a game, a form of currency. Even though she pretended to care for men, she wondered whether she really did. There was this secret feeling of triumph, of victory over them, in having their desires aroused and in withholding her own. While men thought women to be the more fragile and vulnerable, it was actually they, with their bulging member, who were ridiculously exposed. Women pretended to be weak in order to make men feel strong.

I asked Lan whether she felt there was emotional pretending in our relationship as well. She responded that she was uncertain about whether I would still like her if I knew things she had done in the past, or if I would just 'pretend to care' for the money.

As we talked about her associations with dirty money and dirty secrets, Lan began to identify what felt like a cruel part of her own sexuality. There were memories that she had never spoken about and barely thought about. She spoke about her guilt over a brother, eight years younger than herself, who was very important to her as a young girl. Lan had been a mother figure to this younger brother who was often under her supervision. She began to recall how as a puberty-aged girl she had fondled her little brother's genitals and on one occasion had put his penis inside her to 'see what it felt like.' She felt tremendous guilt over this memory, particularly through her later awareness of the issue of sexual abuse as an abuse of power. As her eyes welled up with tears, I felt the urge to focus on the object-relational side of this abusive encounter, on her 'pre-genital' search for deep emotional and bodily contact with someone who loved her. We did explore this memory in the context of both her own sexual abuse by her older brother and her unbearable loneliness. But I also was aware that moving too quickly to redemptive interpretations would communicate my own unease with her position as perpetrator in the story. Feminism meant re-projecting the 'bad' back onto men and casting off the legacy of malignant feminine guilt. My impulse as a feminist therapist to liberate my patient from the chains of her own conscience also carries the risk of foreclosing on how she is making use of this scene from the past to work through a current difficulty. Lan was trying to bear in mind a memory of having violated her younger brother, but she also was making use of this story of abuse to communicate something about current difficulties.

Our exploration of Lan's moments of occupying the hurtful, active position – the one who holds the power to dominate more vulnerable others – led to associations with the Vietnam war. 'I have been reading about Vietnam and the war, lately,' Lan said softly and deliberately. 'I never wanted to think about it before.' I asked her about her remembrances of the war, feeling a vague sense of dread. 'I don't remember much about the war,' Lan went on to say, 'mainly I remember stealing and money. I don't want to be like my parents who were stealing, but this book I've been reading tells how stealing was a way of dealing with poverty, with surviving . . . This is true because Vietnamese people are very generous, they are more so than whites.'

I suggested that 'you are finding something again that is good in the Vietnamese world, something that you had forgotten, and yet you are not sure what is stolen and what is legitimately yours.' Lan commented, 'Well, I've always loved the food. I never felt like you have to steal the food, but the other things of the culture I don't like.' 'Food is the good and abundant side of your Vietnamese world,' I said, 'and this feels so different than the dirty money that is the other side, the bad side.'

Lan responded, 'I don't like the whole success part. You know, Vietnamese people have been invaded so much and yet there is so much emphasis on making money. That is the only important thing, making money, and yet I also know that your country raped my country and before that it was the French. But for my generation, it was the Americans that raped our country.'

At this point, I was very aware of myself in the position of rapist, as part of the world that had reduced her country to having to steal. Stealing came to be associated with the rebellious side of her traditions, and with her own active strivings to find the lost, valuable objects, the reclamation of things that had been taken away. I commented that this memory of being back in Vietnam was also a way of looking for some lost part of herself, something that had been taken away from her.

I asked whether there were times when she hated me too, times when she thought of me as the enemy. This was unsettling for both of us – this moment where she was remembering Vietnam, and feeling loss and longing, while I was located as part of the dominant invading culture, on the other shore. She insisted that it was only for a moment that she felt hate for me. 'Maybe it's that we are both women,' Lan retreated. 'I don't see us as creating war, yet I haven't trusted women before, either, I have always turned to men.' 'With men, you know how to get something back, you know how to bargain,' I responded. 'With women, it has been more difficult, and maybe more disappointing to not find what you are looking for.'

Lan continued. 'During the war, the men were in more danger and we were protected. My mother cried and cried – yet we did win, we stood up to this big country and defeated it. I was talking to Jack about this last night, how we had defeated the United States, even though we were just this little country.' I suggested that 'you are sort of like that little country, you had to learn to fight, and you felt like you were stealing something when you made other people pay attention to your needs.'

During our last months of therapy, Lan would periodically assume a dominating, teaching stance with me. She began to talk about what she had learned about Vietnamese traditions and she became very critical of American ways, particularly the rudeness. I was aware of being the object of her more active desire to influence me – to assert what *she* had that *I* lacked. This may have been a means of externalizing her own sense of what was lacking – of putting back onto me her own burdensome sense of cultural devaluation.

But carried into these transference encounters were earlier developmental struggles and experiences of guilt and defeat. Shifting between our female 'sameness' and our ethnic differences, Lan was reaching toward a new sense of subjective coherence, one that included a less traumatic differentiation between self and other, as well as a capacity for idealization and merger of self and other. In many of her relational struggles, there were active, sadistic moments, and passive, masochistic ones, but these were less frightening or immobilizing than before.

I often found myself rallying in response to Lan's chastisement of American culture, perhaps in an effort to absolve myself of cultural guilt. But beyond this defensive avoidance of guilt, there was an aspect of sharing in her pleasurable triumphs, including her moments of triumph over me.

Conclusions

Therapeutic responsiveness requires entering into a range of shifting states of consciousness while holding the vital connections between present and past. In the case of Lan, dissociated states did signify a numbing response as defense against deprivation, as well as against overt abuse. But dissociated states also may be understood as the emergence of yet-to-be-known aspects of the self. In the course of therapy, Lan's discordant self states registered unsettling desires, fantasies, and memories, organized around shifting identifications with both victim and perpetrator positions. The therapeutic relationship provided a relational framework for not simply 'containing' these disturbing currents of the psyche but in valuing them as essential to the process of becoming a more fully realized person.

In anxiously seeking to locate the source of distress in a discrete event in the past, therapists may prematurely foreclose on these disquieting aspects of remembering. In my work with Lan, it was the murkiness of her recollections – like the ocean she crossed in coming to America – that provided the generative, creative space for self-discovery. This space included recognition of how her memories bore the imprints of her own fears and desires, as much as they did the impact of deeds done to her.

Focusing on the narrative structure of memory and the social uses of stories, rather than on their veridical truth content, does run the risk of downplaying the importance of factual claims. But in recognizing how victim and perpetrator images inhabit the human psyche in complicated ways, a richer realm of self-understandings unfolds than if we focus narrowly on factual claims alone. Once stories acquire social symbolic meaning and go beyond literal representations of past events, they also are open to multiple psychological and social uses. And in making integrative use of such possibilities, it is important to remember that women, no less than men, deserve the freedom to explore – to both create and discover – the dynamic flux that constitutes personal identity and the contours of history itself.

References

Bass, E. and Davis, L. (1988) *The Courage to Heal*. New York: HarperPerennial.
Benjamin, J. (1988) *The Bonds of Love: Psychoanalysis, Feminism, and the Problem of Domination*. New York: Pantheon Books.
Bower, G. (1981) 'Mood and memory', *American Psychologist* 36: 129–48.
Burman, E. (1996/7) 'False memories, true hopes and the angelic: revenge of the postmodern in therapy', *New Formations* 30: 122–34.
Doanne, M. A. (1989) 'Veiling over desire: close-ups of the woman', in R. Feldstein and J. Roof (eds) *Feminism and Psychoanalysis*. Ithaca, NY: Cornell University Press, pp. 105–41.
Eagle, M. N. (1987) 'The psychoanalytic and the cognitive unconscious', in R. Stern (ed.) *Theories of the Unconscious and Theories of the Self*. Hillsdale, NJ: The Analytic Press, pp. 155–89.
Elder, C. R. (1994) *The Grammar of the Unconscious: The Conceptual Foundations of Psychoanalysis*. University Park, PA: The Pennsylvania State University Press.
Ellenberger, H. F. (1970) *The Discovery of the Unconscious: The History and Evolution of Dynamic Psychiatry*. New York: Basic Books.
Freyd, J. J. (1996) *Betrayal Trauma: The Logic of Forgetting Childhood Abuse*. Cambridge, MA: Harvard University Press.

Haaken, J. (1996) 'The recovery of fantasy, memory, and desire: feminist approaches to sexual abuse and psychic trauma', *Signs: Journal of Women in Culture and Society* 21: 1069–94.

Haaken, J. (1998) *Pillar of Salt: Gender, Memory, and the Perils of Looking Back*. New Brunswick, NJ: Rutgers University Press.

Haaken, J. (2003) 'Smart, dumb, or culturally challenged? A social history of the dynamic unconscious', *Politics and Psychotherapy* I: 47–63.

Hacking, I. (1995) *Rewriting the Soul: Multiple Personality and the Sciences of Memory*. Princeton, NJ: Princeton University Press.

Herman, J. (1992) *Trauma and Recovery*. New York: Basic Books.

Hilgard, E. R. (1977) *Divided Consciousness: Multiple Controls in Human Thought and Action*. New York: Wiley.

Kihlstrom, J. F., Barnhardt, T. M. and Tataryn, D. J. (1992) 'The psychological unconscious: found, lost, and regained', *American Psychologist* 47: 788–91.

Lindsay, S. D. (1994) 'Contextualizing and clarifying criticisms of memory work in psychotherapy', *Consciousness and Cognition* 3: 426–37.

Loftus, E. and Ketcham, K. (1994) *The Myth of Repressed Memory*. New York: St Martin's Press.

Loftus, E. J. and Klinger, M. R. (1992) Is the unconscious smart or dumb? *American Psychologist* 47: 761–5.

Middleton, D. and Brown, S. D. (2005) *The Social Psychology of Experience: Studies in Remembering and Forgetting*. London: Sage.

Minsky, R. (1998) *Psychoanalysis and Culture*. Cambridge, UK: Polity Press.

Pendergrast, M. (1996) *Victims of Memories: Sexual Abuse Allegations and Shattered Lives*. Hinesburg, VT: Upper Access.

Reavey, P. and Brown, S. D. (2006) 'Transforming agency and action in the past, into present time: adult memories and child sexual abuse', *Theory and Psychology* 16: 179–202.

Rich, R. (1979) 'It is the lesbian in us', *On Lies, Secrets, and Silence: Selected prose 1966–1978*. New York: W.W. Norton and Company.

Rose, J. (1986) *Sexuality in the Field of Vision*. London: Verso.

Schacter, D. (1996) *Searching for Memory: The Brain, the Mind, and the Past*. New York: Basic Books.

Singer, J. L. (ed.) (1990) *Repression and Dissociation: Implications for Personality Theory, Psychopathology, and Health*. Chicago: University of Chicago Press.

Spence, D. (1982) *Narrative Truth and Historical Truth: Meaning and Interpretation in Psychoanalysis*. New York: Norton.

Toronto, E. L. K. (1991) 'The feminine unconscious and psychoanalytic theory', *Psychoanalytic Psychology* 8. 415–38.

van der Kolk, B. A. and Fisler, R. (1995) 'Dissociation and the fragmentary nature of traumatic memories: an overview and exploratory study', *Journal of Traumatic Stress* 8: 505–25.

Index

Locators in **bold** refer to main entries. Locators in *italic* refer to figures/tables. Locators for main headings which have subheadings refer to general aspects of the topic.

absolute truth 80
abuse, therapy as *23*, 25, 41; *see also* childhood sexual abuse
accounts, memory 20–1
accuracy 181–4, 188; *see also* truth
acting-out memory 9, 105, 107; *see also* alternative memories; behaviour patterns; symptoms
actor-observer error *23*, 24
advocacy groups 45; *see also* British False Memory Society; False Memory Syndrome Foundation
agency: children's 185–6, 188; credibility discourse **76–9**; and material context of memory **132–3**; and material space **133–4**; and spaces of memory **134–9**; *see also* choice
alternative memories 9, **105, 106–9, 124–5**; actively seeking knowledge **119–21**; adult behaviour patterns **110–18**; interpreting spontaneous knowledge **118–19**; research focus **109–10**; symptoms checklist 111–12; therapist guidance **121–4**
ambiguity, childhood 70, 71, 81
ambivalence 137
Antenna TV programme 87
anthropology 5, 43
appearance-reality rhetorical device 28–9
archaeology metaphor 204–5
Aristotle 17
attention-seeking 50, 58
audiotape recordings 20, 22
autobiographical memory 148, 181, 191, 216; learning disabled people 160; and truth 176, 180, 181; *see also* narrative memory

Bantu people 43
behaviour patterns: alternative memories 110–18; learning disabled people 157, 164, 169, 170; *see also* symptoms
beliefs 51, 54, 55, 56, 57, 188
The Best Kept Secret (Rush) 87
BFMS (British False Memory Society) 45, 46, 47, 109
The Bill TV programme 87, 111
biography 43, 47; *see also* autobiographical memory
black swan argument 34–5, *35*
blindspots 34
body memories 9, 10, 105, 107, 164, 218; *see also* alternative memories
boundaries 139, 154
Brass Tacks TV programme 87
British False Memory Society (bfms) 45, 46, 47, 109
Brookside TV programme 87, 94, 95

case histories: alternative memories **110–24**; children's legal testimony 72–3, 76–7; learning disability **157–8**, 160, 161, 166–7, 169; retraction **26–9**, **30–5**, **46–57**; spaces of memory **135–9**; survivors of abuse 185–6, 187, 188, 189; transformative remembering **220–7**
Casualty TV programme 87
catharsis 146
Catholic Church 209
changing one's mind *see* retraction
child witness practice (England/Wales) **64–5, 71–2**, 72–3; *see also* children's legal testimony
childhood ambiguity 70, 71, 81
childhood, concepts of 64–5
childhood sexual abuse (CSA) 1, **66–7**; confronting 92; legitimating 93; media discovery **86–8**; naming/expressing 90–1, 92–3, 167, 217; narrative memoirs **143–9**;

rediscovery **86**; rights/credibility **69–71**; suggestibility **67–9**, 70–1
childhood sexuality 5, 74–8, 201, 223–6
Childline 87, 89
children's legal testimony 4, 8–9, **63–4**, **80–1**; child witness practice **64–5**, **71–2**, 72–3; constructing/realising paradox **79–80**; gender and credibility **72–6**; innocence/agency/gender/credibility **76–9**; methodology **65–6**; rights/credibility paradox **69–71**; suggestibility **66–71**; video recordings 72–3, 75, 79
Childwatch TV programme (Esther Rantzen) 87, 93
choice: children's 185–6; and learning disability 161, 171; *see also* agency
Cisters 109
Cleveland child abuse scandal 87
clinical training **206–7**, **211–12**
codes of practice, professional **198–9**
cognitive dissonance 57
cognitive impairment *see* learning disability
cognitive psychology 165
cognitivist biography 43
collective frameworks 165–8
communication of childhood sexual abuse 90–1, 92–3, 167, 217
conditions of credibility 63, 64, 69, 71, 73, 79; *see also* credibility, children
consciousness raising 96, 180
constructing/realising 65–6, **79–80**; *see also* reconstructive remembering; true/false memory co-existence
constructionism *see* reconstructive remembering
'Constructions in Analysis' (Freud) 204
conversation analysis 23, **46–57**, 65
conversion *23*, 25
countertransference **219**
Courage to Heal, The (Bass and Davis) 111
credibility, children 79, 142; and agency **76–9**; conditions of 63, 64, 69, 71, 73, 79; and gender **72–6**; paradox **69–71**
Criminal Evidence Act (1971) 72
critical discursive research 65
Crybaby! (Williamson) 10, 143, 148–9, **149–53**, 154
CSA *see* childhood sexual abuse
cultural contexts: recovered memory debate **10–12**; therapy **209–10**
Cultural Politics of Emotion (Ahmed) 210

defences 170
delayed memory debate *see* recovered memory debate
denial 31; *see also* dissociation; repression
depression 44, 47, 50, 114
desexualisation: childhood *see* sexuality, children's; learning disabled adults 161
detective work **211–12**
determinacy/indeterminacy 178, 179, 185, 190
developmental psychology 64, 74
disclosure 76–7, 81
discourse analysis 23, **46–57**, 65
dispositional beliefs 30–1
dissociation 19, 33, 41, 144–5, 179; case histories 221, 222; *see also* denial; multiple personality disorder; repression
distancing strategies 218, 221; *see also* denial; dissociation; repression
distortion 181, 191
domestic violence 19
Don't: A Woman's Word (Danica) 149, 151
Down's syndrome 158
dreams 32–3, 34, 217; alternative memories 105, 107, 108, 118, 121–2; collective frameworks 165

ecological approaches to memory 18
Écrits (Lacan) 211
ECT treatment 51
effort after meaning 43, 46, 53, 58, 59
emotional: distress 19, 20; disturbance 169, 170, 171; *see also* neurotic symptoms
epistemic help 27, 33–4
ethics 6, 176, 188, 191; *see also* moral/s
Everyman TV programme 87
evidence-based practice **202–4**; *see also* science of memory
experimental psychology 17–18, 35
expression of childhood sexual abuse 90–1, 92–3, 167, 217
extreme case formulation 27

fact-finding processes 80
false memory syndrome (FMS) 19, 21, 106, 121, 123–4; *see also* recovered memory debate
False Memory Syndrome Foundation (FMSF) 2, 8, 19, 45
false/true memory co-existence 7, 36, 58–9, 125
Father-Daughter Rape (Ward) 87
feeling memory 9, 105, 107, 169; *see also* alternative memories
feminist perspective 1, 3, **4–5**, 5, 11; backlash 200–1; media, role of 98, 99, 100, 101; and therapy 209, 210; transformative remembering 180, 216, **217–18**; truth 176
femininity 44
fixed ideas 18
flashbacks 105, 107, 108, 119, 168; *see also* alternative memories

FMS (false memory syndrome) 19, 21, 106, 121, 123–4; *see also* recovered memory debate
FMSF (False Memory Syndrome Foundation) 2, 8, 19, 45
FMS Foundation Newsletter 23
forensic self **177–81**, 181, 190
Freud, Sigmund 5, 43, 204, 211

gender 12, 75, **76–9**, 98, 176
Glasgow University Media Research Group 88
globalisation 209
Grange Hill TV programme 92
grounded theory 46
guided imagery 19, 119
guidelines, professional **198–9**

harm story 106, 124, 125
healing discourse 106, 124, 125
hermeneutics *see* interpretation
hidden knowledge 119, 124; *see also* alternative memories
historical truth 199, **204–6**
homes, symbolism 133–4, 138
Horizon TV programme 87
hypnosis 3, 18, 19, 145, 218; alternative memories 116, 117, 121, 122, 123
hypodermic effects model 99, 100
hypothesis testing 6; *see also* evidence-based practice; science of memory
hysteria 5; *see also* social hysteria

I Know Why the Caged Bird Sings (Angelou) 87
identity 95–7, 175, 177, 189; *see also* self-constitution
imagistic memory 9, 105, 107; *see also* alternative memories
immigrants/immigration 209, 210, 220
implacement 166–7
implanted memory research 68
incest *see* childhood sexual abuse
Incest: Fact and Myth (Nelson) 87
incest survivor-group therapy 19
indeterminacy/determinacy 178, 179, 185, 190
infantilisation of women 200, 201, 204
inference 43–4
inner child 105, 108–11, 113–20, 201–2, 204; *see also* alternative memories
innocence, childhood 65, 74–9, 81, 145, 200–1; *see also* sexuality, children's
instincts 91
integrity 187, 188, 189, 190; *see also* truth
interpretation 183–7, 188, 189–90; *see also* truth

irrationality 30–1; *see also* evidence-based practice; science of memory

Janus face of truth 180

kettle logic 24–5
Kilroy TV programme 94
Kiss Daddy Goodnight (Armstrong) 87

LA Law TV programme 87
learning disability 10–11, **157–8**, **170–1**; definition **158–9**, 161; memory of abuse **164–70**; power dynamics **159–62**, 168, 170; sexual abuse **162–4**
legal testimony, childhood *see* children's legal testimony
Liar, Liar (film) 94
libido, low 48
literalism 3, 218
litigation 198–9
local moral universe 36
Looking Awry (Žižek) 211
Lost in the Mall study 21

marital problems 47–9, 220
marks of the past 17
mass media *see* media, role of
master narratives 97
material: context of memory 10, **131**, **132–3**; space **133–4**; *see also* spaces of memory
material truth 65
maturity, children 69–70, 78
media, role of 9, **86**, **98–101**; identity and social change **95–7**; 'rediscovery' of child abuse 86, **86–95**; research focus **88–9**
memoirs, narrative **142–3**, **143–9**; *see also* narrative memory
memory: distortion 181, 191; flaws 42; and learning disability **164–70**; and therapy **207–9**; and truth **181–4**; wars *see* recovered memory debate; *see also* alternative memories; narrative memory; truth
Memory Matters (Haaken/Reavey), organization of text **7–12**
moral/s: accounting **35–7**; judgment 17, 18, 21; universe, local 36; *see also* ethics
mother-daughter relationships 221–4
multiple meanings 219
multiple personality disorder 179; *see also* dissociation
multiple perspectives 7, 11, 19, 177–8, 186–7, 190
My Father's House (Fraser) 10, 143–9, 151–4

naming childhood sexual abuse 90–1, 92–3, 167, 217
narrative memory 145, **149–53**, **154**, 177, 187–8; *see also* memoirs, narrative
narrative psychology 46, 49, 59
narrative therapy **143–9**; *see also* naming childhood sexual abuse
narrative truth 199, **204–6**
neuroscience 18, 202, 203
neurotic symptoms 1, 5, 105, 107, 121; checklist 111–12; *see also* alternative memories; emotional disturbance
no smoke without fire 27, 34, 35
Not a Love Story (film) 93–4
'Notes for Practitioners: On Legal Issues Connected to the Practice of Psychotherapy' (UKCP) 198

objective approaches to memory 6, 17–18, 46, 183
objects, psychological 42
ocean metaphor 221, 228
ontological gerrymandering *23*, 24
oppression 191; *see also* power dynamics
Orkney child abuse scandal 87, 89

Pandora (Fraser) 147
past in context of present 43–4
patriarchy 4, 12, 132
philosophy 5
Pillar of Salt (Haaken) 179, 216
Plato 28, 177
politics of remembering **2–4**, 158, 175, 180, 202
post-traumatic stress disorder 42, 198
power dynamics 4, 6, 44, 90, 176, 191; and learning disability **159–62**; in therapy 198; *see also* agency
privacy/private spaces 137–9
private knowledge 89
PROCESS mnemonic 31, 32, 33, 34
professional accountability 197; *see also* guidelines/codes of practice
promiscuity 186; *see also* innocence; sexuality, children's
protection/innocence discourse **76–9**
psychoanalysis/psychoanalytic theory 11, 202, 217, 219; *see also* therapy
psychological objects 42
psychotherapeutic culture **4–5**, 110, 124; *see also* psychoanalysis/psychoanalytic theory; therapy
psychotic symptoms 51–3
public knowledge projects 98–9; *see also* media, role of
'The Purloined Letter' (Poe) 211

qualitative/quantitative methodology 6, 7

rape, pseudo/subjective 100
realism 65–6, **79–80**; *see also* reconstructive remembering; true/false memory co-existence
recollection memories 165
reconstructive remembering 6, 46, 65–6, **79–80**, 180–1; Bartlett's work **42–4**; learning disability **164–70**; retraction **44–57**; theory 42, 58–9; and therapeutic practice 204–6, **207–9**; truth 175–6, 177, 179
recovered memory debate 1–3, 41, 106, 142, 197; claims and counter-claims **7–10**; cultural contexts **10–12**; historical contexts **199–202**; retraction 18–22, 35; *see also* truth
recovered memory therapy *see* therapy; *see also* psychoanalysis/psychoanalytic theory
regression 19, 114, 117
remembering (verb) 12; adaptive role (quotation) 41; children's legal testimony 70–1; gone wrong 45; social construction 37; as social process 45; *see also* reconstructive remembering
reporting traumatic events 41
repression 19, 41, 45, 53–4, 191, 217; sexual 5; social 3; *see also* denial; dissociation
responsibility 186, **189–91**
retraction discourse 18–22, **22–6**, 33; decoupling past/present accounts **30–5**; discursive procedures *23*; moral accounting **35–7**; then/now gap 23–5, **26–9**
retractors 8, **44–6**
rewriting history 24
Rewriting the Soul (Hacking) 179, 181
rhetorical devices 21–2, 23, 25, 27, 33; appearance-reality 28–9; blindspots 34; and moral accounting 35–6
rights, children's **69–71**
road metaphor 185, 190
Rutherford case **30–5**

Salem witch trials 66
schema theory 42, 43
schizophrenia 51
science of memory 18, 21, 36, **181–4**; *see also* evidence-based practice
second order retraction 35
secondary handicaps 170
seduction theory 5
self-abuse 111, 112, 152
self-constitution 176–7, 180–1, **184–9**, 191; *see also* identity
self-help literature 9, 110–11
self-knowledge 191, 217, 219
self-reflection 11, 185, 186

self-respect 187
sense memories 108; *see also* alternative memories
sexual abuse: and emotional disturbance 170; learning disabled people **162–4**; *see also* childhood sexual abuse
Sexual Offences Act (2003) 171
sexual repression 5
sexual violence 19
sexuality: children's 5, 74–8, 201, 223–6; discourse **76–9**; female 132
shared experiences 52
Shattered Subjects (Henke) 146
situational factors 24
skepticism 180–1, 188, 189, 190
social biography 43
social change **95–7**
social construction of memory *see* reconstructive remembering
social hysteria 3–4
social model of disability 159
social science perspective **5–6**
social theory of remembering 8
sociology 5
Something about Amelia TV film 87
The Sopranos TV programme 199
spaces of memory **139–40**; and agency 132–3, **134–9**; material space **133–4**
stake inoculation *23*, 25
storehouse model of memory 43, 178, 179
stories of the past 1, 2, 4, 5, 132, 145; *see also* narrative
suggestibility 2, 19, 21, *23*, 24, 41, 181; childhood sexual abuse **66–71**; definition 67; and retraction 45; and therapeutic practice 198, 205; and truth 191
survey approach 46
symptoms **110–18**, 125; alternative memories **110–18**; learning disability 157, 164, 169, 170; psychotic 51–3; *see also* alternative memories; behaviour patterns; neurotic symptoms

Tense Past (Antze and Lambek) 199
terminological controversy 42
testimony 19, 20, 21, 27; *see also* children's legal testimony
therapeutic ethos **4–5**, 110, 124
therapeutic relationship 219, 228
therapy 175, **196**, **211–12**; cultural contexts **209–10**; dispositional beliefs 30–1; as error producing 24; as form of abuse *23*, 25, 41; guidelines/codes of practice **198–9**; historical contexts **199–202**; historical/narrative truth 199, **204–6**; memory work **207–9**; professional accountability 197; scientific evidence **202–4**; survivor-group 19; transformative remembering **206–7**; *see also* psychoanalysis/psychoanalytic theory; psychotherapeutic culture
third-person accounts 208–9, 212
time: lived 184, 189; sense, and learning disability 168–9
The Times 87
toxic childhood debate 201
traces of the past 17
training, therapist **206–7**, **211–12**
transference 205, 211, **219**, 227
transformative remembering 12, 179, 180, **216–17**, **227–8**; case histories **220–7**; therapy **206–7**; transference/countertransference **219**; unconscious mind **217–18**, 219
Trauma and Recovery (Herman) 144, 145–6
trauma theory 217, 218
traumatic memory 19, 107, 145, 179
traumatic stressors 41–2
true/false memory co-existence 7, 36, 58–9, 125
truth 6, 10–11, 80, 110, 123, **175–6**; absolute 80; **177–81**, 181, 190; historical/narrative 199, **204–6**; and litigation 199; material 65; memory research **181–4**; narrative memory 146, 147, 148, **149–53**, 154; responsibility **189–91**; self-constitution **184–9**, 191; *see also* memoirs, narrative; forensic self

UN Convention on the Rights of the Child 69–71, 77–8
uncertainty 45
unconscious mind 107–8, 123, 216, **217–18**, 219
unspoken childhood sexual abuse 90–1, 92–3, 167, 217

values *see* ethics; moral/s
victimhood 10, 97, 132, 149, 150, 210
video recordings 23, 72–3, 75, 79
vulnerability, children's 74, 75, 76

White Lies (Potvin) 149
women: infantilisation 200, 201, 204; testimony 19
Women's Liberation Movement 98, 100
Woolf, Virginia 131
'Writing aversion' (Williamson) 149

Youth Justice and Criminal Evidence Act (1999) 72